A Reader in Pentecostal Theology

T0339007

A READER IN PENTECOSTAL THEOLOGY

Voices from the First Generation

Edited by
Douglas Jacobsen

Indiana University Press / *Bloomington and Indianapolis*

This book is a publication of

Indiana University Press
601 North Morton Street
Bloomington, IN 47404-3797 USA

http://iupress.indiana.edu

Telephone orders 800-842-6796
Fax orders 812-855-7931
Orders by e-mail iuporder@indiana.edu

The paper used in this publication meets the minimum requirements of
American National Standard for Information Sciences—Permanence of Paper
for Printed Library Materials, ANSI Z39.48-1984.

Library of Congress Cataloging-in-Publication Data

A reader in Pentecostal theology : voices from the first generation /
edited by Douglas Jacobsen.
    p. cm.
  Includes bibliographical references and index.
  ISBN 0-253-34786-6 (cloth : alk. paper) — ISBN 0-253-21862-4 (pbk. :
alk. paper)
    1. Pentecostal churches—Doctrines. 2. Pentecostalism. 3. Theology,
Doctrinal. I. Jacobsen, Douglas G. (Douglas Gordon), 1951–
BX8762.z5.R43 2006
230'.994—dc22

2006004177

1 2 3 4 5 11 10 09 08 07 06

For Fred Schmidt and Bill Trollinger,
Brash thinkers, gentle men of faith, trusted friends

CONTENTS

ACKNOWLEDGMENTS

I AM GRATEFUL to my friends in the Society of Pentecostal Studies who have taught me so much about this fascinating movement and who offered advice on which works to include in this reader. They have helped me understand not only the historical dimensions of pentecostalism but also its inner dynamics.

This book would not have seen the light of day without the assistance of my Messiah College co-workers Gina Hale (assistant for the Biblical and Religious Studies Department) and Seleena Lindsey, Diane Hunsinger, Cathy Weaver, and Helen Winey in the Office of Faculty Services. Their efforts in transcribing these Pentecostal texts into electronic format for publication went far beyond required duties, and I am truly thankful for their conscientious and cheerful assistance.

It has been a joy to work once again with Indiana University Press. The staff there makes everything easy. Elizabeth Yoder, copyeditor for this text, provided insightful suggestions about how to smooth the readings ever so slightly in order to make them more understandable to contemporary readers.

Finally, my deepest word of appreciation goes to my wife, Rhonda Hustedt Jacobsen. Rhonda is a fellow scholar whose fingerprints are all over this book; the places where this book is lacking are likely places where I did not fully heed her advice. Nothing I do would be as good as it is without her help, and life would not be as sweet.

Grateful acknowledgment is made to these sources for permission to reproduce the following images:

Photos of Fred Francis Bosworth, William Howard Durham, Garfield Thomas Haywood, Esek William Kenyon, Charles Harrison Mason, Aimee Semple McPherson, David Wesley Myland, Charles Fox Parham, William J. Seymour, Ambrose Jessup Tomlinson, Andrew David Urshan, and Maria

Beulah Woodworth-Etter appear courtesy of Flower Pentecostal Heritage Center.

Photos of Joseph Hillary King and George Floyd Taylor appear courtesy of I. P. H. C. Archives and Research Center.

Photo of Richard G. Spurling on page 160 appears courtesy of the Hal Bernard Dixon Jr. Pentecostal Research Center.

Photo of Robert Clarence Lawson appears courtesy of Robert C. Spellman.

A Reader in Pentecostal Theology

Introduction: The History and Significance of Early Pentecostal Theology

PENTECOSTALISM IS ALMOST certainly the fastest growing religious movement in history. Though it originated only a hundred years ago, it currently accounts for as much as 25 percent of the global Christian population. In raw numbers this means that approximately half a billion people can now be identified as pentecostal in one form or another. The nearest historical parallel to this stunning pattern of growth is the equally explosive expansion of Islam during the first century following the death of Muhammad (632–732). Pentecostalism's growth is made even more impressive by its having taken place with virtually no political or military support to pave the way, and it has spread despite its opposition to some of the most powerful cultural trends of the era.

This book provides readers with a firsthand introduction to the religious ideas that helped launch this dynamic movement of faith. The writings collected here were all produced during the first generation (roughly 1900–1925) when the movement was still fresh and raw, but many of these ideas continue to define pentecostal faith today. This is partly because many early pentecostal theologians were also institutional leaders who wove their ideas into the practices and ethos of the organizations they led. But the longevity of these ideas is also a function of their inherent power: these writings provide a vision of God, the world, and human existence that many people in the United States and around the world still find compelling today. While Pentecostalism is rightly known for its adaptability and innovation in the areas of religious practice, communication technology, cultural assimilation, and organizational structure, few new ideas have been added to the movement's basic theology since 1925.

Pentecostal Theology: Voices from the First Generation is both an historical introduction to the ideas of early pentecostalism and a general introduction to the agreements and disagreements that continue to define the contours of pentecostal belief today. The purpose of this volume is to make pentecostalism's early theological writings, many of which are now preserved only in out-of-the-way archives, more broadly accessible to those interested in the origins of the movement. The selections have been edited lightly only when necessary to correct obvious typographical errors and sometimes to change the format for ease of reading. The authors appear in rough chronological order, based on the publication dates of the works that are cited.

Persons wanting a fuller description of the contours and context of first-generation pentecostal theology may want to consult *Thinking in the Spirit: Theologies of the Early Pentecostal Movement* (Indiana University Press, 2003), which provides more biographical information about many of these theologians and analyzes their works in depth.

What Is Pentecostalism?

While pentecostalism has become a huge global phenomenon, the definition of exactly what makes a person pentecostal is still to some degree unclear. Pentecostalism is not institutionally defined in the same way, for example, as Roman Catholicism is. Thus, membership or lack of membership in a pentecostal organization is not a sufficient means of differentiating pentecostal from nonpentecostal believers. Pentecostalism also differs from groups like the Lutheran and Reformed churches, which have bodies of normative theological documents such as creeds and catechisms that delineate the belief boundaries of those movements. Pentecostalism is more fluid than either of these alternatives.

The issue of what makes a person pentecostal is also complicated by the ways in which some people within the pentecostal movement try to draw lines between who is and who is not a "real" pentecostal. Thus, some pentecostal believers (and the scholars who study them) want to limit use of the term *pentecostal,* applying it only to a handful of denominations begun during the first two or three decades of the twentieth century. These denominations, including such groups as the Assemblies of God, the Church of God (headquartered in Cleveland, Tennessee), and the Church of God in Christ, are often called the "classical pentecostal" churches. People who restrict the term *pentecostal* in this way refer to other pentecostal-like believers as "charismatic" or "neo-charismatic" or "third wave" Christians. There is historical logic in this division of labels since the classical pentecostal churches represent the first layer of institutionalization that appeared within the movement, but it underplays the considerable amount of similarity and overlap that exists among all pentecostal, charismatic, and third wave believers. In this work, the term *pentecostalism* is accordingly used more broadly to refer to all of these groups.

But we still need to determine what it is that makes any of these groups "pentecostal." What is it that distinguishes them from the wide variety of other Christian traditions that exist in the world? What sets pentecostalism apart?

First, pentecostalism is Spirit-centered faith. It is belief in the present-day power of the Holy Spirit to work miracles and supernaturally change lives. Virtually all Christians believe in the Holy Spirit, but pentecostals sense the Spirit more intensely, and they expect the Spirit to act more visibly and dramatically.

In terms of religious practices, the Spirit-inspired ability to speak in "tongues" (also known as "glossolalia") is what makes pentecostalism different. This is so much the case that pentecostalism has sometimes been referred to simply as "the tongues movement." To outside observers, speaking in tongues can sound like nonsensical babbling, and supporting that view, linguists have never been able to decipher any underlying grammatical structure when studying examples of recorded glossolalia. But pentecostal believers are convinced that speaking in tongues is a special form of communication inspired by God, and they derive profound meaning from the experience. Even if speaking in tongues is not a language in any usual sense of the term, something significant occurs when people engage in it.

Within the broad pentecostal movement, and especially within the older pentecostal denominations, speaking in tongues is often understood to be the visible sign or manifestation of a deeper experience called "the baptism of the Holy Spirit." Different pentecostal groups explain this baptism in different ways, but most agree that the baptism of the Spirit is a distinct and unique inflowing of the Spirit of God that powerfully changes the person who experiences it. When God's Spirit enters a person, it rattles the body as well as the soul.

One of the most famous first-person descriptions of the baptism of the Spirit, accompanied with tongues, comes from the writings of William Durham, who received the experience at the Azusa Street revival in 1906. Durham wrote:

> I was overcome by the mighty fulness of the power and went down under it. For three hours He wrought wonderfully in me. My body was worked in sections, a section at a time. And even the skin on my face was jerked and shaken and finally I felt my lower jaw begin to quiver in a strange way. This continued for some time when finally my throat began to enlarge and I felt my vocal organs being, as it were, drawn into a different shape. O how strange and wonderful it was! and how blessed it was to be thus in the hands of God. And last of all I felt my tongue begin to move and my lips to produce strange sounds which did not originate in my mind, and in a few minutes I heard Brother Seymour, the pastor, say "He is through now."[1]

---

[1] William H. Durham, "Personal Testimony of Pastor Durham," *Pentecostal Testimony* 1, [no. 3?] ([1909?]): 7. (The first page is missing from the only extant copy of this issue of Durham's magazine, so the volume number and date cannot be known for certain.)

Not just the experience of the moment matters, but rather the lasting change wrought by the baptism of the Spirit. Pentecostal believers often speak of a permanent change in their faith and character, of a radically deepened awareness of God's presence in their lives, and of a new sense of empowerment for ministry that does not fade with time.

Of course, not all pentecostals experience that baptism in precisely the same way, and some pentecostals don't even use the term "the baptism of the Spirit" to refer to what they do experience. Many people involved in the more recently developed charismatic and neocharismatic movements that are prominent in the Western world, along with many members of the different pentecostal and pentecostal-like independent churches that have sprung up in Africa and Asia during the last half-century, use the phrase "the baptism of the Spirit" only sparingly. But even if the words differ, there remains in all of these groups a special openness to the work of the Spirit and an expectation that the Spirit can uniquely enter into the lives of individuals in ways that more or less replicate what the traditional pentecostal denominations call the baptism of the Spirit.

In addition to tongues and the baptism of the Spirit, pentecostals also place significant emphasis on what the New Testament calls the "gifts of the Spirit" and other miraculous signs of the Spirit's power. In 1 Corinthians 12:8–10, Paul lists these gifts of the Spirit as wisdom, knowledge, faith, healing, working miracles, prophecy, the discernment of spirits, tongues, and the interpretation of tongues. Another list at the end of the Gospel of Mark (16:17–18) says that followers of Christ will be able to cast out demons, speak in new tongues, pick up snakes and drink deadly poison and not be harmed, and lay hands on the sick to heal them. Pentecostals assume that all of these miraculous powers, and possibly more, are available to Christians today in the same way that the New Testament says they were available to Christians in the first century. The reason that other contemporary Christians do not possess these gifts in the same abundance is simply that they do not seek them.

In short, then, pentecostals are Spirit-conscious, Spirit-filled, and Spirit-empowered Christian believers. In contrast to other groups or churches that emphasize either doctrine or moral practice, pentecostals stress affectivity. It is the *experience* of God that matters—the felt power of the Spirit in the world, in the church, and in one's own life. Pentecostals believe that doctrine and ethics are important, but the bedrock of pentecostal faith is experiential. It is living faith in a living God—a God who can miraculously, palpably intervene in the world—that defines the pentecostal orientation of faith.

The Significance of Theology within Pentecostal Faith

If experience is so central to pentecostalism, what does this imply about the realm of ideas? Are ideas simply superfluous? Is theology in any sense necessary for pentecostal faith? If so, what role does theology play?

Popular portrayals of pentecostalism often imply that theology is virtually absent from this movement. They suggest that pentecostalism's stress on the emotive stands in contrast to the intellectual. The two are at war with each other—the mind versus the heart—and within pentecostalism, the heart always wins. If one accepts such a caricature, the phrase "pentecostal theology" will likely seem an oxymoron.

But the truth is that pentecostal Christians do think about their faith. They always have. They have engaged in theological reflection since the very beginning of the movement, and they continue to do so today. The popular stereotype is wrong.

There is no question that spiritual affections are hugely important within pentecostalism, but that emphasis on experiential faith does not require a concomitant diminution of the intellect or a rejection of theology. In fact, one might even go so far as to argue that, apart from theology, pentecostalism would not exist. It is not necessarily the uniqueness of their experiences that set pentecostals apart; it is the way those experiences are theologically categorized and defined. Other Christians have experienced the power of the Spirit. Others have experienced God's miraculous ability to heal. Others have experienced the filling of the Spirit. Others have even spoken in tongues. What makes pentecostalism different is the way this movement talks about those experiences, naming them and bundling them together in ways that other groups do not.

Religious experience can be extraordinarily powerful, but religious experience alone does not produce a movement. A movement requires words to define what it stands for and words to describe itself to others. Words are often related to experience, but they are not the same thing. Words explain and describe experience, and in doing so, they provide models that can help people assess their own experiences and that can sometimes prompt people to have those experiences. Within religious movements, words also situate experiences within a broader understanding of who God is, how the world is put together, and what it means to be human. All of these uses of words taken together constitute the field of theology, and every religious movement—pentecostalism included—has a theology or theologies to guide it on its way.

But there is a twist. Even though pentecostals use theological words to make sense of their faith, pentecostals have always been simultaneously suspicious of words. In fact, the pentecostal movement was to some degree born as a protest against too much reliance on words. Perhaps more accurately, pentecostalism was a protest against the use of religious words without religious experiences to back them up; it was a protest against theological hollowness. Thus, the leaders of the early pentecostal movement would sometimes mock traditional theology as nothing more than dry "chips, shavings and wind,"[2] and they worried that

---

[2] Untitled, *The Apostolic Faith* 1, no. 7 (April 1907): 3.

too much emphasis on words might even drain the power from their own experiences of the Spirit. The leaders of the Azusa Street Mission, the epicenter of
the early pentecostal movement, once observed that whenever people got too
caught up in "talking thought,"[3] pentecostal fervor seemed to decline.

But despite these dangers, pentecostals knew that words were necessary—
theology was necessary—and however much they may have worried about the
potential for words to displace or replace experience, early pentecostal theologians kept on talking and writing, articulating their own views and correcting the errors of their opponents, competitors, and colleagues. It is that lively
interaction, coupled with the folksy philosophical creativity of the leaders of
the movement, that makes early pentecostal theology so fascinating. There is
a freshness, energy, and honesty that is often missing from more polished and
refined theological treatises.

The Roots of Pentecostal Theology

To a large degree, pentecostalism is an offshoot of American revivalism. The
revivalist tradition in America stresses the immediacy of one's relationship with
God and the importance of conversion. Conversion, understood in this revivalistic sense, takes place in a single moment of time—it is not a process—and
it often takes place in the social context of an extended, emotionally aroused
religious service. Revivalistic conversion includes at least three elements:
the honest confession of sin, a sincere request for divine mercy, and genuine
openness to the transforming power of God made possible by Jesus' death and
resurrection. The result of this kind of conversion is instant and immediate:
the individual is instantaneously "born again." In a moment, a sinner on the
way to hell is transformed into a saint headed for heaven.

Not surprisingly, the revivalistic experience of conversion is often emotional. How could it not be? It involves a huge turnabout in one's life trajec-
tory, an enormous dissolution of guilt, and a tremendous infusion of spiritual
power. During the Great Awakening that took place in colonial America,
people sometimes shook with convulsions, cried out with animal-like grunts
and shrieks, or fell into trance-like states for minutes, hours, or even days.
Similar behavior was associated with the frontier revivals of the Second Great
Awakening during the early 1800s, where it was reported that men would bark
the devil up trees and women would sometimes shudder so violently that their
long hair would crack like a whip as they snapped their heads back and forth.
These kinds of physical manifestations of spiritual struggle and release were
not invented by pentecostals; spiritual physicality is part of the longer history
of revivalism.

---

[3] "To the Baptized Saints," *The Apostolic Faith* 1, no. 9 (September 1907): 2.

Revivalism distilled Christianity to its purest Protestant essence—the face-to-face confrontation of the individual with God and the subsequent submission of that person to God's holy will. That vision of faith provided the ground in which pentecostalism would later grow. The emotional power of conversion, the suddenness of its transformative effects, and the unmediated character of the individual's direct encounter with God became the bedrock of pentecostalism.

If revivalism provided the basic structure of pentecostal faith, the holiness movement of the nineteenth century gave pentecostalism much of its theological vocabulary and categories of thought. Rather than focusing on conversion alone—though of course conversion was seen as very important—the holiness movement turned its attention to what follows conversion. Two concerns were central: purity of life (or sanctification) and spiritual power. How does one become and remain morally pure after conversion? How does one claim the full powers of the Holy Spirit after turning one's life over to God?

Over time, the holiness movement developed a number of different answers to these questions. The influential Phoebe Palmer developed her "altar theology" of spiritual consecration and empowerment in the 1830s and 1840s. A variety of more traditionally Wesleyan understandings of sanctified holiness emerged in the mid-nineteenth century. Keswick theology blossomed in the last few decades of the century, taking its cues at least in part from the Reformed tradition and mixing event and process in its own distinctive view of spiritual development. Alongside these three main alternatives, a variety of other less-organized pietistic groups arose, each touting its own vision of the "deeper Christian life."

In relation to pentecostalism, the theological differences among these groups are less important than their shared concern with post-conversion spirituality. Nineteenth-century holiness Christians, in whatever stripe they came, wanted to press beyond conversion to claim all that God might have for them. Invariably, they turned their attention more and more toward the work of the Holy Spirit. Traditional revivalism had theologically placed most of its emphasis on God as judge and Jesus as savior. The Holy Spirit, while not forgotten, was pushed somewhat to the sidelines in this scenario. In holiness theology, however, the center of gravity shifted away from judgment and forgiveness toward maturation in faith, and that was the purview of the Spirit. It was the task of holiness thinkers to explore this territory, seeking to map its byways, discover its secrets, and pass that information on to others.

One issue that surfaced rather quickly was whether purity and power in the Christian life could be obtained in a single moment of time—in a single event such as conversion—or whether it could only be secured as the result of a life-long process of struggle and growth. Many holiness thinkers ultimately concluded that purity and power were gifts from God, just like forgiveness, and were obtainable in the same way. Thus sanctification, like conversion, could take place at a very precise time on one particular day of one specific year. If that was the case with regard to spiritual purity, why couldn't spiritual power be similarly received? Many people came to believe that the Spirit's empowerment could be acquired in an instant of time, and they began to call such an experience the baptism of the Spirit.

With the question of process versus event decided in favor of event, the next issue to be addressed was just how many post-conversion dramatic experiences one could or should expect. Benjamin Hardin Irwin, the colorful founder of the Fire-Baptized Holiness Association, suggested that after conversion and sanctification one should undergo four other distinct spiritual experiences. Using vivid prose, he called these the baptism of fire, the baptism of dynamite, the baptism of lyddite, and the baptism of oxidite. Irwin's chemically inspired labels were not adopted by anyone else, but the question of how many post-conversion spiritual baptisms might be necessary to arrive at the full maturity of Christian life was left hanging in the air.

The early pentecostal movement took shape amid a flurry of holiness speculation and experimentation about the realm of the Spirit. Rather than supporting Irwin's proliferation of post-conversion experiences, pentecostals generally tended to limit the number of options available. There was diversity of opinion, of course. Some pentecostal groups suggested a threefold pattern as the norm: conversion, followed by sanctification, followed by the baptism of the Spirit. Others reduced the number of separate experiences to two: conversion as "full salvation" (which included sanctification), followed by the baptism of the Holy Spirit. Still other pentecostals clumped all three actions together—conversion, sanctification, and the baptism of the Holy Spirit—into one mega-experience called "the birth of the Spirit." What they all agreed on, however, was that the baptism of the Spirit was the final and culminating event. Surely believers could receive subsequent blessings from God, but those blessings were in a different category than conversion, sanctification, and the baptism of the Spirit. Pentecostals like Charles Parham also offered the holiness movement a simple test for knowing when the baptism of the Holy Spirit had been received: if speaking in tongues accompanied or followed the event, it was genuine and complete; if tongues were missing, the full baptism of the Spirit had not yet been obtained.

While holiness theology and the American revivalistic tradition obviously helped pave the way for pentecostalism, a range of other influences were also at play. For example, the prophecy movement of the late nineteenth century, and the dispensational theology it produced, provided pentecostalism with its framework of history and its expectation of the imminent return of Christ. The various health and healing movements that flourished at the turn of the century gave pentecostalism its deep-felt belief in divine healing and the importance of the body. Similarly, the spiritualism that pervaded nineteenth-century popular American culture was a source of pentecostalism's vision of a world full of spirits and demons and other invisible spiritual realities.

All of these influences and more were blended together in the thinking of early pentecostals. They were open to insights from many sources since they were convinced that as the end of the age approached, God would reveal new truth upon new truth to those who were ready to receive them. They didn't want to miss a thing. Ultimately, everything had to be confirmed by agreement with Scripture—pentecostals evaluated everything they heard and read in the light of the Bible—but pentecostal theologians could be quite creative in their exegesis. Old ideas and new visions were tested side by side to see which rang more true. What seemed false was rejected, often with great vehemence, while the new truths they were discovering were woven together with other previously known truths to produce the many-hued fabric that is pentecostal theology.

The Diversity of First-Generation Pentecostal Theology

While it is convenient to speak of pentecostalism in the singular, the movement has been diverse from the very beginning. The religious landscape of early-twentieth-century America was dotted with spiritual seekers wandering toward truth in many different ways from many different places. Pentecostalism was part of that search. While the Azusa Street revival of 1906 is often cited as the beginning of the pentecostal movement, it was preceded by a stream of pentecostal-like questers who are hard to characterize. Pentecostal scholars have varying opinions about which of these persons, if any, ought to be called pentecostal. After the Azusa revival took place, a whole new cast of characters appeared on the scene. Many of these individuals clearly identified themselves as pentecostals, but others resist easy classification.

The sixteen authors gathered together in this anthology are drawn from across this full spectrum of diversity. Some of them are more obviously pentecostal than others, but each of them played an important role in defining the theology of the movement. The introductions that precede each selection provide important background material on each individual, but first it will be helpful to have an overview of the complex developments of that amazing first generation. (Persons whose names appear in boldface are authors of the sixteen selected readings.)

Maria Beulah Woodworth-Etter was one of the earliest individuals to begin developing a pentecostalistic theology of the Spirit, and she did so well before anything like organized pentecostalism had come into existence. As early as 1894, she was preaching in Ohio, Indiana, and throughout the Midwest that the mighty powers of the Spirit were being newly poured out on the world,

and she believed a full restoration of the signs and wonders recorded in the
New Testament book of Acts would soon follow. Woodworth-Etter did not
formally associate herself with the pentecostal movement until 1912, but her
theology of the Spirit—which includes a strong emphasis on both miracles
and gender equality—shaped and continues to shape the way many pentecostals see the world.

Richard G. Spurling came from a different region of the country and pro-
moted a different vision of faith. In 1897, after participating in an Appalachian
revival that included speaking in tongues, Spurling penned the first draft of
his book *The Lost Link*. (The published version did not appear until 1920.) In
this slim volume he outlines a vision of church history that, like Woodworth-
Etter's, stresses the restoration of the Spirit's influence within the church. In
contrast to Woodworth-Etter, however, Spurling's focus is on the restoration
of mutual love and respect among believers and not on signs and wonders.
As popularly portrayed, pentecostalism is all about signs and wonders, but
Spurling's theology stresses that love is the true fruit of the Spirit and that care
for others takes precedence even over miracles.

Woodworth-Etter and Spurling were important figures, but the significance
of **Charles Fox Parham** is undeniable. In 1901, Parham and his students at the
Bethel school in Topeka, Kansas, formulated the crucial doctrine that speaking in tongues is the physical evidence that one has truly received the baptism
of the Holy Spirit. Parham and his followers came out of the radical holiness
movement, where the idea of the baptism of the Spirit was already part of
the rhetoric. What he added was the doctrine of evidence: that speaking in
tongues was the divine sign that one's experience of the Spirit had finally risen
to the level of the full baptism of the Spirit. Parham asserted that Christians
could experience the Spirit in many wonderful ways, but the baptism of the
Spirit was distinctive and tongues was the evidence.

Despite his watershed insight about the significance of tongues, Parham's
ministry floundered. Then, in 1907, he was accused of sodomy and his support largely collapsed. Rather than becoming the first great organizer of the
pentecostal movement, Parham ended his life in relative obscurity, largely
shunned by those who had adopted his teaching about tongues and the Spirit.
Parham's theology remained influential, but it was no longer associated with
his name.

While Woodworth-Etter, Spurling, and Parham helped pentecostalism
come to life as a new religious vision, the real flourishing of pentecostalism
began with the Azusa Street revival in Los Angeles, which ran from April of
1906 to the summer of 1908. The Azusa revival was a complex and largely
unregulated affair led by **William J. Seymour** and his associates. The main
focus was on the baptism of the Spirit as evidenced by speaking in tongues,
and almost everyone who was anyone within the early pentecostal movement

had some connection with Azusa. It was where people came to get the Spirit, and it was where many leaders of the movement first met each other.

The meetings themselves were open-ended and often continued around the clock, with people wandering in and out at will. Devout believers came by the hundreds, seeking their own "personal Pentecost." Holiness folks stopped by to try to ascertain whether the meetings were inspired by God or Satan. Ministers from the established churches of Los Angeles showed up to criticize the fanatics who had invaded their town. Tourists stopped by to gawk and observe. And religious explorers drifted in and out, trying to pick up a few new insights or techniques that they might be able to incorporate into their own patched-together systems of faith.

The buzzing clamor of the meetings and the diversity of the participants cried out for interpretation. At some point even the most experientially oriented believers must have wondered how to understand the meetings. What was God doing? How was one to make sense of this explosion of spiritual piety and power? What was good and ought to be encouraged, and what was bad and ought to be prohibited? What words best described the Azusa Street vision of God, the pentecostal experience of the Spirit, and the church's mission in the world? These questions demanded theological attention, and soon a variety of leaders felt called to provide the movement with theological answers—answers that quickly demonstrated that there were many pentecostal ways to answer any of these questions.

As pastor of the Azusa Street Mission and chief leader of the revival, Seymour took an early lead in this work, assisted by colleagues like Clara Lum. They used the mission's publication, *The Apostolic Faith*, as the chief means of disseminating their theological views. Seymour had actually studied with Parham, and he shared Parham's tongues-speaking, holiness vision of pentecostal faith. The mission's publications accordingly prescribed a three-step vision of the Christian life that began with conversion, was followed by the experience of full sanctification, and culminated in the baptism of the Spirit as validated by speaking in tongues.

Seymour's was but a bare-bones vision of theology, however, and soon others fleshed out fuller and more systematic visions of pentecostal faith and life. **George Floyd Taylor** and **David Wesley Myland** were the first to publish book-length explanations of pentecostal theology after the Azusa revival was underway.

Taylor was a precisionist who wanted to codify everything into neat and logical explanations of how the Spirit worked. Insisting that God always did things the same way, Taylor asserted that even "deaf mutes" had to speak in tongues when they received the baptism of the Spirit. God made no exceptions for physical limitations. Not only the baptism of the Spirit, but every other operation of the Spirit in the human soul had its accompanying physical manifestation in Taylor's theology. The spiritual and the physical worked together, one reflecting the other. God was a God of order and did things consistently in the same way.

Myland was, in some sense, Taylor's opposite. For him, God was full of surprises and rarely did things in precisely the same way. In fact, Myland claimed to have received different parts of his baptism of the Spirit in two separate experiences that took place sixteen years apart. While Taylor thought theology was supposed to be logical, Myland approached theology as an art. He had no expectation that words could ever capture God's glory. The best way to adequately describe the multifaceted wonder of humanity's encounter with God was through images, layering one on top of the other in aesthetic, not logical, relation to each other.

While Taylor and Myland presented very different versions of pentecostal theology, they never directly clashed with each other. Taylor was a southerner and Myland was a northerner, and their primary networks of association rarely intersected. However, that regionalized state of affairs would soon be challenged by **William Howard Durham,** who wanted all pentecostals everywhere to accept his new "finished work" theology of pentecostal faith. Durham vehemently pronounced that one was either a Durhamite "finished work" pentecostal or one was not really a pentecostal believer at all.

Durham's ministry was rooted in Chicago and the Upper Midwest, but he felt called to become the national leader of the movement, traveling the country incessantly to preach. His new finished-work vision asserted that the pentecostal way of life involved only two dramatic encounters with God (full salvation and the baptism of the Spirit) rather than three (conversion, sanctification, and the baptism of the Spirit). In this schema, Durham compressed conversion and sanctification into one experience; and in doing so, he embraced a more Reformed and much less Wesleyan-holiness understanding of the work of the Spirit. In Durham's own mind, however, this was not merely a difference of theological opinion. He believed that his own finished-work vision of pentecostalism had been given to him as a direct revelation from God, and he accordingly considered anyone who resisted his views an enemy of God.

Pentecostal groups that were steeped in a more Wesleyan-holiness understanding of Christian faith thought it was Durham himself who seemed like an agent of the devil. Broadside attacks on Durham were published in a variety of pentecostal holiness periodicals, with **Joseph Hillary King** emerging as the most judicious and articulate spokesperson for the pro-holiness, anti-Durham position. His book, *From Passover to Pentecost* (1914), is a detailed and extended critique of Durham's theology and also the most comprehensive statement of Pentecostal-holiness views produced during the first generation.

Following this dispute, pentecostalism was divided in half, with one side (represented mainly by the Assemblies of God) supporting Durham's two-step understanding of pentecostal faith, and the other side (represented by groups like the Pentecostal Holiness Church and the Church of God) holding fast to the older three-step model. The division of the pentecostal movement along these theological lines is a fact, but it would be inaccurate to describe this split as fragmentation. Fragmentation implies the breaking apart of a prior whole-ness or unanimity, but pre-1912 pentecostalism never possessed that kind of cohesion. Pentecostalism was never blessed (or cursed) with one authorita-tive founder like Luther for Lutheranism or Calvin for Calvinism. Instead, the movement was a loosely organized association still looking for a theology to guide it. It was only as people like Durham and King spelled out the details of what they thought all pentecostals ought to believe that enough ideas were placed on the table for people to agree or disagree with them. Events like the finished-work controversy represent the flowering of the movement's internally diverse theological impulses more than the fragmentation of an original una-nimity within the movement.

The same diversity of theological impulses drove the second great theo-logical controversy that shook the early pentecostal movement. This dispute, called the "New Issue," was initially about which words should be used dur-ing the ritual of water baptism—whether baptism should be performed "in the name of the Father and the Son and the Holy Spirit" or simply "in the name of Jesus"—but it quickly expanded into a debate over the nature of God and the person of Jesus. Was God a trinity of three persons, as Christianity has tradition-ally affirmed, or was God's essence unitarian? The new proposal was that God was a unity, not a trinity, and that "Jesus" was God's proper name.

The birth of this new "oneness" or "Jesus only" theological perspective is usually associated with a pentecostal camp meeting held at Arroyo Seco (in the Los Angeles area) during the spring of 1913. This gathering took place at a time when concern over the theological and organizational divisions caused by Durham's finished-work theology were still fresh. Maria Woodworth-Etter was the main speaker at the event, and she was deeply troubled by this divide. In fact, the previous year (1912), she and Fred Francis Bosworth had organized a series of revival meetings in Dallas trying to bring the two sides together. She brought that same concern with her to Arroyo Seco.

Woodworth-Etter's hope was that some new revelation or vision from God might bring everyone together, and her sense of anticipation enveloped the gathering. Then a man named John G. Sheppe claimed that revelation had come, and it was that water baptism ought to be performed in the name of Jesus alone and not in the trinitarian names of the Father, Son, and Holy Spirit. Those gathered at the meeting were not sure what to make of this claim, and many simply ignored Sheppe. A small group of pentecostal leaders, however, was convinced that the new message was an important revelation from God, and they left the meeting determined to spread the message of Jesus-only pentecostalism across the country.

Reflection on the significance of baptism in Jesus' name soon prompted a thorough rethinking of the basic nature of God. As a result, many Jesus-only pentecostals began to champion a decidedly unitarian, or oneness, view of the Godhead. They also, following Durham's lead, began to rethink the relationship between salvation, sanctification, and the baptism of the Spirit. In the end, most oneness pentecostals decided Durham's two-step description of the ideal Christian life was not simple enough, and they collapsed conversion, sanctification, and the baptism of the Spirit into one mega-experience that they called "the birth of the Spirit." Ideally this birth would take place in the context of water baptism, where the individual would descend into the water as a sinner and then emerge speaking in tongues as a fully saved, sanctified, and Spirit-filled saint.

The two most articulate early spokespersons for this new oneness theology were **Andrew David Urshan** and **Garfield Thomas Haywood**. Haywood was a leader of the Pentecostal Assemblies of the World (PAW), the flagship oneness denomination in the United States during the first half of the twentieth century. Urshan was also briefly associated with the PAW, but he later helped found a new denomination called Emmanuel's Church of Jesus Christ. Oneness pentecostalism represents a relatively small slice of the overall pentecostal movement in the United States — currently less than 10 percent of the whole — but it has flourished elsewhere, especially in Latin America.

In addition to the finished-work controversy and the rise of oneness pentecostalism, a number of other less-prominent disputes added to the growing diversity of the movement. One event that seemed relatively minor at the time but has subsequently taken on greater significance was **Fred Francis Bosworth**'s public questioning of the necessity of tongues as the physical evidence of the baptism of the Spirit. Bosworth had been a very visible leader in the Assemblies of God, and his decision to question this seemingly cardinal belief of pentecostalism more than raised eyebrows. Under intense pressure from colleagues in the organization, Bosworth withdrew his membership from the Assemblies in 1918.

Bosworth believed that the ability to speak in tongues was a wonderful gift from God but that tongues were not to be forced on everyone and that tongues were clearly not the only valid evidence that one had experienced the baptism of the Spirit. To make a physical sign such as speaking in tongues the only accepted evidence of the baptism of the Spirit was to remove faith from the place of centrality it ought to have. Bosworth's proposal was quickly marginalized within the world of early pentecostalism, but his ideas (even though they were only rarely attributed to him) would be adopted by a broad range of charismatic and neocharismatic pentecostals during the last quarter of the twentieth century.

Bosworth's emphasis on the priority of faith was soon carried even further by **Esek William Kenyon**. Kenyon was never a formal member of any pentecostal denomination, but his ideas about faith were taken, and continue to be taken, very seriously by a number of pentecostal groups. He argued that faith is the key to everything in the Christian life. God-inspired faith produces miracles and brings prosperity to those who believe. Such faith is based on what Kenyon called the Christian's "legal right" to God's power made available by Christ's identification with us. That power already belongs to the believers; it only needs to be claimed. In setting forth this perspective, Kenyon became the father of what has subsequently become known as the "word of faith" movement or, more derisively, as the "name it and claim it" gospel.

Kenyon's ideas were not embraced by many leaders of the early pentecostal movement, but they always hovered around the edges. The views of the many healing revivalists of the mid-twentieth century such as Oral Roberts and A. A. Allen bear some resemblance to Kenyon's, and a number of contemporary television preachers have adopted his understanding of faith. Kenyon's legal-right theology has also become a prominent element within many pentecostal groups in Africa. Most current leaders of America's classical pentecostal denominations have condemned Kenyon's views of faith as heretical, and they have tried to distance their own churches and the whole pentecostal movement from his ideas.

The early pentecostal movement was rife with contention, and race was another area where tensions were evident. On the basis of reports coming from the Azusa Street revival, it was widely assumed that God had washed the "color line" out of the pentecostal movement. Whites, blacks, Hispanics, and people from many nations worshiped together at the Azusa Street Mission side by side, arm in arm, hand in hand. In retrospect, it seems like this idyllic vision of the Azusa revival overstated the racial harmony that prevailed at the mission, but regardless of how racially harmonious the revival may or may not have been, pentecostal believers soon discovered that racism had not been permanently removed from the movement.

The fact that racism existed within the pentecostal movement is hardly surprising. Pentecostalism was born in the heyday of the Jim Crow era, and it would have been literally miraculous for it to have transcended the racist dimensions of early-twentieth-century America. But given the anti-racist hopes inspired by the revival in Los Angeles, it was disappointing, especially for people of color, to discover that racism was still alive within the pentecostal world. In some of his later writings, William J. Seymour, who was an African American, mentioned the problem of race; and occasionally Charles Mason, who led the predominantly black Church of God in Christ, would refer to the blight of racism; but neither of these leaders ever developed a sustained theological critique of racism.

The one person who attacked racism head-on was **Robert Clarence Lawson,** founder of the Church of Our Lord Jesus Christ. In 1925 he wrote a small book entitled *The Anthropology of Jesus Christ Our Kinsman,* in which he developed both an Afrocentric critique of white Western society and a biblically based theology explaining why the church, and especially the pentecostal movement, ought to be explicitly anti-racist. In the early twentieth century, most American Christians would have seen racism as a moral issue, but not necessarily as a concern of theology. Lawson recognized racism as a theological problem long before most other theologians began to include matters like race, gender, and class in their reflections on faith.

The theological reflections of **Ambrose Jessup Tomlinson** focused on ecclesiology—how to understand the nature, purpose, and ideal structure of the church. Tomlinson, the indefatigable leader of the Church of God, worked tirelessly to help his church become the kind of smoothly running organization that would be capable of undertaking whatever tasks God might assign it. His book, *The Last Great Conflict,* sketches his understanding of the place of government in the church, including what he called the Bible's "money system" for the church. Few other pentecostal leaders spent so much time relating theology to the practical matters of church life.

Another important denominational leader was **Charles Harrison Mason,** founder of the Church of God in Christ, the first pentecostal denomination legally licensed to ordain ministers. He remained at the helm of his church until his death in 1961. Mason was not a typical theologian; his schooling was minimal, and his interests were more pastoral than philosophically systematic or logical. A rural believer who understood the folk culture of the farm, he used the natural images of agriculture to make his points, referring to the way God spoke through especially violent storms or through oddly shaped roots and vegetables. He also had a strong sense of his own apostleship over his church, and he defended his proper authority. This theme of apostleship would later recur in various pentecostal groups.

Finally, the inimitable **Aimee Semple McPherson** was perhaps the best-known pentecostal preacher of the entire century. She had a dramatic flair and an easy way of putting faith into words. The content of her theology was not particularly unique—and she never claimed that it was—but the tone of her sermons and publications was distinctive. She could be both forceful and irenic at the same time, and she had a genuine concern for Christian unity that few if any other pentecostal leaders could rival. Although she was the founder of a denomination, the International Church of the Foursquare Gospel, she was not a denominational partisan. In fact, her ministry was in many ways a precursor of the nondenominational charismatic pentecostalism that is so popular today.

Taken together, these sixteen figures represent a cross-section of the theological options that were present in early pentecostalism. Their voices exemplify the complexity of pentecostal origins and provide points of reference that mark out that uneven terrain. But the writings that follow are not only of historical interest. Many of the ideas first articulated by these theologians remain influential, making these selections essential reading for anyone seeking to understand global pentecostalism today.

CHAPTER ONE

Maria Beulah Woodworth-Etter
(1844–1924)

I N MANY WAYS Maria Beulah Woodworth-Etter was a typical nineteenth-century Midwestern woman. Born in 1844 and married to a returning Civil War veteran, she had given birth to six children by the time she was thirty-five, though only the firstborn survived. Then her life changed. She received a call from God to preach, a call that included a vision of grain ready for harvest and the experience of being immersed in the "liquid fire" of God's presence. Her husband was not thrilled with Maria's newfound desire to preach, but eventually he relented and Woodworth-Etter began what would be more than four decades of evangelistic work.

During the early years of her ministry, Woodworth-Etter was eclectic in her churchly associations. At different times she was connected with the Friends (Quakers), the Methodists, the United Brethren, a group called Bible Christians, and most consistently with the Church of God founded by John Weinbrenner and headquartered in Findlay, Ohio. Later, after the Church of God withdrew her credentials, she struck out on her own, unencumbered by ties to any denomination.

Almost from the start, she was noted for the strange physical manifestations that took place at her meetings. People would be healed, they would cry out with strange sounds, and quite often they would fall into trances or trance-like states. Woodworth-Etter herself would sometimes be taken up into a spiritual trance or vision of God for minutes or hours while leading services. All of this took place long before the pentecostal movement emerged on the scene, and neither Woodworth-Etter nor those who participated in her meetings knew quite what to make of these manifestations. They accepted them as the work of God but did not try to make theological sense of what was going on. Retrospectively, Woodworth-Etter would interpret her entire career in a pentecostal light, seeing these occurrences as precursors of the larger pentecostal movement that would follow.

Woodworth-Etter's own transition from holiness preacher to pentecostal spokesperson is somewhat obscure. Just a short while before the Azusa revival erupted in Los Angeles, Woodworth-Etter more or less disappeared from view. For a seven-year period starting in 1905, she hardly preached at all. Then in 1912 she burst back onto the American religious stage as a full-blown pentecostal in a series of meetings co-sponsored with Fred Francis Bosworth in Dallas, Texas. After that, Woodworth-Etter was a regular speaker on the pentecostal circuit until she died in 1924.

The selections reproduced here represent both the pre-pentecostal and pentecostal stages of her career. The first, taken from *The Life, Work, and Experience of Maria Beulah Woodworth* (1894), provides a sense of her pre-pentecostal, but very pentecostal-like, vision of the world, stressing divine power, spiritual battle, and the end of the world. The other two passages come from *Signs and Wonders God has Wrought in the Ministry for Forty Years* (1916) and focus on Woodworth-Etter's defense of the right of women to preach and why trances and visions are needed as part of the contemporary experience of the church.[1]

The following selection is taken from *The Life, Work, and Experience of Maria Beulah Woodworth, Evangelist*, revised edition (St. Louis, Mo.: Maria Beulah Woodworth, 1894).[2]

Chapter XLI

. . . We read with wonder the supernatural displays of God's power and glory, but how many comprehend that we, too, may behold them? The people seem to think that these manifestations were for the early followers. We do not find any such teachings in the word of God. Lord, help us to know that our God is the same forever. God would ever dwell with his people. He does not want to live apart from them. His delight and pleasure is to ever be with them.

---

[1] For more information, see Wayne Warner, *Maria Woodworth-Etter: For Such a Time as This* (Gainesville, Fla.: Bridge-Logos, 2004).
[2] I am thankful for the help of Wayne Warner of the Flower Pentecostal Heritage Center in selecting these passages.

He would walk with them; and wherever the footsteps of God have been among his people he has left a beautiful pathway of light and glory.

God delights to reveal his arm of power; he rejoices to show forth his glory. He maketh a way in the sea, and a path in the mighty deep. His glory is for his people. He wants to bestow it upon them. O, that his people should reject it! O, that he should come unto his own, and his own receive him not! God has ever desired to manifest himself unto his children. In the ancient days he made himself known in various manifestations of his power. He descended upon mount Sinai in fire and smoke, and a cloud of glory covered the mount; his voice was heard in the thunder; he revealed himself in the lightning; he went before Israel in a cloudy pillar by day, and hovered over them in a pillar of fire by night, and the glory of his presence was with them. In the apostolic days God revealed himself, through the blessed Holy Ghost, in many miraculous ways. He came to Saul of Tarsus in the brightness of the noonday sun, and changed him from a bold persecutor to a bold preacher. He came to the amazed disciples upon the transfiguration mount, and the Old Dispensation and the New held heavenly converse. He came upon the church with such magnifying power that she presented, not simply one of the phenomena, but the grand phenomena of history. In all these exhibitions of his power the people recognized the presence of God and gave him the glory. That there came a time when there was an interruption of the communication of God with his people, was not due to God's plan. God has told the people that if they would hearken unto his voice he would give them counsel. But they apostatized, and God withdrew himself. God will never dwell with an apostate people, nor will his voice be heard in their midst. God never speaks in the heart where the whispers of Satan are heard. It is only the pure in heart who shall see the manifestations of God.

We are living in the last days, and the glorious times of the early pentecost are for us. If, as in the days of Samuel, there could be a return of the "open vision" and the interrupted communication of God with his people restored, the great decline of the power of the church would be arrested. The Holy Ghost is no longer with us in primitive pentecostal power. Instances of marked faith-power, of unction in preaching, of wondrous displays of the Holy Ghost, are painfully inconspicuous and exceptional. The church is merely a negative barrier in restraining the floods of wickedness, when she should be a positive, aggressive force in driving back evil. Sorrowfully we must acknowledge that the glory of the former days has departed.

Now, there is a reason why we do not see the wonderful displays of God's power among the people. There is a hindrance. The trouble with the people today is, that they believe that this power was for the early church only, and we have taken the views of our ancestors and abided by them. We have not tested God and met his conditions, and seen whether he would pour down his Spirit.

We have not met the conditions, such as would ask God to display his power. We have believed that God has taken this power from the church; and when one does put forth the faith and believes these days may be for us now, such a one is called a crank, a hypnotic, etc.

The glory of God was withdrawn from the temple because they had abandoned him. He told them that so long as they would obey his laws he would be with them; but it was because they forsook God that he withdrew his presence from them. The Lord is always ready to do his part. Though his true believers may be few, he will be to them a mighty host. "Fear not, thou worm Jacob, and ye men of Israel, and I will help thee," saith the Lord. God's people are in the minority. Wherever God's people were engaged in warfare the numbers of the Lord were the smallest. But whenever the battle was fought in the strength of the Lord, then God fought the battles for them and delivered them. God will make the minority victorious when the fight is in the strength of the Lord.

The masses of the people are not looking for signs and wonders today. They do not want to see them. The preaching of God is foolishness to them that believe not. We preach the gospel as the Lord gives it to us. Bless God, his people obey the spirit, and where the spirit is they recognize it. Where you see these manifestations—the lame leap as an hart, the sick healed, people stricken down with the power, etc.—it is a visible sign of God's wonderful presence. . . .

The following selections are taken from *Signs and Wonders God Wrought in the Ministry for Forty Years* (N.p.: Maria Beulah Woodworth-Etter, 1916).

Chapter XXXIV: Sermon—Women's Rights in the Gospel

. . . "And suddenly there came a sound from Heaven as of a rushing mighty wind, and it filled all the house where they were sitting.

"And there appeared unto them cloven tongues like as of fire, and it sat upon each of them.

"And they were *all* filled with the Holy Ghost, and began to speak with other tongues, as the Spirit gave them utterance." (Acts 2.2–4.)

There was a wonderful excitement; the people came rushing in great multitudes from the city to see what was the matter. They saw these men and women, with their faces shining with the glory of God, all preaching at once; all anxious to tell what God had done for them and a dying world. Conviction went like daggers to their hearts. And, just as it is today, when the power of God is manifest, instead of yielding, they cried out, "Too much excitement," and began to fight against God; they said, "These people are mad, are drunken with new wine," and mocked them.

Peter gets up to defend the cause of Christ. He refers to Joel 2.28–29. "And it shall come to pass in the last days, saith God, I will pour out of my Spirit upon all flesh; and your sons and your daughters shall prophesy, and your young men shall see visions, and your old men shall dream dreams, and on my servants and on my handmaidens I will pour out in those days of my Spirit; and they shall prophesy." (Acts 2.17–18. I. Cor. 14.22–26; and I Cor. 1–5. Paul speaks as if it were very common for women to preach and prophesy.

"Every woman that prayeth or prophesieth with her head uncovered dishonoreth her head." (I. Cor. 11.5.) "The same man had four daughters, virgins, which did prophesy." (Acts 21.9; Eph. 4.11.)

Paul worked with the women in the gospel more than any of the apostles; Priscilla and Phebe traveled with Paul preaching and building up the churches. (Acts 18.2–18–26; Romans 16.)

He and Phebe had been holding revivals together; now she is called to the city of Rome; Paul cannot go with her, but he is very careful of her reputation, and that she is treated with respect, he writes a letter of recommendation: "I commend unto you Phebe, our sister, which is a servant of the church (which signifies a minister of the church) at Cenchrea, that ye receive her in the Lord as becometh saints and that ye assist her in whatsoever business she hath need of you, for she has been a succourer of many and of myself also." (Rom. 16.1.)

This shows that she had authority to do business in the churches and that she had been successful in winning souls to Christ. He is not ashamed to say she had encouraged him; he speaks in the highest praise of a number of sisters who had been faithful workers in the work of the Lord, who had risked their lives in the effort to save souls, and not he alone, but all the churches of the Gentiles sent their thanks.

Paul said, "Let your women keep silent in the churches." So saith the law. We are not under law but under grace. "And learn of their husbands at home." What will those do who have no husbands? Do you suppose they will remain in ignorance and be lost? And if some women had to depend on their husbands for knowledge they would die in ignorance.

Paul referred to contentions in the churches. Paul says you had better not marry. How many agree with Paul? How many obey? He is referring to contentions in the churches, that it is a shame to bring up questions and have jangling in the house of God. He writes to the brethren, "I hear that there be divisions among you, and I partly believe it." (I. Cor. 11.18.)

"Help those women which labored with me in the gospel, with Clement also, and with my other fellow laborers whose names are in the book of life." (Phil. 4.3.) There were also several women who were prophetesses. (Luke 2.36; II. Kings 22.13–15.) Huldah, the prophetess, the wife of Shallum, dwelt in Jerusalem, in the college, and they communed with her, and she said unto them, "Thus saith the Lord God of Israel."

Exodus 15:20; Micah 6.4 "I sent before thee, Moses, Aaron and Miriam."

Judges 4.4. "Deborah, a prophetess, the wife of Lapidoth she judged Israel at that time." See the responsible position that God gave her, to sit and judge the hosts of the children of Israel. The children of Israel had sinned and God would not fight their battles, and for twenty years the nations arose against them and defied them to come out to battle. Barak dared not meet the enemy unless Deborah led the van. This brave woman, ever ready to defend the cause of God, said, "I will surely go." God's people must not be taken by the enemies. Oh, no; call out the armies of the Lord. Sisera's mighty host is gathering. Every soldier to his post. See the brave woman riding with Barak, the commander, at the head of the army cheering on the hosts to victory, shouting victory as she led on the armies, sweeping through the enemies' ranks carrying death and destruction till the king leaped from his chariot and fled for his life, but was captured and killed by a woman. Every man was put to the sword; not one was left to tell of the defeat.

The mother of Sisera looked out of the window for the return of the king, her son, from the battle, and cried, "Oh, why does he not come, why is his chariot so long in coming? Why, oh, why does he tarry so long?" While she is weeping for her son's return he is lying cold in death in the tent where he has been captured and killed by a woman.

Queen Esther intercedes at the king's court, and the sad decree of the king is reversed, so that her life and the life of the Jewish nation are saved.

Paul says there is no difference, but that male and female are one in Christ Jesus. (Gal. 3.28.) Let us take Jesus for our pattern and example and see no man, save Jesus only.

Women were called and commissioned by the Angel sent from Heaven, and by the Lord Jesus Christ, to preach the gospel (Matt. 28.5–10.)

The cowardly disciples had forsaken the Saviour and fled. Peter denied the Saviour and swore he never knew him, but many women followed him and stood by the cross, and went to the sepulchre and saw the body laid away; the great stone was rolled against the door. (Matt. 27.55–61.) These women went home sad and broken-hearted, but they returned to pay a last tribute to their dear friend. They spent the night in preparing spices to embalm the body of their Lord. They came to the sepulchre as it was coming day. The grave was empty. The Lord was not there. As they stood weeping two Angels stood by them and said: "Fear not ye, for I know that ye seek Jesus, which was crucified. He is not here, for he is risen, as he said. Come, see the place where the Lord lay. And go quickly, and tell his disciples that he is risen from the dead; and, behold, he goeth before you into Galilee; there shall ye see him; lo, I have told you."

They started at once with joy and rejoicing. They could not walk fast enough; they ran to hunt up the brothers, to tell the good news. As they were going Jesus met them and they fell at His feet and worshiped him. He said: "Be not afraid; go tell my brethren that they go into Galilee and there shall they see me." It was not only the twelve that were to tell the good news. There were several hundred brethren; yes, thousands of followers at this time. They never thought of blood-thirsty soldiers who had put their Master to death and were seeking for his friends who would dare to defend him.

Observe the wonderful mission that Jesus had intrusted to these weak women to preach the first resurrection sermon; to risk their lives in gathering together the followers of Christ, where the wonderful meeting was to be held. But just like many today, they would not believe. Peter said, "I will not believe your report." Thomas said, "I will not believe except I see the prints in his hands and feet."

In the midst of all these discouragements they went on with the work and had grand success. Jesus met with and preached to them; they were all made to rejoice. They were called by Angels, and the Lord from glory, and sent to preach the gospel. The names of four women were given and there were many others.

God is calling the Marys and the Marthas today all over our land to work in various places in the vineyard of the Lord; God grant that they may respond and say, "Lord, here am I; send me." This call was made after Christ had risen. Turn also to John 4.10–29–39–42.

"I will pour out in the last days of my Spirit"; that refers in a special manner to these last days in which we are now living. God is promising great blessings and power to qualify His hand-maidens for the last great harvest just before the notable day of the Lord comes. We must first be baptized into Christ by the one Spirit, that is, to be born of the Spirit; then we ought to be anointed with power and wisdom. The Spirit ought to be poured out like oil on our heads, to give us knowledge of the deep thing[s] of God. The Lord says we shall prophesy.

"Paul says desire spiritual gifts, but rather that ye may prophesy." (I. Cor. 14.1.) It makes no difference how many gifts we have, if we have not the gift of talking, and teaching, it will not avail us much. The Lord has promised this greatest gift to his handmaidens, and daughters. In the third verse Paul explains what it is to prophesy. He that prophesieth speaketh unto men to edification and exhortation, and comfort. He that prophesieth, edifieth the church. No one can talk for God [except] by the enlightening power of the Holy Ghost. Moses said, "Would God that all the Lord's people were prophets, and that the Lord would put His spirit upon them." (Numbers 11.29.) . . .

My dear sister in Christ, as you hear these words may the Spirit of God come upon you, and make you willing to do the work the Lord has assigned to you. It is high time for women to let their lights shine; to bring out their talents that have been hidden away rusting, and use them for the glory of God, and do with their might what their hands find to do, trusting God for strength, who has said, "I will never leave you."

Chapter XXXV: Sermon on Visions and Trances

. . . On the day of Pentecost, when the Holy Ghost was seen, heard and felt, thousands were brought into the spiritual kingdom of God. Peter stood up in a blaze of Holy Ghost power and glory, and said when God poured out His Spirit on His sons and daughters they would see visions and dream dreams and prophesy. He told them that these signs would be sure to follow the out-pourings of the Spirit.

The Lord said to Miriam, "If there is a prophet among you, I, the Lord, will make myself known unto him in a vision and speak to him in dreams." Moses said, "Would to God all the Lord's people were prophets and all would prophesy."

Peter says we will all prophesy when we have the spirit of God, and visions is one of the signs that we have the Spirit.

The Lord says if we are prophets He will make himself known to us in visions. The heathen, or gentiles, were perishing; they knew nothing of the religion of Jesus.

God used two visions to bring about a great revival, where the whole con-gregation was converted and filled with the glory of God. This was the first Holy Ghost revival among the heathen. It was a sample of all that was to follow. When the people saw the visible signs of the presence of God in their midst, and He revealed himself to them, everyone felt they were in the pres-ence of God, and sinners came rushing to the loving arms of Christ and were saved from the awful doom that awaits the unsaved.

"Where there is no vision the people perish."

Those who are opposing the demonstration of the spirit today say we do not need these things, that we are progressing with the age, that we want an intellectual religion, that we must explain and present the word from a human standpoint in a scientific way.

In these last days the masses of so-called religious teachers belong to the class Paul said, who have a form of Godliness but deny the power. From such, turn away. They will not endure sound doctrine, will turn the people away from the truth.

These false teachers are in a worse condition than the Jews were. They are sinning against much greater light. They are willingly blind, and are teaching their followers to hide behind a refuge of lies, trusting to doctrines, and tradi-tions of men, "In vain do they worship me," saith the Lord.

The judgments of God in the most awful way are coming upon the false church. . . .

Saul, who was one of the best scholars of his day, and had a polished form of religion, would not believe in or accept visions, or visible demonstrations of the power of God; so when he saw the glory of God, and heard Stephen tell the wonderful vision he had seen, when the howling mob gathered around Saul helped them on, and consented to his death.

Now the great persecution commenced. Saul, like a blood-hound, who had got the smell of blood, followed the trail, filling the prisons, and putting the Saints to death. (Acts 26–12.)

While on his way to Damascus to take the Saints from prison to put them to death, about noon, when the sun was shining in all its strength, this man who did not believe in the visible power of God, said he saw a light from Heaven above the brightness of the sun, "Shining round about me and them which journeyed with me."

He and all of his party were struck to the earth as dead men. There was no loud praying or singing, or religious excitement to put these strong men in that condition. God had sent a shock from the battery of Heaven.

Saul, who had hated demonstrations of the Spirit, saw at once he was lost and on the way to hell. The Lord showed him while lying under the power off the Holy Ghost, that he must preach the Gospel, and wherever he went he must tell about all he had seen and heard, and things that the Lord would show to him in the future. Jesus appeared to him then and talked to him face to face, and many times after in vision.

The Lord used three visions to bring about the conversion of Saul, one of the brightest scholars of the Jewish Church. He was under deep conviction, neither ate nor drank for three days and nights. He counted the cost. When he accepted Christ he was filled with the Holy Ghost. The first thing he did was to preach a living Christ, and to throw open the prisons and stop the awful persecution, and show the despised followers of Jesus that he was their friend and brother. The Churches all had rest, and the waves of Salvation swept over all the land.

See the glorious results to the Church and the world. All brought about by three visions.

"Where there is no vision the people perish."

Paul never doubted the power of God nor any demonstration. He knew more about the personality of the Holy Ghost, and his many offices, gifts, visions, revelations, divers operations, leadings, teachings and power; and taught more about these things than any, or all the rest of the apostles, and he proved clearly that all this power would be for the people of God forever.

The Book of Revelations is the most wonderful of all in the Bible. Christ appeared to John in person and gave him one vision after another. He showed him the Heavenly City, the Great City, the City of Gold, and the jasper walls. The City lieth four square—fifteen hundred miles high, as long and wide as it was high. He was told about the climate, the inhabitants, and their occupation. He had visions of the great judgment day, of the lake of fire and brimstone and all the lost that were swept into it. The Lord told him to write all that he saw and heard, and show it to the Churches, and they were to show it to the world.

The prophet said, the time would come, if any one had a vision, when they would be ashamed to tell it. That time is here. The masses of church leaders look upon everything supernatural as a disgrace and cry out, "Hypnotism," "Excitement," "Drunkenness," or some other power. Just like the Jews, progressing with the age, they are satisfied with dead form.

The churches are filled with unconverted people. Where there are no visions the people perish. *If there is not power enough for visions, there is not enough to save a soul.*

The gift of visions was especially promised in the last days. "And it shall come to pass in the last days, saith God, I will pour out my Spirit upon all flesh: And your sons and your daughters shall prophesy, and your young men shall see visions, and your old men shall dream dreams;

And on my servants and on my handmaidens I will pour out in those days of my Spirit; and they shall prophesy." (Acts 2.17–18.)

Thank the Lord, those days are here, and God is revealing Himself to those who come to Him in the right way in special gifts, in healing all manner of diseases, in all the fullness of the Holy Ghost power. Hundreds are having wonderful visions, and wherever these signs follow the word, all classes flock to Christ.

CHAPTER TWO

Charles Fox Parham
(1873–1929)

CHARLES FOX PARHAM was born in Iowa, grew up in Kansas, and spent most of his life in the central region of the United States. He had a public school education and then went on to attend several years of college with the goal of becoming a physician, but in matters of faith he was almost entirely self-taught.

Parham was very much a believer in the Bible, but he bluntly rejected the notion that Christian "orthodoxy" should set any limits on his own interpretation of that book. He could be quite creative in his thinking and also, at times, controversial. Among his other views, Parham rejected the idea of an eternal hell as out of keeping with God's character; he believed in divine healing; he advocated Christian care for the poor in a way that presaged some of the concerns of the Social Gospel movement; and he was a convinced racist. He was clearly eclectic in his thinking—at times, his views were quite eccentric—but he was also a systematizer of sorts who truly wanted to help others understand the mysterious ways of God in the world.

Parham is sometimes called the "father" of pentecostal theology because he was the first person to clearly articulate the thesis that speaking in tongues was the necessary physical evidence of the baptism of the Spirit. The first selection included here, chapter 3 from his book *Kol Kare Bomidbar* (1902), is his original published explanation of that proposition. This piece needs to be treated with care, however, since it has often been read out of context. Like many of Parham's writings, this selection focuses on the end of history, the perils of the coming "tribulation," and the return of Christ. Within this "end times" scenario, Parham believed that the baptism of the Spirit provided recipients with special protection from Satan and also special powers to aid in preaching the gospel. Speaking in tongues was one of those powers. This gift of tongues was given to Spirit-filled Christians in order to allow them to preach the gospel in other human languages that they had never learned. In contrast to many later pentecostals, Parham did not make a distinction between tongues as a sign of the baptism of the Spirit and tongues as a spiritual gift. He thought there was only one phenomenon of tongues, defined as the miraculous ability to speak in foreign languages without prior study.

The second selection, chapter 2 of his book *The Everlasting Gospel* (1911), focuses on the key pentecostal question regarding how to interpret one's spiritual experiences, and in particular, how to recognize the differences that separate the baptism of the Holy Spirit from both sanctification and the anointing of the Spirit. While Parham believed the baptism of the Spirit was the ultimate Christian experience that superseded all others, he was convinced that there were many other ways to experience the Spirit (both before and after receiving the baptism of the Holy Spirit), experiences that provided their own wonderful and miraculous powers. Using vocabulary that pentecostals would later discard, Parham called these powers "psychic" and "occultic."[1]

The following selection is taken from *Kol Kare Bomidbar: A Voice Crying in the Wilderness*, 1902. (Reprint, Baxter Springs, Kans.: Robert L. Parham, 1944.)

Chapter Three: "Baptism of the Holy Ghost. The Speaking in Other Tongues and Sealing of the Church and Bride"

Since there are so many teachings today of self-ordained leaders of more or less human unction and truth, yet who fall into dreadful errors, it behooves us to "try the spirits," to prove all things by the Word of God. That error is the most dangerous which contains the most truth. Yea, error would fall on its own weight if not upheld by pillars of truth. We also find that wherever error exists it is marked by the intensity of propagation and seeming blindness of its disseminators to its utter unscripturalness.

The Word of God is perverted to suit their own convenience, until onward rushing through deserts barren or mountain wildernesses, they are lost to sight

---

[1] For more information, see James R. Groff Jr., *Fields White Unto Harvest: Charles F. Parham and the Missionary Origins of Pentecostalism* (Fayetteville: University of Arkansas Press, 1988); and Douglas Jacobsen, *Thinking in the Spirit: Theologies of the Early Pentecostal Movement* (Bloomington: Indiana University Press, 2003), 16–50.

of sane and wiser men, wrecked on the crater of modern seething religious volcanic disturbances.

Many dear sheep of the tender Shepherd's fold, failing to find proper food either through the narrowness of self appointed leaders, or through failing to take the true teaching and light from men sent of God, have done what this little anecdote illustrates. Down in Texas there is difficulty in getting sheep over sloughs. A goat is sent ahead. The sheep nearly break their necks in following. So God's sheep are today led by goats into many arid pastures; starved, bleating flocks are eating the wool off each other, proselyting, denouncing all others who do not feed in the same pasture as themselves, while they feed upon the cacti and sage brush of wildest fanaticism, led by men whose so-called "divine revelations" are vain as mad-man's dreams, the unction of over-wrought imaginations of self-exaltation and esteem.

We have found the sweet relief of being shut away with the Word of God, where we may learn what He says and hear Him speak.

There are so many today claiming divine leadership, who say they are sealing the Bride, setting the true church in order by the baptism of water, etc. We feel led to declare the sealing of the Bride and setting the Body, the Church in order, is the work of the God-head, not man's work.

Let us view the Scripture on this point. This very precious fact is noted, the sealed ones escape the plagues and wraths of the last days. Now is the seal of such a nature as to cause us to know when we are sealed, not to be deceived by the fallible sealings of men? Counterfeit sealings being abroad assures us it is time for the true sealing to take place. Wherever the counterfeit exists, the real must also. When we heard and studied the pretended claims of Medical, Mental, and Christian Sciences, hypnotism, etc., we said: God has the real of which these sorceries are the counterfeit. We found Him who bare our sicknesses (Matt. 8:17) and was lifted up for us even as Moses lifted up the serpent in the wilderness, (for healing). (John 3:14.)

When beholding the power of spiritualism, for though 99 per cent of it is slight of hand it does contain certain forces, as the possession of mediums, speaking under the control of evil spirits, etc. We said, God has the real of this; and, lo, when the power of Pentecost came, we found the real, and everyone who has received the Baptism of the Holy Spirit has again spoken in tongues, having the same confounding evidence of Acts 2nd chapter, also 10:44-48 and 19:6.

Again, when like the Witch of Endor, they materialize spirits, we said, God has the real, that He may be glorified, and we find this in our coming redemption.

For years we have prayed for this present truth given in this book, simply that again we might throw down the rod of God's truth like Aaron of old—to utterly confound these workers of magic; leaders of anti-Christian seditious iniquity, the leaven of which worketh exceedingly now, preparing the way of the Anti-Christ.

Note where the 144,000 are sealed. (Rev. 7.) These are considered by nearly all students of the Scripture to refer to the Bride. This sealing is not accomplished by man or water baptism, or the following of certain leaders, but is accomplished by the Baptism of the Holy Ghost as recorded in Acts 2.

Now He which established us with you in Christ and hath anointed us in God; who hath also sealed us and given us the earnest of the Spirit in our hearts. (2 Cor. 1:21–22.)

And grieve not the Holy Spirit of God whereby ye are sealed unto the day of Redemption. (Eph. 4:30.)

After that ye believed, ye were sealed by the Holy Spirit of promise, which is the earnest of our inheritance. (Eph. 1:13 & 14.) These verses clearly prove that it was the Holy Spirit promised.

Behold, I send the promise of the Father upon you, but tarry ye in the city of Jerusalem until ye be endued with power from on high. (Luke 24:49.)

This promise, when fulfilled was followed by such unmistakable evidence that no one can doubt it who has received it. Thousands of Christians profess this sealing as well as the Baptism of the Holy Ghost, yet the Bible evidence is lacking in their lives. We want to say it is unscriptural to call mighty convictions, floods of joy, unctions or anointings, the Baptism; there is but one. Jesus said, John truly baptized with water; but ye shall be baptized with the Holy Ghost not many days hence. (Acts 1:5.)

But ye shall receive power after that the Holy Ghost has come upon you, and ye shall be witnesses unto me both in Jerusalem, and in all Judea, and in Samaria, and unto the uttermost part of the earth. (Acts 1:8.)

Now all Christians credit the fact that we are to be the recipients of the Holy Spirit, but each have their private interpretations as to His visible manifestations; some claim shouting, leaping, and falling in trances while others put stress upon inspiration, unction and divine revelation. Probably the greatest mistake has been of thinking "the anointing that abideth," (1 John 2:27), which the disciples received in the upper chamber when Christ breathed upon them, (John 20:22), the real Baptism of the Holy Spirit. But by a careful study of Acts 1:8, we find that the power was to make them witnesses. The modern idea of shouting, groaning and screaming, performed in imitation of supposed drunken disciples, is a misinterpretation of their actions; because the disciples by speaking various languages which were not understood by many in the audience—speaking as the Spirit gave them utterance—sounded like the mutterings of drunken men. These Galilean fishermen were not only witnessing to their own nation, but to the uttermost parts of the earth. The assembled Jews from different countries heard them speak the marvelous works of God in their own tongues wherein they were born.

This scene being true the same evidence would follow today as at that time, if we also are privileged to be recipients of the Baptism of the Holy Ghost; proving they did receive this promised power, for which they tarried. How much more reasonable it would be for modern Holy Ghost teachers to first receive a BIBLE EVIDENCE, such as the disciples, instead of trying to get the world to take their word for it. And how much better it would be for our modern missionaries to obey the injunction of Jesus to tarry for the same power; instead of wasting thousands of dollars, and often their lives in the vain attempt to become conversant in almost impossible tongues which the Holy Ghost could so freely speak. Knowing all languages, He could as easily speak through us one language as another were our tongues and vocal chords fully surrendered to His domination and in connection realize the precious assurance of the sealing of the Holy Ghost of promise, knowing it by the same evidence as received by the one hundred and twenty on the day of Pentecost, of Cornelius and his household, and of the church at Ephesus.

Modern Reception of the Holy Ghost

Since the days of the Apostolic church a few authentic cases of the Baptism of the Holy Spirit are recorded.

We have found that the early Catholic Fathers upon reaching the coast of Japan spoke in the native tongue; that the Irvingites, a sect that arose under the teachings of Irving, a Scotchman, during the last century, received not only the eight recorded gifts of 1 Cor. 12, but also the speaking in other tongues, which the Holy Ghost reserved as the evidence of His oncoming. A gentleman and his wife, whose names we have forgotten, received their Pentecost and spoke in the Italian language. Jenny Glassey of St. Louis, after a special time of tarrying received her Pentecost and was enabled to speak, sing, write and interpret certain African dialects. After being a missionary in Africa she became a resident of Jerusalem.

A very pious man, member of the Baptist Church, Marshaltown, Iowa, received the Baptism of the Holy Spirit. His church not honoring the presence and power of the Holy Ghost in their midst, he was gathered in by the Spiritualists who persuaded him that his Pentecostal power was but a manifestation of their nefarious mediumship. Losing his salvation and spiritual power, he became sick and afflicted, lost his mind and is today a complete wreck. How many like cases there are in this world we know not, but we do know that the narrowness of modern church Christianity, by refusing to believe and receive true Bible doctrines has driven many thousands unto Spiritualism, Theosophy, Christian Science and infidelity.

Thousands have received what they termed and supposed was the Baptism of the Holy Spirit, but which was in reality the anointing that abideth. The

first teaching on this subject that we became conversant with was that the witness of our sanctification was the Baptism of the Holy Spirit. The fallacy of
this is easily proven. For by one offering He has perfected forever them that
are sanctified. Whereof the Holy Ghost also is a witness unto us. (Heb.
10:14–15.)

The word "also" in the 15th verse precludes the teaching that the witness to
our sanctification is the Baptism of the Holy Spirit, for it proves that the witness
to our sanctification is given by the Holy Spirit the same as our justification,
and if we should claim the one at sanctification to be the Baptism of the Holy
Spirit, the word "also" would force us to claim the witness of justification to be
the Baptism of the Holy Spirit.

The fact is in justification and sanctification, the Holy Spirit witnesses to our
hearts of the inwrought work of the atonement, His personal work as the third
person in the trinity which is a gift not a grace, is not obtained in justification
or sanctification.

Later came a wave of teaching that the Holy Spirit was really a gift not
received at the time of sanctification. Accordingly hundreds sought for the
Holy Spirit in this way, receiving a special anointing such as the disciples
received in the upper chamber, when Jesus breathed upon them saying:
Receive ye the Holy Ghost. (John 20:22.) Therefore having the anointing that
abideth and teacheth like the disciples upon whom Jesus breathed, their eyes
were opened, the teaching of the Scriptures became clear and precious, the
reception of the Holy Ghost as their Anointer and Teacher. (Luke 24:45.) The
disciples obtained all that modern Holy Ghost people have, and yet this occur-
rence was ten days before Pentecost. Hungering and thirsting for the realization of the same mighty power in God's people today, which is theirs by divine
light for we truly are in the days of the restitution of all things which God has
spoken by the mouth of all His holy prophets since the world began. (Acts
3:21), we made a study of all teachings upon this subject and found none had
really the experience of Acts 2.

Pursuing our studies, we visited institutions of deep religious thought, which
were reported as having the power of the Holy Ghost; yet these all failed to tally
with the account in Acts. After careful study, we returned from an extended
trip through the east and Canada with profound conviction that no one in
these days was really enjoying the power of a personal Pentecost, while many
were anointed above measure. We ourselves had known the power of the Holy
Ghost in our lives to a wonderful degree for many years, and had such wonderful anointings that we were carried far beyond ourselves, many times for ten,
fifteen and twenty minutes words of living truth (Our minds took no part, but in
which we became an interested listener) flowed from our lips; yet this was but
the anointing that abideth, not the Baptism of the Holy Ghost as many declared
it to be. This anointing is sufficient under all circumstances for needed inspi-

ration when speaking in our tongue, but if you desire a personal Baptism of the Holy Ghost, the sealing power, escaping plagues, and putting you in the position to become a part of the Body, the Bride or the Man-Child, seek the Holy Ghost.

It was prophesied: With men of other tongues and other lips will I speak unto this people, and yet for all that will they not hear me, saith the Lord. (1 Cor. 14:21.)

Many say to us, if we were going to a foreign land we should need to speak in other tongues, what need have we of it among our own people? According to the above prophecy, God intends to use the speaking in other tongues in preaching to our people. For centuries men have been sent preaching in their own tongues to their own nation, until the people have come to believe that they are simply propagating some self-constructed creed or ideas for their pecuniary benefit.

In the close of the age, God proposes to send forth men and women preaching in languages they know not a word of, which when interpreted the hearers will know is truly a message from God, spoken through lips of clay by the power of the Holy Ghost. This is truly the Acme of inspiration, prayed for every Sabbath and desired by all true ministers of God.

Do you mean to say that John Wesley and others since, did not have this Baptism? Exactly; he and many since have enjoyed a mighty anointing that abideth, and spoke like the holy men of old as they were moved by the Holy Ghost but the power of this Pentecostal Baptism of the Holy Spirit is a different thing entirely.

The Baptism of the Holy Spirit is especially given now as the sealing. Therefore the sureness of the last days.

On Oct. 15, 1900, we were led to open in Topeka, Kansas, a Bible School which became widely known sometime later as "the College of Bethel." Its unique features and teachings became subjects of the daily papers throughout the land. Its only text-book was the Bible; its only object utter abandonment in obedience to the commandments of Jesus, however unconventional and impractical this might seem to the world today. About forty students entered . . .

Nearly all of the students had been religious workers of considerable spiritual growth and attainment. Like many of our readers, [they] said they had received the Baptism of the Holy Ghost a number of years ago, but in spite of this we continued to teach what we believed to be in the Word of God, and in the mind of Jesus; a mighty Baptism such as the disciples received of old, to make His saints today world-wide powers for good, to the end that this gospel might be preached to all the world as a witness; "To remove the covering cast over all the face of the earth," for we believe this to be the will of God, and the accomplishment of the same well pleasing in His sight.

In the closing days of the fall term of 1900, we had our examination on Repentance, Justification, Consecration, Sanctification and Healing. As there yet remained a few days before the opening of the New Year, the students were required to carefully study the subject of the Baptism of the Holy Spirit. The main object of this study was to discover the real Bible evidence of this Baptism so that we might know and obtain it, instead of being confused by the chaotic claims of modern Holy Ghost teachers.

On New Year's night, Miss Agnes N. Ozman of Beatrice, Neb., a missionary lady who had attended several Bible Schools and done considerable religious work; one who had had mighty anointings and had for years the "anointing that abideth" which she mistook for the Baptism was convinced of her need of a personal Pentecost. She desired hands laid upon her that she might receive the gift of the Holy Ghost. During invocation of hands prayer was offered, she was filled with the Holy Ghost and spake with other tongues as the Spirit gave utterance. Upon beholding this marvelous restoration of apostolic power in our midst, all became hungry, earnestly desiring a personal realization of the same in our lives; remembering that Peter had said, This promise is to you and to your children, and to all that are afar off, even as many as the Lord our God shall call. (Acts 2:39.)

Scarcely eating or sleeping, the School with one accord waited upon God. On the night of the 3rd of January, 1901, we were all assembled in an upper room. A most wonderful power pervaded the atmosphere, and twelve students were filled with the Holy Ghost and began to speak with other tongues as the Spirit gave them utterance; while several in the room saw above their heads, cloven tongues of fire, as in the days of old. Thus was the Church militant again permitted to realize the Baptism of the Holy Spirit, which has since then been given to not only others in the School but to those in other cities and states.

Like seekers for justification, sanctification and healing some then and others since, have sought for and failing to obtain the Baptism, turned back, saying it was either not for them or deriding it as mere bramble which had no special import or value. The fact remains that it is the Baptism of the Holy Spirit of promise, that seals the Bride and the same Baptism that puts us in one Body, (the Church).

We wish here to give a little advice: No one in the school or in our work or meetings since, who protested that they had received the Baptism of the Holy Spirit, have ever obtained it; while those who have freely acknowledged and given glory to God for all His wonderful anointings, manifestations and gifts of the Spirit, humbly surrendering the claim to this Baptism, have obtained the power desired, and gone forth speaking in tongues as the authoritative evidence.

Many in our meetings have said: "Oh, I have had the baptism of the Holy Spirit for years," and many with an extra boast of human unction: "I have received the Baptism of fire."

We have heard of a Bible School that made most marvelous claims in regard to the Baptism of the Holy Spirit. Like many individuals above spoken of in different meetings, said: We have received the Baptism of the Holy Spirit, but as we are bent upon the world's evangelization, we must have this. This Bible School sought in vain, month after month for the speaking in other languages.

Now we want to say to private individuals or to schools, that the speaking in other tongues is an inseparable part of the Baptism of the Holy Spirit distinguishing it from all previous works; and that no one has received Baptism of the Holy Spirit who has not a Bible evidence to show for it. As pardon is received as a result of sincere repentance, restitution and surrender; sanctification received as the result of entire consecration; so the speaking in other tongues is received as the result of this Baptism. The Holy Spirit, thru witnessing to the work of Calvary in our lives, in justification and sanctification, reserves the speaking in other tongues as evidence of His own incoming.

The following selection is taken from *The Everlasting Gospel* (Baxter Springs, Kans.: Charles F. Parham, 1911).

Chapter II: Address by Charles F. Parham

What Is Spirit?

There are several meanings to the word. Man has a spirit. God is a spirit. There are psychic waves of influence, spirit influences that emanate from each one of us, sometimes so strong that when sitting in a room, with no knowledge that there is another individual in the room, his presence is felt; one may become so responsive to these influences that when blindfolded in the presence of different people they are differentiated purely by the atmosphere, or aura. Madam Guyon says in her memoirs that when Father LaCombe came to see her, her husband would not allow her to speak to the priest, but that such a radiating influence proceeded from that holy man of God that strength came to her when he came to talk with her husband. What we need as Christians is a sanctified influence, a sanctified spirit, so that the people with whom we come in contact with will feel a benign, a beneficial influence flowing out from us to them. Then others will feel and know the power of that spirit life, because out from our inward parts will flow streams of living water to our fellow men, imperceptibly, and which cannot be resisted. Then the influence of our life upon others will be such as to win them to God, and parents will have an influence over sons and daughters never dreamed of before. Oh, for a sanctified spirit in every Christian!

Sanctification is the second work of grace and also the last work of grace. Sanctification is a cleansing to make holy, and is an act of God's free grace. Sanctification begins in the inner man and reaches out until the soul is sanctified entirely; then comes the sanctification of the body from all inbred disease, and from the inbred principle of disease. Disease came with the fall, "When dying thou shalt die" was pronounced upon the body as well as the soul. But when the body is sanctified from its inbred tendency and predisposition to disease, as well as all other forms of inbred sin and carnality, when the spirit influence of our lives, whether it covers only the radius of our own families or whether that influence shall reach out to our neighborhood, or shall become world-wide, we shall send forth a sanctifying influence wherever that tide of influence reaches, and its power shall be for good—it shall be a sanctifying influence.

Sanctification Is Not Pentecost

The disciples were God-fearing, Godly, justified men before Jesus met them. Make note of that. The moment that Jesus called them to consecrate their lives they did not stop at sentimental consecration; they made one hundred-fold consecration, such as is scarcely known in these days, and followed Him every step of the way. For three years and one-half they followed Him. The disciples were sanctified before the day of Pentecost. "Now ye are clean through the Word which I have spoken unto you."—John 15:3; 13–10.

Too many confuse the grace of sanctification with the endowment of power, or the Baptism of the Holy Spirit; others have taken "the anointing that abideth" for the Baptism, and thus failed to reach the glory and power of the true Pentecost. The great difficulty with modern "holiness" teachers has been that they have tried to make holiness the bone, marrow, fiber, tissue, and muscle, of our faith. Should we build a church on the coming of the Lord, or on Divine healing, or any other thing? It would be just as reasonable as to build on holiness; for holiness is but one step in the plan of God's great salvation. When people get side-tracked and narrow and hobbified on a subject, everything begins and ends with that subject; just as some people have set their minds on "tongues," and can see nothing in this Pentecost movement but "tongues."

The witness to sanctification is the same power that witnesses to our conversion, no more, no less; but you have a cleaner life, you have a maturity, a conquering power; the carnal nature has been cleansed, the flesh purified. The witnessing power of the Holy Spirit has the same character it had in conversion, witnessing to what has been done by the blood of Jesus Christ. The

Holy Spirit witnesses in justification and sanctification; you are forgiven and cleansed, and you have the protection of the blood of Jesus Christ. But you are not sanctified by the Holy Spirit; the Bible does not teach it, neither does the Word say that the Gentiles were sanctified by the Holy Spirit. Read carefully, and you will see that they are legally sanctified or set apart, making it possible for them to receive the Gospel, and it was not a process of purification. "For, by one offering he hath perfected forever them that were sanctified. Whereof the Holy Ghost is also a witness to us." — (Heb. 10:14, 15)

The Baptism of the Holy Spirit is a gift of Power upon the sanctified life; so when we get it we have the same evidence that the disciples had on the Day of Pentecost (Acts 2:3–4) in speaking new tongues. (See also Acts 10:45–46; Acts 19:6; I Cor. 14–21.)

If sanctification were Pentecost you would get the same result as in the second chapter of Acts. How dare anyone claim to have the same evidence as in the second chapter of Acts unless the result agrees! The witness to your sanctification bears out the work of cleansing through the power of the blood of the Lord Jesus Christ. God gave His only begotten Son that we might be converted, but Jesus gave Himself to the Church that he might sanctify and cleanse it by His precious blood. It was Jesus who gave himself for your sanctification.

Wherever justification is mentioned in the Bible it refers to your sins; where sanctification is mentioned, it speaks of the cleansing power. It is God's business to clean you up, and when you are wholly set apart, He will sanctify you.

The Anointing of the Holy Spirit

I want to distinctly nail one thought. The teaching that one has not the Holy Spirit at all until one gets the speaking in tongues is absolutely untrue and not borne out by the Scriptures. As we have previously stated, the Holy Spirit enlighteneth every person born into the world; the Holy Spirit convicts individuals, witnesses to conversion, and witnesses in sanctification.

The anointing of the Holy Spirit takes precedence to the Baptism of the Holy Spirit. When the vessel is cleansed and prepared as an instrument, then it needs something else. Soon after His resurrection Jesus came where His disciples were assembled, "the door being shut," and He breathed on them, and said: "Receive ye the Holy Ghost," and they did; but it was seven weeks before Pentecost fell. (John 20:19, 22.)

Many Christians, preachers, and people have had the experience for years. God comes to them from time to time in what we may term occasional anointings. The anointing of the Holy Spirit is sometimes given even before sanctification comes. When people tell you that you should not work before you get tongues, they are putting a premium on tongues that will tempt people to make guttural sounds and simulate a speaking in tongues, which leads to many false and injurious things under the guise of the Holy Spirit. I want to say that unless you use all that you have got in your justified experience you will never get sanctified. It is the fruit bearing branches He purges. If you want sanctification you have got to bear fruit, got to be purged and cleansed, and if you want Pentecost, you have got to obey the commandments before He will send the Comforter. Have you spiritual discernment enough to know whether you are in that place of position where the travail of your soul is really going to give birth to a new experience? If you have not, then there is work that you must do before you receive the blessing.

A man passing down the road saw a little boy in the field plowing some corn that was yellow and thin.

"Son," he said, "it does not look like your corn would amount to much; it is so yellow."

"Yes," said the boy, "father planted the yellow kind."

"It doesn't look as though you have much of a crop."

"No," was the reply, "father planted on shares."

That is the trouble with so many people's religious experience. Their time is taken up with the world, the flesh, and the Devil, and the Lord gets only a little share of it; unless you are living up to all the light you have in your consecrated and sanctified experience, you are not ready for Pentecost.

The anointing of the Holy Spirit is given to illuminate His Word, to open the Scriptures, and to place the spiritual man in direct communication with the mind of God; man will be in instant communication with the mind and will of God, and not only so, but to directly connect this mind with your spirit. This is occultic in the sense that the mind of the spirit in you becomes the receptacle for the thought waves of wisdom that have been let loose by the minds of the church of the past ages, until the wisdom of the ages, floating ever upon the waves of ether, are at your command to draw from. This is a profound, though little understood, truth.

But let us get this one simple thought: Let us realize that it is not this poor, spongy brain that has absorbed a little modern wisdom—the thought of other people—but let us know that it is possible for God to speak through the subconscious mind by His Holy Spirit's power, until, trained and in touch with the power of Divinity, beautified and enhanced in spirituality, it is tuned to catch the deeper thoughts of God and of the ages and transmit them to others.

CHAPTER THREE

William J. Seymour
(1870–1922)

W ILLIAM SEYMOUR spent his first twenty-five years of life near his birthplace in Centerville, Louisiana. His parents were Catholic, but they attended the Baptist church as well, and they encouraged the intense spirituality that was evident in the dreams and visions of their young son. In his adult life, Seymour was a seeker, moving through a variety of holiness groups before finally connecting with Charles Parham in 1905 at a Bible school Parham had just established in Dallas, Texas.

Because Seymour was an African American, Parham would not let him sit in the classroom, but he did allow him to listen from the hall. What Seymour heard changed his life. Convinced that he needed to be baptized by the Holy Spirit, he began single-mindedly to seek that experience and the sign of tongues that Parham said would follow. Before he had received the experience, however, he was called to a pastorate in the booming West Coast town of Los Angeles.

At his new preaching post, Seymour began to proclaim a Parham-style pentecostal gospel, and the church almost immediately locked him out of the building. Seymour had the support of a small remnant of the church, however, and they continued meeting for prayer in their homes. Finally, the power of the Spirit fell on Seymour's little flock, and he, along with all the others, received the baptism of the Spirit and began to speak in tongues. Word of what had taken place spread quickly, and soon a new place of worship was required in order to accommodate the crowds. A shabby warehouse on Azusa Street, which had formerly been an African Methodist Episcopal church, was purchased by the group, and the Azusa Street revival was off and running.

Seymour's theological education consisted of a few classes he had taken at an institution called God's Bible School in Cincinnati along with the additional insights he had gleaned while sitting in the hallway of Parham's school in Dallas, but he found himself needing to give theological guidance to a mushrooming movement of pentecostal faith. Seymour and his associates at the Azusa Street Mission used their monthly newspaper, *The Apostolic Faith*, as their teaching medium, and soon a rudimentary theology was being formulated for the movement as a whole.

In contrast to Parham's apocalyptic orientation, Seymour's concern was pastoral: how to explain to ordinary folks in the pew what it means to be a Christian and what one can expect from God. Articles excerpted from this newspaper provide a sense of Seymour's pastoral orientation. They answer simple questions with straightforward prose: What is the atonement? How do you receive the baptism of the Holy Ghost? What are the gifts of the Spirit and how are they obtained?

The heyday of the revival in Los Angeles lasted only a few years, and then developments moved elsewhere. Instead of being the epicenter of the movement, the Azusa Street Mission became just one more small, predominantly African American pentecostal congregation. The final document reprinted here, which is taken from a manual of doctrine and discipline that Seymour published in 1915, comes from this later period of his career. Seymour's pastoral disposition is still clearly evident, but there is a new pragmatism in these passages along with a hint of sadness: racial discord is bemoaned, differences with other pentecostals groups are outlined, and, perhaps most significantly, speaking in tongues is no longer emphasized in the same way.[1]

The following selection is taken from *The Apostolic Faith* 1:1 (September 1906).

The Precious Atonement

Children of God, partakers of the precious atonement, let us study and see what there is in it for us.

First. Through the atonement we receive forgiveness of sins.

Second. We receive sanctification through the blood of Jesus. "Wherefore Jesus also that he might sanctify the people with his own blood, suffered

---

[1] For more information, see Jacobsen, *Thinking in the Spirit*, 61–84.

without the gate." Sanctified from all original sin, we become sons of God. "For both he that sanctifieth and they who are sanctified are all of one: for which cause he is not ashamed to call them brethren." Heb. 2:11. (It seems Jesus would be ashamed to call them brethren, if they were not sanctified.) Then you will not be ashamed to tell men and demons that you are sanctified, and are living a pure and holy life free from sin, a life that gives you power over the world, the flesh, and the devil. The devil does not like that kind of testimony. Through this precious atonement, we have freedom from all sin, though we are living in this old world, we are permitted to sit in heavenly places in Christ Jesus.

Third. Healing of our bodies. Sickness and disease are destroyed through the precious atonement of Jesus. O how we ought to honor the stripes of Jesus, for "with his stripes we are healed." How we ought to honor that precious body which the Father sanctified and sent into the world, not simply set apart, but really sanctified, soul, body and spirit, free from sickness, disease and everything of the devil. A body that knew no sin and disease was given for these imperfect bodies of ours. Not only is the atonement for the sanctification of our souls, but for the sanctification of our bodies from inherited disease. It matters not what has been in the blood. Every drop of blood we received from our mother is impure. Sickness is born in a child just as original sin is born in the child. He was manifested to destroy the works of the devil. Every sickness is of the devil.

Man in the garden of Eden was pure and happy and knew no sickness till that unholy visitor came into the garden, then his whole system was poisoned and it has been flowing in the blood of all the human family down the ages till God spoke to his people and said, "I am the Lord that healeth thee." The children of Israel practiced divine healing. David, after being healed of rheumatism, (perhaps contracted in the caves where he hid himself from his pursuers,) testified saying, "Bless the Lord, O my soul, and all that is within me bless his holy name, who forgiveth all thine iniquities, who healeth all the diseases." David knew what it was to be healed. Healing continued with God's people till Solomon's heart was turned away by strange wives, and he brought in the black arts and mediums, and they went whoring after familiar spirits. God had been their healer, but after they lost the Spirit they turned to the arm of flesh to find something to heal their diseases.

Thank God, we have a living Christ among us to heal our diseases. He will heal every case. The prophet had said, "With his stripes we are healed," and it was fulfilled when Jesus came. Also "He hath borne our grief," (which means sickness, as translators tell us.) Now if Jesus bore our sicknesses, why should we bear them? So we get full salvation through the atonement of Jesus.

Fourth. And we get the baptism with the Holy Ghost and fire upon the sanctified life. We get Christ enthroned and crowned in our hearts. Let us lift up Christ to the world in all His fullness, not only in healing and salvation from all sin, but in His power to speak all the languages of the world. We need the triune God to enable us to do this.

We that are the messengers of this precious atonement ought to preach all of it, justification, sanctification, healing, the baptism with the Holy Ghost, and signs following. "How shall we escape if we neglect so great salvation?" God is now confirming His word by granting signs and wonders to follow the preaching of the full gospel in Los Angeles.

The following selections are taken from *The Apostolic Faith* 1, no. 5 (January 1907).

"Receive Ye the Holy Ghost"

1. —The first step in seeking the baptism with the Holy Ghost, is to have a clear knowledge of the new birth in our souls, which is the first work of grace and brings everlasting life to our souls. "Therefore being justified by faith, we have peace with God." Every one of us that repents of our sins and turns to the Lord Jesus with faith in Him, receives forgiveness of sins. Justification and regeneration are simultaneous. The pardoned sinner becomes a child of God in justification.

2. —The next step for us is to have a clear knowledge, by the Holy Spirit, of the second work of grace wrought in our hearts by the power of the Blood and the Holy Ghost. Heb. 10, 14, 15, "For by one offering, He hath perfected forever them that are sanctified, whereof the Holy Ghost also is a witness to us." The Scripture also teaches (Heb. 2, 11) "For both He that sanctifieth and they who are sanctified are all of one; for which cause He is not ashamed to call them brethren." So we have Christ crowned and enthroned in our hearts, the tree of life. We have the brooks and streams of salvation flowing in our soul, but praise God, we can have the rivers. For the Lord Jesus says, " 'He that believeth on me, as the Scripture hath said, out of his innermost being shall flow rivers of living water.' This spake He of the Spirit, for the Holy Ghost was not yet given." But, praise our God, He is now given and being poured out upon all flesh. All races, nations, and tongues are receiving the baptism with the Holy Ghost and fire, according to the prophecy of Joel.

3. —When we have a clear knowledge of justification and sanctification, through the precious Blood of Jesus Christ in our hearts, then we can be a recipient of the baptism with the Holy Ghost. Many people today are sanctified, cleansed from all sin, and perfectly consecrated to God, but they have never obeyed the Lord according to Acts I. 4, 5, 8 and Luke 24, 39 for their

real personal Pentecost, the enduement of power for service and work and for sealing unto the day of redemption. The baptism with the Holy Ghost is a free gift without repentance, upon the sanctified, cleansed vessel. II. Cor. 1, 21–22, "Now He which establisheth us with you in Christ, and hath anointed us, is God, who hath also sealed us, and given the earnest of the Spirit in our hearts." Praise our God for the sealing of the Holy Spirit unto the day of redemption.

Dearly beloved, the only people that will meet our Lord and Savior Jesus Christ and go with Him into the marriage supper of the Lamb, are the wise virgins — not only saved and sanctified, with pure and clean hearts but having the baptism with the Holy Ghost. The others we find will not be prepared. They have some oil in their lamps but they have not the double portion of His Holy Spirit.

The disciples were filled with the unction of the Holy Spirit before Pentecost, that sustained them until they received the Holy Ghost baptism. Many people today are filled with joy and gladness, but they are far from the enduement of power. Sanctification brings rest and sweetness and quietness to our souls, for we are one with the Lord Jesus and are able to obey His precious Word, that "Man shall not live by bread alone, but by every word that proceedeth out of the mouth of God," and we are feeding upon Christ.

But let us wait for the promise of the Father upon our souls, according to Jesus' Word, "John truly baptized with water, but ye shall be baptized with the Holy Ghost not many days hence. . . . Ye shall receive power after that the Holy Ghost is come upon you; and ye shall be witnesses unto me, both in Jerusalem and in all Judea, and in Samaria, and unto the uttermost part of the earth." Acts 1:5, 8. Glory! Glory! Hallelujah! O worship, get down on your knees and ask the Holy Ghost to come in, and you will find Him right at your heart's door, and He will come in. Prove Him now. Amen.

Gifts of the Spirit

"Now concerning spiritual gifts brethren, I would not have you ignorant."

Paul was speaking to the Corinthian Church at this time. They were like Christ's people everywhere today. Many of His people do not know their privileges in this blessed Gospel. The Gospel of Christ is the power of God unto salvation to everyone that believeth. And in order that we might know His power, we must forever abide in the Work of God that we may have the precious fruits of the Spirit, and not only the fruits but the precious gifts that Father has for His little ones.

Dearly beloved, may we search the Scriptures and see for ourselves whether we are measuring up to every word that proceedeth out of the mouth of God.

If we will remain in the Scriptures and follow the blessed Holy Spirit all the way, we will be able to measure up to the Word of God in all of its fulness. Paul prayed in Eph. 3. 16, "That He would grant you, according to the riches of His glory, to be strengthened with might by His Spirit in the inner man; that Christ may dwell in your hearts by faith; that ye being rooted and grounded in love, may be able to comprehend with all saints, what is the breadth, and length, and depth, and height, and to know the love of Christ which passeth knowledge; that ye might be filled with all the fulness of God. Now unto Him that is able to do exceeding abundantly above all that we ask or think, according to the power that worketh in us."

Many people say today that tongues are the least gift of any that the Lord can give, and they do not need it, and ask What good is it to us? But by careful study of the Word, we see in the 14th [chapter] of Corinthians, Paul telling the church to "follow after charity and desire spiritual gifts." Charity means Divine love without which we will never be able to enter heaven. Gifts all will fail, but Divine love will last through all eternity. And right in the same verse he says, "Desire spiritual gifts, but rather that ye may prophesy," that is to say, preach in your own tongue, which will build up the saints and the church.

But he says in the next verse, "For he that speaketh in an unknown tongue, speaketh not unto men, but unto God, for no man understandeth him, howbeit in the Spirit, he speaketh mysteries. . . . But he that prophesieth speaketh unto man to edification, exhortation and comfort." He that prophesies in his own tongue edifies the church; but he that speaks in unknown tongues edifies himself. His spirit is being edified, while the church is not edified, because they do not understand what he says unless the Lord gives somebody the interpretation of the tongue.

Here is where many stumble that have not this blessed gift to use in the Spirit. They say, What good is it when you do not know what you are talking about?

Praise God, every gift He gives is a good gift. It is very blessed, for when the Lord gets ready, He can speak in any language He chooses to speak. You ask, "Is not prophecy the best gift?" Prophecy is the best gift to the church, for it builds up the saints and edifies them and exalts them to higher things in the Lord Jesus. If a brother or sister is speaking in tongues and cannot speak any English, but preaches altogether in tongues and has no interpretation, they are less than he that prophesies, but if they interpret they are just as great.

May God help all of His precious people to read the 14th [chapter] of I. Cor., and give them the real interpretation of the Word. May we all use our gift to the glory of God and not worship the gift. The Lord gives us power to use it to His own glory and honor.

Many times, when we were receiving this blessed Pentecost, we all used to break out in tongues; but we have learned to be quieter with the gift. Often when God sends a blessed wave upon us, we all may speak in tongues for awhile, but we will not keep it up while [the] preaching service is going on, for we want to be obedient to the Word, that everything may be done decently and in order and without confusion. Amen.

The following selections are taken from *The Doctrines and Discipline of the Azusa Street Apostolic Mission of Los Angeles, Cal. with Scripture Readings* (Los Angeles: William J. Seymour, 1915).

The New Birth

St. John 3:5, 6; Rom. 8:7, 8; Tit. 3:5; Salvation comes through the blood of Jesus Christ. When we get it, we will know it, and if we lose it we will know it. There is only one way to get it: It is by repenting and believing the Gospel. St. Mark 1:15.

Salvation is not feeling; it is a real knowledge by the Holy Spirit, bearing witness with our spirit. . . .

Some people to-day cannot believe they have the Holy Ghost without some outward signs: that is Heathenism. The witness of the Holy Spirit inward is the greatest knowledge of knowing God, for he is invisible. St. John 14:17. It is all right to have the signs following, but not to pin our faith to outward manifestations. We are to go by the word of God. Our thought must be in harmony with the Bible or else we will have a strange religion. We must not teach any more than the Apostles [taught]. I Cor. 12:1–34; I Cor. 13:1–13; I Cor. 14:1–40.

   1. The Character of the Church.—A church constitutes a kind of spiritual kingdom in the world, but not of the world; whose king is Christ; whose law is his word; whose institutions are his ordinances; whose duty is his service; whose reward is his blessing.

In all matters of faith and conscience, as well as in all matters of internal order and government, a church is "under law to Christ": (I Cor. 9:21) but as men and citizens, its members must "submit themselves to governors" (I Peter 2:14) like other men, so far as shall not interfere with, or contravene, the claims of the divine law and authority upon them—they must "render unto Cesar the things that are Cesar's, and unto God the things that are God's," (Matt. 22:21) remembering that God's claims are supreme, and annihilate all claims that contradict or oppose them.

2. The Design of Church.—The evident design of our Saviour in founding and preserving the church in the world, was, that it should be a monument in the midst of guilty men, bearing perpetual witness against the wickedness of the world, and to the goodness of God. But especially that she should be living testimonies to the work of redemption, "the light of the world," and "the salt of the earth." Matt. 5:13, 14.

The Church constitutes the effective instrumentality by which the will of God and the knowledge of salvation through Christ are made known to men; at the same time she form[s] homes for the saints on earth; sheep-folds for the safety of the flock, and schools for the instruction and training of the children of the covenant; while she encourages the penitent and warns the careless. The church should well understand her "high calling," and seek to accomplish it, "according to the will of God." Gal. 1:4.

3. The Authority of the Church.—The authority of a church is limited to its own members, and applies to all matters of Christian character, and whatever involves the welfare of religion. It is designed to secure in all its members a conduct and conversations "becoming godliness."

This authority is derived directly from God; not from states, nor princes, nor people; not from its own officers, nor its members, nor from any other source of ecclesiastical or civil power or right. But Christ "is head over all things to the church" (Eph. 1:22) and also as of right, "the church is subject to Christ" (Eph. 5:24). . . .

Apostolic Address

To the Members of the Apostolic Faith Church.

Dearly Beloved Brethren: We esteem it our privilege and duty most earnestly to recommend to you this volume, which contains the Doctrines and Discipline of our Church, both of which, as we believe, are agreeable to the word of God, the only and the sufficient rule of faith and practice. Yet the Church, using the liberty given to it by its Lord, and taught by the experience of a long series of years and by observations made on ancient and modern Churches, has from time to time modified its Discipline so as better to secure the end for which it was [founded].

We believe that God's design in raising up the Apostolic Faith Church in America was to evangelize over these lands. As a proof hereof we have seen since 1900 that time of an extraordinary work of God extending throughout all the United States and Territories, and throughout the whole world.

In 1906 the colored people of the City of Los Angeles felt they were led by the Holy Spirit that they decided to have Elder W. J. Seymour of Houston, Texas, to come to Los Angeles, Cal., and give them some Bible teaching. He came Feb. 22nd, and started Feb. 24th, 1906. From his teaching one of the greatest revivals was held in the city of Los Angeles. People of all nations came and got their cup full. Some came from Africa, some came from India, China, Japan, and England.

Very soon division arose through some of our brethren, and the Holy Spirit was grieved. We want all of our white brethren and white sisters to feel free in our churches and missions, in spite of all the trouble we have had with some of our white brethren in causing diversion, and spreading wild fire and fanaticism. Some of our colored brethren caught the disease of this spirit of division also. We find according to God's word [that we are] to be one in the Holy Spirit, not in the flesh; but in the Holy Spirit, for we are one body. I Cor. 12:12–14. If some of our white brethren have prejudices and discrimination (Gal. 2:11–20), we can't do it, because God calls us to follow the Bible. Matt. 17:8; Matt. 23. We must love all men as Christ commands. (Heb. 12:14). Now because we don't take them for directors, it is not for discrimination, but for peace, [t]o keep down race war in the Churches and friction, so they can have greater liberty and freedom in the Holy Spirit. We are sorry for this, but it is the best now and in later years for the work. We hope everyone that reads these lines may realize it is for the best; not for the worse. Some of our white brethren and sisters have never left us in all the division; they have stuck to us. We love our white brethrens and sisters and welcome them. Jesus Christ takes in all people in his Salvation. Christ is all and for all. He is neither [a] black nor white man, nor Chinaman, nor Hindoo, nor Japanese, but God. God is Spirit because without his spirit we cannot be saved. St. John 3:3–5; Rom. 8:9. . . .

Sound Doctrine

We must have sound doctrines in our work. We don't believe that the soul sleeps in the grave until the resurrection morning. The next we don't believe in being baptized in the name of Jesus only. We believe in baptizing in the name of the Father, and the Son, and the Holy Ghost, as Jesus taught his disciples (Matt. 28:19–20). We do not believe in keeping Saturday as the Christian Sabbath, we do not believe in dipping a person three times in order that he may be properly baptized. We believe in burying the candidate once in the name of the Father, and in the Son, and in the Holy Ghost, Amen. We don't believe in the Fleshy Doctrine of the male and female kissing and calling it the Holy Kiss. It hurts the cause of Christ, and caused our good to be evilly spoken of. We believe in the Holy Brethren greeting the Brethren, and the Holy Sisters greeting the Holy Sisters with a kiss.

The Support of the Ministry

Our ministers that labor in the work of the Lord and give all their time to the Gospel should be supported by the Gospel. I Tim. 5:17–18. Those that labor in Doctrine and giving the word should be nicely carried, for they are worthy of it. I Cor. 9:7–11. We must support the Gospel or the Gospel will die on our hands and the enemy will get in and destroy the flock of God. How would a man know that he was born of the Spirit, if he did not have the inward witness? He would have to look for some outward sign. But God's word says he that believeth on the son of God, hath the witness in himself. I John 5:10. How do we take the gift of tongues? We believe that all God's children that have Faith in God can pray to God for an out pouring of the Holy Spirit upon the Holy sanctified life and receive a great filling of the Holy Spirit and speak in new tongues, as the spirit gives utterance. But we don't base our Faith on it as essential to our salvation. Someone will ask: How do you know when you will get the Holy Ghost? He, the spirit of truth, will guide you into all the truth. St. John 16:13. The gift of the Holy Ghost is more than speaking in the tongues. He is wisdom, power, truth, holiness. He is a person that teaches us the truth.

How does our doctrine differ with the other Pentecostal brethren? First, they claim that a man or woman has not the Holy Spirit, except they speak in tongues. So that is contrary to the teaching of Christ. Matt 7:21–23. If we would base our faith on tongues being the evidence of the gift of the Holy Ghost, it would knock out our faith in the blood of Christ, and the inward witness of the Holy Spirit bearing witness with our spirit. Rom. 8:14–16.

CHAPTER FOUR

George Floyd Taylor
(1881–1934)

G EORGE FLOYD TAYLOR was a North Carolinian. Born in the town of Magnolia in 1881, Taylor faced so many difficulties as an infant that people thought it was a miracle he survived. He struggled with a variety of physical disabilities for the rest of his life. Taylor was a fighter, however, and he succeeded against odds that might have discouraged others.

His original plan was to become a respectable Methodist minister, but after a year at the University of North Carolina (1901–1902), he dropped out to join the new, radical, and decidedly not respectable Holiness Church being organized by Albert Blackmon Crumpler. Taylor's abilities and his indefatigable spirit soon drew him into the top leadership core of the new denomination. His educational plans were temporarily set aside, but Taylor eventually finished his bachelor's degree at UNC in 1928 and went on to obtain a master's degree in history in 1930.

When Taylor joined Crumpler's Holiness Church, it was not yet pentecostal; in fact, pentecostalism was still an unknown entity in North Carolina. Once the Azusa revival got underway, however, news spread quickly through the holiness networks of the South, and Taylor felt compelled to examine the new movement. He was soon a confirmed believer, receiving the baptism of the Holy Spirit in January of 1907. Taylor never did anything halfway, and once convinced of the truth of pentecostalism, he became one of its most ardent champions. Soon he was denouncing anyone in the Holiness Church who refused to accept the new pentecostal message. The church split in two, with some members determined to hold onto their older holiness views, while another cohort, Taylor included, left to start their own Pentecostal Holiness denomination.

Taylor was perhaps the most finicky theologian of the early pentecostal period. He insisted that there was one and only one best way of describing God's activity in the world, and it was his goal to get that description right. While his theology could take on a polemical tone, and while he never hesitated to criticize views he thought were inaccurate or wrong-headed, his central aim was simply to get it right—to construct a theology for the pentecostal movement that left no room for debilitating ambiguity or inarticulate conviction.

The readings below include four chapters taken from Taylor's book *The Spirit and the Bride*, published in 1907. These selections illustrate Taylor's precisionism at its best. In clear and unambiguous terms he explains the person and character of God and then discusses the different ways in which God's power is and is not manifest in the world today. Early pentecostalism could be quite fluid in both its practices and its beliefs. Taylor's goal, at the very beginning of the movement while the Azusa revival was still underway, was to set up a system of theological boundaries that would help channel, direct, and control the hot, crackling spirituality of the movement and keep it from drifting off into heresy.

Being theologically precise, however, did not prevent Taylor from being creative at the same time. The two chapters reproduced from his book *The Second Coming of Christ* (1916) represent this other side of Taylor's theology. These chapters summarize Taylor's view of human history as a struggle between God and Satan. In a very interesting way he links Satan with the Old Testament figure of Nimrod (who built the tower of Babel) and then argues that this same Nimrod will someday reappear as the Antichrist of the final days. To explain how this can happen, Taylor develops a theory of demonic reincarnation that sounds almost Hindu in the way he articulates it. Taylor's writings—and this is true of other early pentecostal theologians as well—can take you by surprise. He was interested in exploring truth wherever that might take him and despite what other theologians might say, as long as that exploration did not contradict what he took to be the plain meaning of Scripture.[1]

The following selections are taken from *The Spirit and The Bride: A Scriptural Presentation of the Operations, Manifestations, Gifts and Fruit of the Holy Spirit in His Relation to the Bride with Special Reference to the "Latter Rain" Revival* (Dunn, N.C.: George F. Taylor, 1907).

Chapter I. The Spirit—A Person

. . . God, in the most hidden absoluteness of His being, in which the whole Godhead and all things stand, is indescribable; but there are embodied

---
[1] For more information, see Jacobsen, *Thinking in the Spirit*, 84–110.

in this Godhead three blessed personages, each of which is indescribable, and each of which is God; and yet the three together are still the indescribable One.

We read in John 4:24 that "God is a Spirit"; but we also read in I Cor. 15:44; "There is a natural body, and there is a spiritual body." So we find that the Scriptures speak of the different parts of the Father's body. "The clouds are the dust of his feet" (Nah. 1:3); "Eyes of the Lord" (Zech. 4:10); "Behold, the Lord's hand is not shortened, that it cannot save; neither his ear heavy, that it cannot hear" (Isa. 59:1).

We know that the Son has a body, for He "was made Flesh, and dwelt among us" (John 1:14). "And was made in the likeness of men" (Phil. 2:7). When He ascended to heaven He took His body with Him.

There is no Scripture which seems to teach that the Holy Spirit has a body; and yet He is the Personal God, and as much so as God the Father or God the Son; forming with the Father and the Son a unity in trinity and the Trinity in unity. He is as eternal as the Father and the Son; we read of Him from the beginning. "And the Spirit of God moved upon the face of the waters" (Gen. 1:2). As He was one in the councils (Gen. 1:26) of the Trinity in the eternal past, as He is now and ever will be in the advancement of God's kingdom, so was He one with Christ during His earthly ministry. The Holy Spirit was personally at one with the Son of Man from the time of His conception throughout His whole earthly life. Listen at the wondrous annunciation made to the Virgin Mary: "The Holy Ghost shall come upon thee, and the power of the Highest shall overshadow thee; therefore also that holy thing which shall be born of thee shall be called the Son of God" (Luke 1:35). At His baptism, the Holy Spirit in form like a dove came upon Him. Jesus said, "If I cast out devils by the Spirit of God, then the kingdom of God is come unto you" (Matt. 12:28). Thus He clearly sets forth their entire cooperation. Jesus said again, "I and my Father are one" (John 10:30). So these three persons, Father, Son, and Holy Ghost, form the Trinity in unity. The Father has a body and Son has a body, but the Holy Spirit dwells in the body of the Father and in the body of the Son, thus uniting the Father and the Son and making One of the three.

The Spirit is not a vapor or an influence, as many suppose, but a real Person going forth from the Father and Son, and serving in their behalf. He is God himself imparted to work in His children the good pleasure of His own will, making his grace avail in them and for them, helping their infirmities, witnessing to their salvation, and carrying into effect all the divine administrations of the kingdom of grace.

Since the Holy Spirit has no body, God has to reveal Him and His work to us through material emblems . . .

Chapter III. The Seven Spirits of God

In Revelation 1:4; 3:1, and 4:5, we read of the seven Spirits of God; while in Ephesians 4:4 we are told that there is but one Spirit. Harmony exists between these Scriptures in the fact that there is but one Spirit, yet the Holy Spirit, as sent forth for the illumination, comfort and edification of all the subjects of God's redeeming grace, is represented to our finite minds by sevens. This does not infer that the Spirit is divided, but He is the one Spirit in whatever way He may operate in us.

Doctor Seiss says, "There is a sacred significance in numbers: not cabalistic, not fanciful; but proceeding from the very nature of things, well settled in the Scriptures, and universally acknowledged in all the highest and deepest systems of human thought and religion."

Three represents the Trinity—Father, Son and Holy Ghost.

Four represents humanity.

Seven is the union of three and four, hence it represents salvation, or the Christ-life in His saints. It is connected with whatever touches the covenant between God and man. It also signifies dispensational fullness. It is complete in that which is temporal. Thus we are not surprised to find that the Holy Spirit, in His offices, administrations, operations, and in whatever way He may deal with man, is presented to our minds in the number seven.

We have already seen that there are seven symbols which the Spirit uses to present to our finite minds the different ways He operates in our hearts, and now we are to see that there are seven operations of the Spirit. May the Holy Spirit help us to a proper understanding of these mighty things.

1. The Spirit Strives (Gen. 6:3). It is the office of the Spirit to convict of sin, both actual and inbred. The Holy Ghost often strives with careless Christians to move them out into active service for God.

2. The Spirit Regenerates (John 3:5–8). To be born again or from above is to receive a new heart. This change in the heart and life is wrought by and through the power of the Holy Ghost.

3. The Spirit Sanctifies (I Pet. 1:2). Sanctification is the destruction of the old man—the taking away of the old heart—the eradication of the carnal mind. "Jesus, that He might sanctify the people with His own blood, suffered without the gate." The Holy Ghost applies the blood of Jesus to the heart, and the heart is sanctified. The blood is the means by which we are sanctified, while the Holy Ghost is the Agent.

4. The Spirit Witnesses (I John 5:6). He witnesses to our justification (Rom. 8:16), to our sanctification (Heb. 10:15), to divine healing, to answer to prayer, etc.

5. The Spirit Teaches (John 14:26). The Spirit must teach the sinner how to be saved. Every saved soul realizes his need of divine guidance,

of divine illumination, of that wisdom which is from above, and to every such soul there comes the blessed assurance that he will be so guided and led. The Spirit enables him to understand the Scriptures, to perceive spiritual things, to know God's will, and to receive divine wisdom. "For we know not what we should pray for as we ought: but the Spirit himself maketh intercession for us with groanings which cannot be uttered" (Rom. 8:26). Into all the details of the ministry of the gospel the Holy Spirit enters. It was by the direction of the Spirit that Philip was sent into the desert to preach to and baptize the Ethiopian eunuch (Acts 8:29–39). The Spirit suffered not Paul and Silas to go into Bithynia when they desired of themselves to do so (Acts 16:7). And it was the Spirit that sent Peter to preach to Cornelius (Acts 10:19 and 11:12). And so all through the ministry of the apostles they were directed by the Holy Spirit.

6. The Spirit Anoints (Ps. 23:5 and Acts 4:31). The purpose of these anointings is to prepare us for service, or to enable us to undergo some particular trial. Many miss all the sweetness of a trial by failing to tarry before God until He anoints them for that trial.

7. The Spirit Baptizes (Matt. 3:11). This is the culmination of the offices of the Spirit; it is the grand climax. This is the seal of the Spirit of promise, by which seal we are designated as the Bride of the Lamb.

Thus I have given the seven offices of the Holy Spirit with reference to man's salvation. There may be others, but it seems to me that they can be enumerated under these seven. It may be that "the anointing" spoken of in I John 2:27 is the same as the Baptism, but there is no doubt that we may several times, either before or after our Baptism, receive "an anointing" of the Spirit to prepare us for special service or trial (Acts 4:29–31). But be all this as it may — consider that there are seven, less than seven, or more than seven operations of the Spirit, or explain "The Seven Spirits of God" as you may — it still remains a fact that the Spirit does operate in man's behalf, and that "there are diversities of operations, but the manifestation of the Spirit is given to profit withal." So any arrangement you may wish to make of the operations or offices of the Spirit with reference to man's salvation, any theory you may wish to build, will not at all affect the main truth upon which we take our position in this book.

"For He whom God hath sent speaketh the words of God: for God giveth not the Spirit by measure unto Him" (John 3:34). I draw from this that the Spirit is given to no man in His full embodiment, but always by measure. I mean to say that Jesus had the Holy Ghost in all of His operations, in all of His administrations, in all of His gifts, and in all of His power as far as the relation between them existed; and therefore the symbol chosen in the case of Jesus was that of a dove; but that our capacities are too small to receive Him rather than by measure, though we may be filled with Him; hence He never comes upon us as a dove. Just as one drop of water contains the fullness of water, and as much so as a barrel, and yet the barrel cannot contain all water; even so we may have all the fullness of God, or we may be filled with all the fullness of God; and yet we can receive Him only by measure. . . .

Chapter IV. The Manifestation of the Spirit

"And there are diversities of operations, but it is the same God which worketh all in all. But the manifestation of the Spirit is given to every man to profit withal" (I Cor. 12:6, 7).

It appears to me from the above Scripture that there is a manifestation which follows each operation of the Spirit in our hearts. I also gather from other Scriptures that each operation of the Spirit includes two kinds or phases of manifestation. First, there are the invisible and internal influences or manifestation; and second, the visible and external manifestation: and since there is profit in the manifestation, it is given to every man in whom the Spirit operates.

1. We know that when the Spirit strives with a man, there is an uneasiness in his soul, and a troubled look on his face (Dan. 5:6; Acts 24:25; Ps. 42:5).

2. Justification brings the invisible manifestation of peace (Rom. 5:1), and the visible manifestation of a new life (Eph. 2:1–5; Gal. 5:22, 23; 2 Cor. 5:17).

3. Sanctification brings the invisible manifestation of joy (Luke 24:50–52), and the visible manifestation of fruit unto holiness (Rom. 6:22).

4. The witness of the Spirit brings an internal manifestation of confidence towards God (I John 3:20–22), and an external manifestation of testimony to the world (Rom. 10:10).

5. A person who is taught by the Spirit has an internal manifestation of an insight into the words of Jesus (John 14:26), and an external manifestation of wisdom, especially in regard to the Christ-life, and the hidden things of God (Gen. 41:37–40; Dan. 1:19, 20; Acts 4:13; 18:24–26).

6. A person who receives an anointing of the Spirit has an internal manifestation of an insight into God's dealings with His children (Ps. 23:5, 6), and an external manifestation of boldness and liberty (Acts 4:29–31).

7. The Baptism of the Spirit brings an invisible manifestation of living water (John 7:37–39), and a visible or external manifestation of tongues (Acts 2:3, 4).

There are other manifestations of the Spirit which I have not mentioned, but as far as I have gone I have tried to build upon the Word. It is possible that I have made some error in giving the manifestation following each of the first six operations; for in regard to these the Word is not so clear. I will therefore give my readers the liberty to rearrange these manifestations if they choose; but you must remember, "the manifestation of the Spirit is given to every man" in whom He operates, and also your manifestation must be Scriptural. But when we come to the manifestation following the Baptism of the Spirit, we have a "thus saith the Lord." We may think for many years that we have the manifestation of the Spirit following any or all of the first six operations, and then find out that we have been mistaken; but not so in regard to the visible manifestation of the seventh. . . .

Here let me say that there is quite a difference between "the manifestation of the Spirit" and emotions. A person may have emotions without "the manifestation," or he may have "the manifestation" without emotions. An emotion is caused by the spiritual overcoming the physical. But such is not the case with regard to speaking with tongues. Of course, a person may be emotional while speaking with tongues, but neither is the other, nor does either cause the other. Leaping, shouting, dancing, etc., are emotions, while speaking with tongues is "the manifestation."

Many people to-day are claiming the Baptism of the Spirit without the manifestation, and are advancing every theory and argument they can to convince the world that they really are baptized with the Holy Ghost; and these theories are, no doubt, satisfying thousands of people who otherwise would be seeking for and obtaining the Baptism of the Spirit. . . .

Chapter VI. The Gifts of the Spirit

"Now, concerning spiritual gifts, brethren, I would not have you ignorant."

"Now there are diversities of gifts, differences of administrations, diversities of operations, but the manifestation of the Spirit is given to every man to profit withal" (I Cor. 12:1, 4–7).

Here we count: "gifts," "administrations," "operations," and "the manifestation," each of which is different, separate, and distinct from the others. We are told that there are diversities of the first three, but the fourth is in the singular number "the manifestation." While the Spirit distributes the first three, He always gives with each gift, with each administration, with each operation, not manifestations, but "the manifestation," to profit withal. God has given all these things to work together in the salvation of man. The Spirit divides these among us, not with respect to persons, but as we prepare ourselves for them. He will perform the same operation in each heart, if each will prepare for that operation. He will impart to each heart the same administration, when He sees each heart prepared for that administration. He will bestow upon any of us any gift we desire, when He sees we have reached the degree of grace where we can use that gift for the glory of God.

In a preceding chapter we spoke of seven operations of the Spirit; perhaps there are many more. We will not here give you our ideas of the administrations, but pass on to consider the gifts. I am persuaded that much more is implied by these gifts than most sanctified people ever dreamed of. Let us approach the subject with an open heart, longing to understand the Scriptures.

Let us notice that what is said in verses 8, 9 and 10 (I Cor. 12), rests upon the conjunction *"for,"* which connects these verses—not with verse 7, but with verse 4.

"Now there are diversities of gifts, but the same Spirit. For to one is given by the Spirit the word of wisdom; to another the word of knowledge by the same Spirit; to another the faith by the same Spirit; to another the gifts of healing by the same Spirit; to another the working of miracles; to another prophecy; to another discerning of spirits; to another divers kinds of tongues; to another the interpretation of tongues."

1. Wisdom. James says, "If any of you lack wisdom, let him ask of God, that giveth to all men liberally, and upbraideth not; and it shall be given him" (Jas. 1:5). All Christians have wisdom, some in a greater degree than others. Who has reached that degree as that it may be said of him, he has "the gift of wisdom?" Solomon had "a gift," but not "the gift." I am persuaded that the manifestation of "the gift of wisdom" should far exceed Solomon's wisdom.

2. Knowledge. This is insight into divine truth. Therefore this is the gift which we all need to understand the Bible. All have knowledge, some more than others; but who has the gift? Methodist, Baptist, Holiness, Universalist, etc., all claim it, but who has it?

3. Faith. All Christians have faith, but all have not the gift. To the one who has the gift "nothing shall be impossible."

4. Healings. "Both of these nouns (gifts of healings) are in the plural number, because there is a diversity of gifts, as well as an infinite multiplicity of diseases to be healed."—*Godbey.* The Word says, "To another"—one person—"is given the gifts of healings." So a person who has received this should be able to heal any disease or affliction unless the healing would be contrary to God's will. The gifts of healing are quite different from the "prayer of faith." A person to whom has been intrusted the gifts of healings, need never pray for the sick. The power is in him (not his own power, but the power of God imparted), and he simply bids the sick, "Be whole." Examples of the manifestation of this may be seen in the following Scriptures: "Silver and gold have I none; but such as I have give I thee; In the name of Jesus Christ of Nazareth rise and walk" (Acts 3:6). "Insomuch that they brought forth the sick into the streets and laid them on beds and couches, that at the least the shadow of Peter passing by might overshadow some of them. There came also a multitude out of the cities round about unto Jerusalem, bringing sick folks, and them which were vexed with unclean spirits; and they were healed EVERY ONE" (Acts 5:15, 16). "So that from his [Paul's] body were brought unto the sick handkerchiefs or aprons, and the diseases departed from them, and the evil spirits went out of them" (Acts 19:12).

5. Miracles. Doctor Godbey says the Greek here is *"energemata dunam-con,"* which means the inward workings of dynamites. He says that a more literal translation would be MANIPULATIONS OF DYNAMITES. He concludes that it refers to spiritual miracles, and not to physical. I do not know, however, but that both may be included. If it does refer only to spiritual, or only physical, or to both, it does not affect our position in this book. One thing is clear, it is a gift added after the Baptism of the Spirit; for in Acts 1:8, the literal reading is, "You shall receive dynamite of the Holy Ghost having come on you." So you see we receive *dynamite* when we receive the Holy Ghost, but the gift is *manipulations of dynamites.* Momentous conception!

6. Prophecy. This word originally meant to bubble up like a boiling spring or an artesian well. The application seems to be that of speaking under the immediate inspiration of the Holy Ghost, unfolding to men the counsels of God, especially as contained in the way of salvation through Christ, and at times unfolding future events.

7. Discerning of Spirits. This gift, I doubt not, will put us to the place where neither men nor devils can deceive us.

8. Tongues. On the day of Pentecost the one hundred and twenty spoke in languages as the Spirit gave utterance. A person who has only the manifestation of tongues can speak in another language only as the Spirit gives utterance, but a person who has the gift of tongues can speak other languages at will, and, no doubt, several different languages. Neither has that person who has learned them in college the gift of languages, but the gift is imparted by the Holy Ghost independently of the human intellect.

9. Interpretation. This is quite different from translation. Translation from one language to another is accomplished by a knowledge of the vocabularies and syntax of those languages; but interpretation is accomplished, while we listen to an unknown tongue, by the Holy Ghost speaking the same in our heart in a known tongue; thus we are enabled to give it out to others. All who have this gift, I doubt not, are able to understand any language which they may hear spoken under the power of the Holy Ghost, and also recognize its nativity.

I am sure that people have been claiming these gifts for years, while the manifestations have fallen far short of the Bible standard. I do not believe that anyone has ever received any of these gifts in their normal state until he received the Baptism of the Holy Spirit; neither do I believe that all or any of them often come with the Baptism, but must be sought for and obtained afterwards. It is one thing to say, I have the gift of wisdom, or of knowledge, or of faith, or of prophecy; but it is another thing to really possess it. I believe when a person receives any of these gifts that he will know it that moment, and that it will so manifest itself that others will soon find it out. The Spirit has these gifts, and He has them for us. He imparts them to those whom He sees can use them for the glory of God. I believe that it is the will of God that each of us should have all these gifts, but because all of us are unable to use all or any of them properly, they are withheld. . . .

The following selections are taken from *The Second Coming of Jesus* (Falcon, N.C.: Falcon Publishing Company, 1916).

Chapter XVIII. The Antichrist

. . . All specimens of the spirit of antichrist sprang from the devil. We must not suppose, however, that every act of the devil is, strictly speaking, from the spirit of antichrist. In the spirit of antichrist we see only one special feature of the devil's work, and this feature of his work can be easily traced through the ages of the world's history.

As we pursue our course we shall see that this spirit manifests itself chiefly along two lines, viz., religious and political. Religion and politics are two elements found in every government. No government can exist without a religion. More than that, the laws of any people are based upon the religious convictions of that people. There is a religion of the Lord Jesus Christ and there is a religion of Antichrist. The religion of Christ has always been in some way associated with blood; the religion of Antichrist has always been without blood. The covering of man's nakedness through the shedding of blood (Gen. 3:21) was the impartation of the religion of Christ; the covering of his nakedness without the shedding of blood (Gen. 3:7) was the religion of Antichrist. Abel had a religion which was connected with blood (Gen. 4:4), and hence, the religion of Christ; Cain had a religion with which was associated no blood (Gen. 4:3), and hence, the religion of Antichrist. Noah's ark rose above the earth, and carried animals across the flood, that were slain in sacrifice on the other side of the flood (Gen. 8:20), and hence, it set forth the religion of Christ; Nimrod's tower rested on the earth (Gen. 11:4), and had no blood in connection with it, and hence, it set forth the religion of Antichrist. It is in connection with Nimrod's tower that we first notice the political element coming in connection with the religious element of the spirit of Antichrist. In fact, Nimrod was the first person who ever instituted a government this side [of] the flood. If there were any governments before Nimrod's day, they surely fell at the time of the flood. . . .

If God had not hindered Nimrod, I believe that the kingdom of Antichrist would have been fully established at that time. Nimrod had certainly started a government like unto that one which the Scriptures teach will be in the time of the final Antichrist. God saw what would be the outcome, of course, and said, Now they have begun, "nothing will be restrained from them, which they have imagined to do."—Gen. 11:6. This certainly sounds like the beginning of the government of Antichrist, for it is stated that when Antichrist does come he "shall do according to his own will."—Dan. 11:16. Nimrod had started out on this wise, but God, seeing what the outcome would be, defeated him in his work. (Gen. 11:8.)

The defeat of the kingdom of Babel, however, did not mean the final over-throw of Antichrist government. Far from it. The devil is very persevering. After the dispersion of the people from Babel, the devil began to work to bring about another confederation, and to imbibe the spirit of antichrist into all the governments of the world. . . .

Chapter XXVIII. Beelzebub

Taking the Bible definition, Beelzebub is the "Prince of the devils." However, we are still far from anything definite concerning him, unless we can determine just what is meant by "devils." This may prove to be a difficult task. When once this question is settled, the identification of Beelzebub will present no great difficulty. It is the purpose of this chapter to give a clear presentation of the identity, of the character, and of the work of Beelzebub.

There is a great deal of confusion in the minds of Bible readers concerning "devils." Our common version of the Bible increases the confusion rather than diminishes it. The Greek word for "devil" is "diabolos." This is the word applied to Satan himself. The Greek in Matt. 12:24, as also in many other places where our common version reads "devils," is "daimonion." This last word classically denotes a subordinate divinity, [a] supernatural being. In Scripture this word always has its evil sense. The word "demons" is a far better translation of this term, as it distinguishes this class of spirits from Satan. The Scriptures everywhere distinguish demons from "the devil," but our English version continually calls them "devils." Properly speaking, there is but one devil, whereas demons may be numbered by billions.

Just what demons are is to some extent an unsettled question. That they are in existence today, and that they are present among the human family, no one with any degree of spirituality will deny. Every Christian on the globe is conscious of a daily contact with them. Just what they are, and just from where they came, however, is hard to determine. There are chiefly two theories concerning their origin. The one theory is that demons are fallen angels; the other is that they are the souls of dead men, particularly the spirits of those who bore a bad character in this life. There are strong arguments presented by the advocates of each side of the question in favor of their position.

In my mind, this has always been an unsettled question. It might not involve any serious danger to say that the term "demons" applies to both fallen angels and souls of wicked men. However, I am almost persuaded that this term applies more directly to the latter. "The angels which kept not their first estate, but left their own habitation, he hath reserved in everlasting chains under darkness unto the judgment of the great day." — Jude 6. This verse with others (Rev. 9:1, 14; 2 Peter 2:4) indicates that the fallen angels are chained now in hell. Of course, Satan himself, though chained, is allowed to roam the earth (1 Peter 5:8), and yet to hold his throne in the atmosphere (Eph. 2:2). Yet, it seems more plausible to me that the millions of spirits that inhabit our atmosphere, the emissaries of Satan with whom we meet so often, are the souls of bad persons who once lived on earth. It is a noticeable fact that, whoever these demons are, they are always seeking refuge in some human beings; and this is a strong argument in favor of their identity as human souls. By this, I do not mean to teach that all men who have died in wickedness are roaming about the earth as demons but that certain classes of them are so doing. . . .

If we are correct in our identification of demons as human souls, it follows that Antichrist himself is no more than a demon. The Scriptures clearly state that Antichrist is one who did live, is today in the bottomless pit, and will be resurrected during The Great Tribulation. Perhaps one reason why the people will so readily worship him when he appears is because the most of them are worshiping him already. If men have been so inclined to worship demons all through the ages, it is easy to see how they will yield themselves to a demon that has been resurrected and placed before their eyes. As stated above, it appears that not all wicked men who have died are roaming the earth today as demons. Some are so terrible in their nature and work that God, in His mercy, withholds them from the habitation of man. There is coming a day, however, when the worst of them shall be let go, shall be manifested in the flesh, and shall be made rulers of this world. Of all of those who shall be so manifest, Antichrist will be the chief or prince.

This brings us to a logical conclusion that Beelzebub and Antichrist are the same. If demons be fallen angels, then I cannot believe that Beelzebub will be the Antichrist; but if demons be the souls of the wicked dead, then I can not see how anyone can fail to see that the two are one. . . .

Baalzebub is the original form of Beelzebub. Baalzebub was the Ekron god of flies. Before this we have stated that one phase of anti-Christian religion consists in the worship of bugs, flies, etc. There were certain animals, bugs, and flies that this class of worshipers held sacred. They believed that their gods dwelt in the bodies of insects. Closely related to this doctrine was the doctrine of the "Transmigration of Spirits." By this is meant that the human soul passed from one body to another. In other words, it meant that at death the human soul passed into the body of an animal or insect; at the death of that animal or insect the soul passed on to another body, and so on. "Zebub" means "dwelling." "Baalzebub" means "lord of those dwelling in bodies originally not their own." The "Transmigration of Spirits" closely resembles the Bible doctrine of demons. Antichrist himself is to be resurrected, is to transmigrate from one body or state to another. He is the lord of those who transmigrate, the prince of demons, the Baalzebub of the Old Testament, and the Beelzebub of the New Testament. Hence, we see the vivid contrast between Baalzebub and the Lord drawn in the text last quoted.

"Baalzebub" is a title applying to Baal, as it is easy to determine from the word itself. "Baal" is a word coming from the same [word] from which "Babel" is derived. As we have said before, "Baal" is a title applied to Nimrod after his death. While Nimrod lived, he was believed to be a god; after he died, he was reckoned among the "immortals." For years he was worshipped as "Baal Nimrod." Afterwards "Nimrod" was dropped, and he became known as only "Baal." It seems probable that thousands of Nimrod's followers died and became "demons." These demons began seeking refuge in human bodies. Then it was that Baal became "Baalzebub," or "lord of dwellers."

CHAPTER FIVE

David Wesley Myland
(1858–1943)

D AVID WESLEY MYLAND believed that words could never truly define or describe spiritual realities and that most certainly one particular formulation of theology could never apply to everyone. God acted in whatever way God wanted to, and theology had to acknowledge that divine freedom. His own approach to theology was thus more poetic and more empirically oriented than it was systematic.

Myland's own life story was the primary source of this more flexible and pragmatic approach to theology. We know little of his early religious experience, except that his mother, on her deathbed, laid hands on her son and dedicated him to the ministry. Myland himself was not necessarily convinced that pastoral work was for him, preferring to run the family retail business. Eventually, however, he decided God was indeed calling him into ministry via a message he could not ignore: the business was failing. Myland later concluded it was always better to heed God's call quickly because "it will cost you more the more you put it off."

While Myland entered the ministry with some reluctance, he was soon convinced that it was his life vocation. He began as a Methodist, but after a series of physical crises and subsequent healings, he developed a more dynamic form of faith that eventually led him into the Christian and Missionary Alliance (CMA). In 1890, he left the Methodist Church and joined the CMA, though he tried hard to remain on good terms with all his Methodist colleagues.

Myland's move to the CMA was an important step in his journey toward pentecostalism, but it was not his first move in that direction. A year earlier, a powerful religious experience had changed his life. He explains very little of exactly what took place, but he later referred to it as "the beginning" of his baptism in the Spirit. The completion of that baptism—or, as Myland called it, the reception of the missing "residue" of that earlier experience—did not take place until 1906, a full sixteen years later.

Myland said this completion of his spiritual baptism happened just before he heard about the pentecostal revival that had broken out at the Azusa Street Mission in Los Angeles. That is symbolic. Myland always thought of his own pentecostal faith as separate from, but compatible with, the theology coming out of Azusa, and he never felt compelled to adopt the theology of Azusa verbatim. In fact, Myland even felt free to largely ignore the phrase "the baptism of the Holy Spirit." His own preferred way of talking about the pentecostal experience was to refer to it as the "fullness of God" or the "fullness of Pentecost."

These selections, all taken from his *Latter Rain Covenant* (1910), exemplify this flexibility in Myland's thought. For Myland, pentecostal fullness could take different forms. A person could possess more or less of that fullness or possess it in unique ways. These passages also reflect Myland's belief that developments in the natural world often presage or parallel developments in the spiritual world. In particular, he was convinced that the increase of physical rainfall in the Holy Land signaled that a spiritual rainfall was about to fall on the earth as a whole. And finally, Myland's theology emphasized love. This makes perfect sense, given his lack of trust in tightly defined theological formulas. For Myland, belief was important but secondary; theology was ultimately a matter of how one lived.[1]

The following selection is taken from *The Latter Rain Covenant and Pentecostal Power with Testimony of Healings and Baptism* (Chicago: Evangel Publishing House, 1910).

Chapter IV. Its Fulness and Effects

This afternoon's lecture brings us to the *fifth* division in the subject of the Latter Rain, *The Fulness and Effects of Pentecost* itself. When I left home God said to me on the train, "Tarry in Chicago until Pentecost." I had no idea then of giving these special addresses, but somehow in God's providence they were thrust upon me just at a time to bring us to this phase of the subject on

---

[1] For more information, see Jacobsen, *Thinking in the Spirit*, 110–33.

this, the anniversary of the day of Pentecost. Nobody planned this, but all the Spirit's leadings, all my praying, and all God's communications to me have led up to this very point.

Literal and Spiritual Latter Rain

The latter rain was once literally restored to Israel's land after the seventy years of captivity, but that rain largely ceased. God is bringing it back the second time to the land which is shown by the reports from the weather bureau in Jerusalem. Since 1860 the measurement of rain in Palestine has been recorded very accurately at Jerusalem, and shows a great increase, especially of the latter rain. It is a generally understood fact that for many centuries the rain-fall in Palestine was very small. During comparatively recent years the rain has been increasing. The official record of rain-fall, which was not kept until 1860, divides the time into ten-year periods, and the facts are that forty-three per cent more rain fell between the years 1890 and 1900 than fell from 1860 to 1870.

Spiritually the latter rain is coming to the church of God at the same time it is coming literally upon the land, and it will never be taken away from her, but it will be upon her to unite and empower her, to cause her to aid in God's last work for this dispensation, to bring about the unity of the body, the consummation of the age, and the catching away of spiritual Israel, the Bride of Christ. God said He would bring back this latter rain "as at the first" and He is doing it. The *early* rain was for the sowing and the *latter* for the harvest; one for the beginning and the other for the end; one for the introduction and the other for the consummation of the dispensation. . . .

Now we begin to understand this great prophecy: "I will pour out My Spirit"—literally on Israel, spiritually on God's church, dispensationally to bring in the consummation of the ages and open the millennium, the age of righteousness. To this great point we are converging, and we see enough now that ought to make anybody willing to go through life a continual sacrifice to help hasten that day. I am surprised at men and women who say they believe these things and then hold back their time, their talent, and their money. If the Lord should burst through the air today with the sound of the trump and the voice of the archangel, many who profess to believe these truths could not go up to meet Him because they are bound down by bank stocks, bonds, and real estate—these are weights upon them. Oh, you must be light; you must have laid aside the weights and the sin that doth so easily beset you—the sin that is so common among us, the sin of unbelief, of not being sharp and quick in our faith. Our questions, doubts, fears, and misgivings—let us lay them aside.

"Oh for a faith that will not shrink
Though pressed by every foe,

That will not tremble on the brink
Of any earthly woe."

"God is able to make all grace abound toward us, that we always having all
sufficiency in all things, may abound to every good work." Glory to His Name!
If God has His way, men and women who have come up to these meetings
will find new places in God's earth to serve Him and bring forth fruit. Beloved,
will you take time to get a vision of the Almighty? Will you take time to let
God project in you, through you and upon you the vision of His purpose for
you? If you do, some will soon find themselves in the uttermost parts of the
earth. Then there will be people living in Chicago united so closely with those
God has sent to foreign lands that they will be living one life, one laboring
here and one laboring there; one working here that the other might prosper
there. This is the *intent* of Pentecost, that my heart might be bound with men
and women in Africa; in Japan, in the fastnesses of Tibet; that my spirit might
be bound with men and women in India and we are made one in working out
the purposes of God. When we come up to meet Him it will be like one man,
developed into the fulness of the stature of Christ, because we have come by
the love of the Spirit, into the unity of the Spirit, through the wisdom of the
Spirit, into the unity of the faith that works as one, believes as one, labors, and
toils, and suffers as one.

Fulness of the Godhead

Pentecost then is *this*, and "this is *that.*" Jesus is at the right hand of the Father
"shedding forth that which ye see and hear"; for He said, "I will ask the Father
and He will give you another Comforter," and I will pour Him out upon you. It
was well-pleasing to the Godhead that in Him should all the fulness dwell. Col.
1:19. He is made Head over all things, to the church which is His body, "the fulness of Him that filleth all in all." Eph. 1:23. He is Head over all principalities
and powers. He can take care of the things that hinder. He is the Head; let Him
have the body and He will take care that it shall be full of him. Fulness!

That is how I always like to see Pentecost. His fulness! Pentecostal fulness! If
it is a tongue let it be the fulness of the tongue; if it is discernment let it be the
fulness of discernment; if it is interpretation let it be in its fulness; if healing or
faith, let them all be in fulness; whatever the display, let it be in its *fulness.* We
must never stop short of that. But first, Pentecost was the promise of the Father,
foretold by Joel, and reiterated by Christ. In Luke 24:49 Jesus said, "Behold!"
that is, look for the promise of the Father, I am going to send Him upon you;
"but tarry ye in the city of Jerusalem, until ye be endued with power from
on high." He didn't say, "Behold, I send the promise of the Father on you, but
tarry ye at Jerusalem until you speak in tongues!" Now I am no modifier of

tongues, please remember that, nor am I a stickler about tongues, you never had any too much tongues for me, but I will not, I cannot, and I *shall* not magnify tongues out of its legitimate place, its scriptural setting, and its value compared with other gifts of the Spirit. Tongues is the least of all the gifts, and subordinate to other gifts, and when it is not kept so, there is some trouble.

Now that is the strongest statement I have ever made on this phase of the subject, but I say again, it is the least of all the gifts and subordinate to the others. And when it is not, there is sure to be trouble. It is least because it is last, and because it is physical, and because it is dependent upon other gifts. Three of the gifts are spiritual, three in the psychical realm, and three in the physical. Satan can manifest all the three physical gifts. They are all gifts of God, but I am talking about the region in which they operate: miracles, healings and tongues are physical, that is, they operate in the natural realm. Satan can imitate each of these three, but he cannot give you wisdom, nor can he give you intuitive knowledge. Satan cannot give you discernings of spirits nor true interpretation of tongues; nor can he give you true prophecy. Satan works from the physical, from the lower up. God works from the spiritual down. The spiritual must dominate the psychical and the psychical the physical; in other words, the spirit must control the soul and the soul the body.

Keep in consonance with all the Godhead and His revealed will and you will never have any trouble. Tongues is a great gift; I will never minimize it, never modify it, but I will give all the gifts their proper setting.

Do not think that all these displays are of the Spirit alone; the Father is there, the Son is there, and the Holy Spirit is there. Whenever God has come to anyone, the whole Godhead is manifested therein; it is the dynamics of the Godhead; the things of the Spirit are displayed in His sovereign working. This movement must be saved from saying that there is never any Spirit until there is Pentecostal fulness, and also after we get Pentecost, from saying it is the Spirit only. It is God! the Father, the Son and the Holy Spirit. Read Christ's own words in the fourteenth chapter of St. John, twentieth verse: "Ye shall know that I am in My Father, and ye in Me, and I in you." Twenty-third verse: "If a man love Me, he will keep My words: and My Father will love him, and We will come unto him and make Our abode with him." It is God now in the house, moving around as He pleases, through your eyes, your lips, your tongue, your hands, your feet; it is God dwelling in mortal flesh; "I will dwell in them and walk in them," and speak through them. It is God—Spirit, Son, Father, the fulness of the Godhead bodily.

The Promise of Pentecost

Now Pentecost is first a *promise*. He charged them that they should not leave Jerusalem, but "wait for the promise of the Father, which, said He, ye have heard from Me." Acts 1:4–5. "Ye have heard about it in My paschal sermon; ye shall be immersed, or submerged in the Holy Spirit and in fire not many days hence. Behold, I send the promise of the Father upon you."

Preparation for Pentecost

"But tarry ye in the city of Jerusalem until ye be endued with power from on high." Tarry! Wait! That is for preparation; that is not so much that God has a time and that He cannot give it before, but you must tarry for your own *preparation*. Historically, there had to be a completion of the scriptures. The work had to be completed by Christ; He had to go to the Father and get the Godhead power put into Him. Peter comprehended it aright when he said, "being by the right hand of God exalted, and having received of the Father the promise of the Holy Ghost," (this great fulness of the Godhead) "He hath shed forth this which ye now see and hear." So we have the promise coupled with the demonstration in its realization. Seeing then that Pentecost results from the absolute oneness of the Godhead, what oneness and unity ought it to produce in us *who* have received! It ought to make us as one body, and it will do it. I am one with everybody that is at all one with God. I simply cannot help it. The only thing that can keep me from being one with others is some work either of the flesh or of the devil. Will you throw away your little scruples and colorings and shades of opinion? When Christ pours out the Godhead fulness upon us, who are we, as Peter said, that we should withstand God? This preparation moves us on into one accordness; and when it is complete through yieldedness, prayer, trust, obedience, and praise, He will flood you; yes, He will. The floods from above will meet the floods from beneath and there will be a blessed shower. Oh, it is wonderful! You will know it is real.

Position of Pentecost

Then you will know it is "*upon* you." You are immersed into the Spirit. The Spirit is upon you. He has been "*with* you," and has been "*in* you," and now He is "*upon* you." You cannot eliminate from your New Testament these three prepositions, "with," "in," and "upon," and understand truth in its right relation regarding the Spirit. We have seen the *promise*, the *preparation*, now here is the *position*. He is "upon you," making you a witness, and thank God, you cannot escape. In this sense the witness is in the "witness-box." You do not fix up things any more, saying—I guess I will do this for the Lord, I guess I will pray, I guess I will give a testimony. The thing goes and it is God. You cannot help it. He has thrust you right out. Everybody sees it. Jerusalem found them with the goods on them: "They spake in *tongues* as the Spirit gave utterance." I wish we could catch more of them that way today. There are lots of people saying, "I have had my baptism," but one that He fully baptizes today shows the sign, and the best of it is, you cannot stop it. Tongues, in one sense, is the advance agent, the tell-tale of Pentecost. That is where it is valuable as a gift when nothing else will do. But you need a baptism of interpretation when you get a baptism of tongues, and some need a baptism of discernment, and some will need, especially the leaders, a baptism of wisdom, and you will have to have a baptism of knowledge and a great baptism of faith to lead this kind of life, or you will have a great deal of trouble. And so when we get all these ministries together we can make some sort of complete assembly, but, like the Corinthians, we may get too much of the gift of tongues and not enough wisdom to balance it, and then it works weakness. We may have too much "caution" also, and so come to neglect even tongues. If we do we shall not see God display Himself in freshness and newness thus subduing the human. Every little while it requires the outburst of a tongue to subdue things and make us mind our business and look to God. We are too well acquainted with the old English tongue, and we can play fast and loose with that; but not when God begins to talk. The people begin to get near to God and say, "What meaneth this?" How we need perfect assemblies where all the gifts are in operation! I am praying day and night for this. The great deficiency in this movement is interpretation of tongues, and discernment of spirits, and these are the fundamental parts of Pentecost.

Profusion of Pentecost

"They were all filled," overflowing. Everywhere you find that word in the New Testament it means the *"overflow."* They were overflowing with the Holy Ghost. That is the first thing that is said about Pentecost, and the second was, "they began to speak in other tongues as the Spirit gave them utterance." It manifests itself through the organs of speech apart from any mentality—that is its profusion, its fulness. And so above everything else, we must look for *fulness, overflow of God in whatsoever manner He pleases.* We needn't know much about it; just enough to take the first step. No "yesterdays" and no "tomorrows," but moment by moment in His will, realizing His fulness.

God, as you read in the fourth chapter of Ephesians, is above all, through all and in you all. Don't forget that the God who is in you wants to go through you. He wants to diffuse Himself through all, and then He will be over all. He is in you to reveal Himself, He is *through you* to manifest Himself, and He is *over you* to control you. All these things God will do.

Penetrance of Pentecost

Then there is that *penetrance* of God which every soul may have, which is mentioned in Acts 1:8: "Ye shall receive power"—*dunamis*, the dynamite, we like to call it, for dynamite is both *explosive* and *expulsive*; it breaks into bits and throws the bits wherever it pleases. But it is also the *dynamics*, and that is the better word, for it is the divine display, heavenly theatricals. It is the *pneumatikos*, the *spirituals* of I Corinthians 12:1, the *dynamics* of the Spirit. The word "gifts" is in italics, having been supplied by the translators. It might better read "spirituals," a word similar to our "victuals." In this chapter there are nine kinds of "spirituals," which means things of the Spirit, dynamics, outward displays of the Spirit. There are nine of them. Which will you have? Do not seek any more, just sit down at the table; the Head of the table, who is Christ, the Dispenser, the Baptizer, with the *pneumatikos* — "the things of the Spirit," will give you just what He wants you to have. I sat down at the table and He gave me just what I wanted. I took it and I am thankful for it, as He who distributed also worketh it according to His own will. Don't try to work your healing; don't try to work your faith; don't try to work your wisdom; don't try to work your tongue; don't try to work discerning or interpretation. Listen! Let it work you! Faith will put people to work, and faith works by love. Love is the atmosphere in which faith and work live, and if you do not give them a good, big, pure atmosphere, they will soon die, some by disease and some by suffocation; still others will die by perversion. Oh, it is love that is the life of every gift, and without this it dies.

CHAPTER SIX

William Howard Durham
(1873–1912)

WE KNOW LITTLE of William Howard Durham's early life. He was raised in Kentucky and his family were members of the Baptist church, but Durham said he never felt any real "joy or peace or knowledge of salvation" during his time as a Baptist. He seems not to have liked Kentucky very much either, because he left home as soon as he could. When he was seventeen, he headed first to Chicago and then to Tracy, Minnesota. It was there, in 1898, that Durham finally turned his life over to God at a revival service sponsored by the World's Faith Missionary Association. Three years later, he would become a licensed preacher with that organization.

For the first five years or so of his ministry, Durham behaved very much like every other itinerant holiness minister in the country. He preached both conversion, the first work of God's grace in the human heart, which provided forgiveness, and sanctification, God's second work of grace, which purified the heart and took away the root cause of sin. The only way in which he really stood out was his hyperactive travel schedule. Indicative of this is the fact that when he and Bessie Mae Whitmore married in 1905, they spent the first three months of their wedded life on the road, completing three thousand miles on the preaching circuit before settling down in Chicago.

Durham heard about the Azusa Street revival in the summer of 1906 and, in his typical fashion, he immediately jumped on a train to Los Angeles to see firsthand what was going on. He attended the meetings, met Seymour, received the baptism of the Holy Spirit, and then took the train back home as a newly minted pentecostal preacher. In terms of theology, this meant he now added the baptism of the Holy Spirit to conversion and sanctification as the third and final life-changing experience every Christian should seek from God.

Durham's preaching was fiery, and his reputation within the pentecostal world spread quickly. He was becoming one of the best-known national leaders of the movement. But inside, Durham was struggling with his beliefs about sanctification. Eventually he concluded that the traditional holiness doctrine of sanctification was mistaken, and he began to preach a new simplified version of the Christian life. In his new theology, conversion and sanctification were blended together into a single "finished work" experience of full salvation, and this was followed by the separate experience of the baptism of the Holy Spirit. The intervening "second work" experience of sanctification was jettisoned.

In 1909, when he first began to express this position in public, the pentecostal world exploded into dispute. People were forced to choose. Everyone had to take a side. Were you for or against Durham and his message? Tension soared, and the rhetoric boiled hot until Durham's sudden death in 1912 (most likely from tuberculosis). Even after his death, the controversy continued to shake and reshape the movement. The creation of the Assemblies of God denomination in 1914—a church largely defined by Durham's views—was the most visible institutional development, but the ripple effects of this controversy spread far and wide.

The following selections are taken from Durham's magazine, *Pentecostal Testimony*, which he used to publicize his views. These essays capture both the clarity of his arguments and his combative spirit. They also reflect Durham's absolute belief in the doctrine of evidential tongues. In fact, it was this commitment that convinced many pentecostals to follow him. Even though they may have had some questions about his new theology, they admired him as an unflappable defender of the faith when he spoke and wrote about tongues.[1]

The following selection is taken from *Pentecostal Testimony* 1:8 (Summer 1911):

Sanctification

The Bible Does not Teach that It Is a Second Definite Work of Grace.

. . . To my mind the second work theory is one of the weakest, and most unscriptural doctrines that is being taught in the Pentecostal movement, and therefore ought to be ruled out as damaging.

---

[1] For more information, see Edith L. Blumhofer, "William H. Durham: Years of Creativity, Years of Dissent," in *Portraits of a Generation: Early Pentecostal Leaders*, ed. James R. Groff and Grant Wacker (Fayetteville: University of Arkansas Press, 2002), 123–42; and Jacobsen, *Thinking in the Spirit*, 136–64.

The Word of God is so clear in regard to this matter that no one need be in confusion about it. In fact when one's attention is called to the teaching of the Scriptures on the subject, there is nothing plainer.

If sanctification were a second definite work of grace, the Scripture would certainly contain instances where some one received such an experience. But while one instance after another of conversion and receiving the Holy Spirit is recorded, not one single case is recorded where any one got sanctified as a second, instantaneous work of grace. The reason is, no such thing ever happened. There is none to record. Nor do the advocates of the second work theory today attempt to prove it from the Scriptures. Some of them attempt to prove it by misapplication or misrepresentation of Scripture. Most of them however simply refer us to the teaching of Mr. Wesley, or some other good man, and seem to expect that we will accept them as authority, whether their teaching is Scriptural or not. Many seem to expect that we will accept their personal testimony instead of the plain teaching of the Word of God. Now we believe Mr. Wesley and many others who have taught the second blessing doctrine were real men of God, but we believe that they were mistaken in this matter. We believe God raised up Mr. Wesley to preach holiness unto the Lord, and that his message was a great blessing to the world, but we do not believe that God sent him to preach that holiness or sanctification was and could be received only as a separate and distinct work of grace. Again I can nowhere find where Wesley ever taught dogmatically that sanctification is and must be a second instantaneous work.

In his Plain Account of Christian Perfection, he admits that one can come into a state of sanctification in the first work of grace, and also that it may be entered by a gradual process. Further, almost all of his teaching on this line, so far as we have had time to examine it, is based upon experience, and not upon the Word of God. In other words, experience, and not Scripture, is used to prove the experience of sanctification, and the way it is received and kept. So it is today. Folks say, "Your teaching is not like my experience." Many who will admit that what we teach is Scriptural, say they have trouble in making it harmonize with their experience. Others say it does not harmonize with what they have been taught by some great leader or other. Now the trouble lies in the fact that these recognized great leaders have failed to grasp and teach the truth on this subject, and therefore many of us have called our experiences by the wrong name. Many of us have singled out some particular experience or blessing we have had, and called it a second work of grace, when the truth is, if we would admit it, as many of us have done, we were either backslidden and got reclaimed, or we called one of our many blessings sanctification, when we had no more grounds for doing so than we had for calling many other experiences the second blessing. It is a sad thing that so many who never had any experience that they could call a "definite second work of grace" have been rejected and refused fellowship or started to seeking for an experience that is not to be found in the Word of God. Many have gotten into awful confusion on account of this very thing and it is high time the truth was taught and the people undeceived. It is too bad for people to be started to seeking for something as an experience that is not taught as such in Scripture.

Sanctification is a state, and an experience or life as well. In conversion we come into Christ, our Sanctifier, and are made holy, as well as righteous. When one really comes into Christ he is as much in Christ as he will ever be. He is in a state of holiness and righteousness. He is under the precious Blood of Jesus Christ and is clean. Every sin has been washed away. This is the state one enters at conversion. If he keeps there he will continue to be holy and righteous. There is no reason why he should not remain in the state he is brought into in conversion. The Scripture clearly teaches that a converted person is to reckon himself dead, Rom. 6:11. Such a one is exhorted to present himself to God as alive from the dead, Rom. 6:13, not to seek for a second work of grace. In fact all the teaching of Scripture on the subject is that in conversion we become identified with Christ and come into a state of sanctification, and we are continually exhorted to live the sanctified life in the Holy Spirit. Living faith brings us into Christ, and the same living faith enables us to reckon ourselves to be "dead indeed" and to abide in Christ. It is a sad mistake to believe that any one, or even two experiences, as such can ever remove the necessity of maintaining a helpless continual dependence on Jesus Christ, and bearing our daily cross, and living the overcoming life. The mistake of the age has been omitting to clearly teach the overcoming life. In other words, young and even old, converts have been told that what they needed was a second work of grace, when they should have been told that what they needed was to get back under the Blood and reckon themselves dead, and live the overcoming life. Instead of telling folks that there is an experience that removes the necessity for bearing the daily cross, they should have been taught that the Christian life is a battle from conversion to glorification. We come into Christ by faith, and it is only by faith that we abide in him. It is by faith that He abides in our hearts. We are saved by faith, and by faith we keep saved. The new covenant is conditioned on faith alone, therefore, as soon as a man believes, he is saved, but it requires just as much faith to keep right with God as it did to get right in the first place.

This is the reason there are so many up and down experiences. People are saved, and the glory and power of God fills their souls, but they grow careless and lose the joy of their salvation, and often get in to darkness and confusion. They are often told, while in this state, that they should seek to be sanctified. This is of course true. They need to be sanctified, but reclamation would be a much better name for it. But if one is made to believe in such a case that his need is a definite second work of grace, and is then reclaimed, and brought back into the same blessed state he was in when he was first saved, he will contend that he was sanctified as a second work of grace. Of course the truth is, if he had staid in the place he was in conversion, he would have had no need of his second experience, and it is a fact, too well known to be disputed, that very few people ever become really established in one or even two experiences. Most people have the mortification of more failures than that. This is no proof however, that more than one experience is necessary. God will restore us over and over, if we truly repent when we fail, but it must be an insult to Him for us to teach that it takes more than one work for Him to save us from all sin if we meet His conditions faithfully.

The following selections are taken from *Pentecostal Testimony* 2:2 (May 1912):

The Finished Work of Calvary—It Makes Plain the Great Work of Redemption

The confusion and misunderstanding in the religious world today is largely due to the fact that the simple Gospel of Christ is not taught and understood. Christ's great work of redemption is the sure foundation on which real Christianity rests. "Other foundation can no man lay than is laid which is Jesus Christ." If the great work of redemption and atonement wrought by Christ on the Cross of Calvary is left out, it is hard to see that Christianity is very far superior to some other religions. Satan knows this, and is leaving no stone unturned in his unceasing effort to blind the eyes of the people to this great fact. It is a fact that cannot be denied, that he has very largely succeeded in doing so. Only a remnant remain who see and cling to Christ as their personal Savior and Redeemer.

The surest possible way to overturn a building is to remove its foundation. The basic truths of the Gospel are that Christ became a substitute for sinners and died in their stead, and that men are saved by faith in Him. If this teaching be not true, then the whole Gospel or Christian structure is built upon an absolutely false foundation, Christ was a false teacher and an impostor and all who have trusted in Him are lost. The time has come that God will have the truth go forth and men will be called to decide one way or the other. God will have His simple, primitive Gospel preached in all the world exactly as it was in the days of the Apostles, so that all men can decide whether they wish to stand for Christ and His Gospel or for the foolish theories of men.

This makes the battle to largely center around the glorious truth of the "Finished Work of Christ on Calvary," which is the most glorious and powerful truth of the Gospel. Yea, it is the very center and heart of the Gospel. When once this truth is established it clearly draws the line so that no one need be mistaken as to where he is. Thousands of people, who are trusting in morality, legality, philanthropy, humanitarianism, church membership, the brotherhood of man and the hundreds of other silly things in which men are being made to trust by false teachers who are influenced by the devil, will have their eyes opened to the fact that if the Gospel is true, all these things combined could never save a single soul. And all will be made to know that if any or all other things combined could ever save even one soul, then the Gospel is not true and Christ is dead in vain. In this decade the Gospel will be proven true. It will be confirmed by the signs that follow it. The establishment of the truth of the Gospel will explode every theory of men in existence concerning the salvation of lost men.

Many who are in the Spirit see clearly the great battleground and the point at issue. When the truth of the "Finished Work of Christ" was first sounded forth through *PENTECOSTAL TESTIMONY*, a large number saw what a conflict it would cause. None saw it clearer than the editor who wrote the articles on the subject. How could it be otherwise? The Finished Work is by far the most important teaching in the Bible. What could we expect but that the enemy would oppose with all his power? One brother after another was convinced by the Word of God itself. Nothing else could have convinced them, as they had had the other thing drilled into them for years, and like myself, well knew that it would mean the loss of friendship of all who did not see it, and who would still cling to the second work theory. One after another under challenge said, "I will find it in the Word of God, and convince Durham that he is wrong." They would then begin the most careful search of the Scriptures and after days would be compelled to acknowledge to themselves and others that they could not find sanctification taught as a second definite work of grace in the New Testament, nor anywhere else, as to that. Then they would write and ask our forgiveness for having opposed us, and inform us that they had taken their stand for the Finished Work.

Some have tried to make it appear that people have simply accepted my teaching without investigation. Nothing could be further from the truth. No truth which I ever presented has ever been so carefully investigated as this one. Many have been forced to acknowledge that they could not find their theory taught in the Scripture long before they would accept the truth. Others have declared they would never go back on some experience they had, no difference what the Bible taught. By far the greater number of all who have heard this teaching, however, have accepted it, however prejudiced they may have been against the truth and those who preached it. In fact it is a truth that is so clear and convincing that once one's attention is called to it he cannot help but see it unless he simply closes his eyes and turns away.

The doctrine of the Finished Work, brings us back to the simple plan of salvation. Christ died for us. He became a substitute for every one of us; for He tasted death for every man. Here is a truth so simple and yet so great that it is wonderful. We are not saved simply because we are forgiven our sins. We are saved through identification with our Savior Substitute, Jesus Christ. We are given life because He died for us and rose again. But some one may ask. "How do we become identified with our Substitute?" We answer, "By faith alone." We are condemned and sentenced to death. Christ, the Blessed Son of God, stepped in and took our place and died in our stead, thus paying the death penalty that we might go free. When the truth is preached and we tremblingly fall at His feet and cry out, "What must I do?" the word comes back, "Believe on the Lord Jesus Christ, and thou shalt be saved." This does not, as we have been taught, mean that we shall be partly saved by having our outward sins forgiven. This would not be salvation. Salvation is an inward work. It means a change of heart. It means a change of nature. It means that old things pass away and that all things become new. It means that all condemnation and guilt is removed. It means that the old man, or old nature, which was sinful and depraved and which was the very thing in us that was condemned, is crucified with Christ. This makes Christ all in all as Savior, and faith the only means by which we can become identified with Him.

How different are the theories preached today, compared with the Gospel preached by the Apostles. On every side men are telling us today that there is no saving virtue or merit in the Blood of Christ, but that He was a very great teacher, and that He was our example of a perfect man. They deny that we are saved through the merits of His precious blood, and set at nought His blessed work of redemption. They deny His Deity and make him a mere man. They tell us the world needs a religion of love, one that recognizes the brotherhood of all men, and that there is good in all religion. Thus they rob us of our Blessed Redeemer. They entirely rob us of the Gospel of Christ which the Apostles preached and which we find in the Bible. No religion ever taught or advocated by any one could ever teach and enjoin more love and good works than the religion of Christ. The point is that we are not taught that we are saved by these things. Imagine, if you can, one of the Apostles going forth preaching and telling men that they were to believe that Jesus was a great and good man, and that this coupled with good works would save them. A thousand times no! They declared that He was the Son of God, and that God had raised Him up from the dead. They declare that He died for our sins and that we were saved by grace through faith. They made everything to center in Christ, declaring Him to be our only hope. They exhorted to a clean, separate, holy life, fruitful in every good work, separate from the world, lived in fellowship with God, not as a means of being saved, but as a sure proof of salvation already received by faith in Christ. It has remained for modern theorists to rob the Son of God of His title of World's Redeemer, and thus of His right to the title of Savior, leaving Him a mere man.

So persistent has been the work of Satan along the line of deceiving the people, and blinding their eyes so that they would not see the great truth concerning the sacrifice of Christ on Calvary, that, not only have the eyes of the people of the world been blinded, but a large percent of those in the churches as well. People have been made to look to so many other things that Christ has largely been lost sight of. They have turned to theories and creeds, experiences, blessings, works of grace, states of feeling, standings in churches, acceptance of certain truths, and so many other things that their vision of the Blessed Christ of Calvary has been dimmed. God has sent the Blessed Holy Spirit to His Children in these last days, to witness clearly in their hearts that the Gospel of Christ, as contained in the Scripture, is true. Men, doctrines, experiences and churches have been exalted in the earth for centuries. In the end of the age the Holy Spirit has come to exalt Jesus Christ, and give Him His rightful place in the hearts and lives of all God's children, as well as in the assembly. Never has such a fight been made for men and the things of men as is being made in these days. These are days that try men's souls. These are days when God is sifting and bringing to light. These are days when the theories of men are being tried by the Word of God, and shown up in their true light. They are weighed in the balance and found wanting. Men are proving their loyalty to their theories and their disloyalty to God, by clinging to their old theories after they are exposed by the Scriptures. They are in many instances fighting the truth of God with all their power. Most of them are not even attempting to bring Scripture to prove their position. They have none to bring; so they try to stop the progress of truth by denouncing those who bring the truth. This method of warfare is sure to fail. What God undertakes, He does. He has undertaken to establish the truth concerning the Finished Work of Christ and the baptism in the Holy Spirit, and He will certainly do it. No power will ever prevent His doing so.

One thing is sure, and all would do well to recognize it. Time can never change nor interfere with the plan of God. The Gospel of Jesus Christ is exactly the same today that it was in the beginning. A man is saved today on exactly the same terms he was in the days of the Apostles. Men change, customs change, churches change, very greatly, both as to their faith and practice, but the Gospel of Christ and God's plan of salvation remain exactly as they were in the beginning. If Jesus Christ ever was the Redeemer of mankind He is such today. If man ever needed redemption he needs it today. If repentance and faith were necessary in the days of the Apostles they are necessary today. Not in even one place in the New Testament is it ever taught that there is any other way of salvation except through Jesus Christ. Over and over again it is declared that there is no other way, no name except His great name that has salvation in it. The same thing is true today. Millions are deceived by the devil into believing that they will be saved in some other way, only to wake up in the end to see that in reject-ing Jesus Christ and setting at naught God's plan, they sealed their own doom and missed the glories of eternal life.

No doubt the second work of grace theory has done more to blind the eyes of people to the simple truth of the Gospel than any other one theory that was ever taught. It has come to thousands of truly saved people, declaring that they are not saved, and that, instead of men coming into Christ and receiving eternal life in conversion, all they get is pardon of their outward transgressions. They are told that when God pardoned them He left them full of sin and cor-ruption, and that it requires a second work of grace to save them from hell. Bishop Horner, in his book "The Root," makes the astounding statement that a converted person has enough sin in him to damn a nation. Of course, if this loathsome doctrine were true, no man is saved till he receives a second work of grace. If the Word of God taught any such thing we would heartily sanction it, and declare to all that unless they had had the second work of grace they were just as much on the way to hell as they ever were. Such teaching is so unscriptural, unreasonable and damaging that by the grace of God we will show it up in its true light, regardless of the way its adherents rage against us. Let them come forward and defend this thing with the Scripture. God's Word makes it plain that when God saves a man He cleanses him. A saved man is saved no matter what the theorists say. He is saved from sin, death and hell, is a real child of God, possesses eternal life, does not need another work of grace, but needs to abide in Christ, receive and walk in the Spirit, hold fast the faith, grow in grace and in the knowledge of God and of Christ.

The simple truth is that a sinner is identified with Adam. A believer is identified with Jesus Christ. No man is identified with Adam the first and Adam the second at the same time. A sinner is in Adam and Adam is in a sinner. A believer is in Christ and Christ is in a believer. A sinner is condemned in Adam. A believer is free from condemnation in Christ. A sinner has condemnation and a believer has peace. A man is not in Adam and Christ at the same time. Christ and Adam are not in a man at the same time. When Adam fell the old creation was dragged down with him. When Christ arose from the dead, the new creation came up with Him. A sinner is in the kingdom of darkness and sin. A believer is in the kingdom of Jesus Christ. Before conversion a man is in "nature's darkness." In conversion he is translated out of nature's darkness into the Kingdom of God's dear Son. It is in conversion that a man receives Jesus Christ, the glorious Son of God, and is made a new creature in Him, and old things pass away and all things become new. As these glorious truths grip our souls they put real strength in us, and we become established in our Blessed Lord and Savior, Jesus Christ. These are the real truths of the Gospel. The Spirit witnesses to them when they are preached. The signs follow when this Gospel is preached.

Speaking in Tongues Is the Evidence of the Baptism in the Holy Spirit

For six years the question of whether speaking in other tongues as the Spirit gives utterance is the evidence of the baptism in the Holy Spirit, has been much agitated. The real question is, "Do all who receive the gift of the Holy Spirit speak in tongues as at Pentecost, at the time?" Perhaps no point of doctrine has ever been more bitterly contested. It is also doubtful if any other point of doctrine was ever so shamefully compromised, as this one has been by some in the movement. It would be impossible to calculate what the work has suffered, as a result of this point of truth's being compromised. The work has never suffered from the effects of the opposition of those who stood on the outside of the movement, and bitterly opposed this and other truths. It has suffered from the effects of those who claim to be Pentecostal people, and at the same time deny this great distinguishing truth of the movement.

Now it is not to be supposed that this truth is opposed just simply as an ordinary point of doctrine is opposed. Men in this day, as a rule, are not concerned enough about a small point of doctrine to fight against it, as this doctrine has been fought. This is one of the penetrating truths of God, such as He often sends, that locates every man that hears it. If God did not send His plain, pointed messages and truths into the world occasionally, men would have a much smoother time of it. But just about the time men get settled down to rest in carnal security, on their highly prized but false theories, God sends a plain message of truth, that simply puts every soul on the face of the earth in a corner. In all past time both the message of God and His messengers as well, have been rejected and opposed. By very far the greatest majority of the messengers God has sent to the world have been utterly rejected, and a great per cent of them have been slain.

God's message puts men under conviction, and, unless they are willing to give heed to it, there is nothing left for them to do but to try to get that which disturbs them out of the way. It has been no exception with this truth. While no one, so far as we know, has been killed for preaching it and for the results that have followed, on every side we have seen it stir up the same spirit that was manifested in those who have murdered the saints and martyrs in the past. We have heard it said over and over again, that our ministers ought to be hung, or killed, or sent to jail. We have been threatened, and heard others threatened. Some have been assaulted and shamefully entreated. The most bitter and scathing articles have been published and circulated against the truth and those who preach it. In a word, there has been a very determined and united effort to exterminate this point of doctrine.

We do not believe that all those who have opposed this doctrine have understood fully what they were doing. We believe that most of them, if they would own the truth, would acknowledge, however, that they hate this truth, because it says to them, in so many words, that they have not the baptism. We believe it is because they are located. Of one thing we feel certain: The devil knows exactly why he hates it and opposes it so. It is because it exposes every false theory that he ever got men to believe. He knows that, if every person he has ever deceived and made satisfied with a theory, and thus robbed of the baptism, should see this truth and tarry for the baptism, they would receive it. He knows that just as soon as men see this truth, they will begin to seek God, and will never be satisfied again till they get the real baptism. He knows just how it stirs men up. He knows this is the one thing that represents the genuine, Scriptural baptism in the Holy Spirit. Therefore he knows the importance of getting it out of the way. He knows that, even among Pentecostal people, as soon as he gets them to lose interest in this great Pentecostal truth, they will settle down, and that in a little while people will quit seeking and receiving the Holy Spirit. One thing one need never be in doubt about; and that is the attitude of the devil toward this truth, or whether he fully understands it.

As small a thing as the speaking in tongues seems to many to be, it is marvelous what a stir it has made in the world. When six years ago it was first preached on the Pacific Coast that the speaking in tongues was the evidence of the baptism, it met with bitter opposition from the holiness people. The most of the people who heard did not believe it. Therefore they branded it as a false doctrine, and the man that preached it as a false prophet. But some tarried and the Lord met them. In a short time most of those who had opposed them were seeking and most of them received. Then those who had been so confident that they had received the Holy Spirit before, and thus had opposed this teaching, knew two things: first, that they never had had the baptism before; second, that the doctrine that the tongues is the evidence was true.

Right here the line began to be drawn. When the people saw the power of God coming on the people, and heard them speaking in tongues, those, as a rule, who were acknowledged as the most spiritual among them recognized that it was God, and took their stand for it. The other class said they did not believe it was God, continued to oppose, and none of them ever received the baptism. On the other hand those who saw and believed that it was God and became seekers, almost without exception, received the glorious baptism and spoke in tongues. The writer of this article has had this glorious experience for over five years, and has heard all that could be said against it. He gladly places himself on record today as believing, beyond a doubt and without a single misgiving, and more strongly, if possible, than ever before, that this is the genuine, Scriptural baptism in the Spirit, and that in glory and blessing it eclipses all other experiences. No experience is, or could be more valuable except conversion, which is of course the experience on which all other experiences of the Christian life are built. The writer knows today, as he has known from the first, that when the blessed Holy Spirit, the third Person in the Trinity, comes in to take up His permanent abode, He speaks in other tongues.

So far as our knowledge extends, every one that went forth for the first year or two stood firmly for the truth that the tongues are the evidence of the baptism. Wherever they went this simple truth put people in a corner, and either drove them away or started them to seeking. The result was, scores received. The instructions were as simple as they could have been. "Just yield yourself up to the Lord and trust the Blood and wait," they would say. As souls did this, the Spirit would fall on them. The results were the same in all localities. When the power would come upon people they would often fall helplessly to the floor. Generally they would be shaken more or less violently. This was a trying experience to some who never felt the power before and who of course did not understand it. "Just let Him have His way," the workers would say, and soon the person who was under the power would begin to speak in tongues. No person ever had a stranger experience than those who speak in tongues for the first time. No one could ever describe it. To me it was the strangest, most glorious and wonderful experience I had ever had. The power, which has already overcome and which shakes the person's body, simply moves to his vocal organs and begins to operate on them and, if yielded to, soon produces a language. After a person had spoken in tongues we pronounced him through. By this we meant his baptism was completed. Many would have the power on them and not get through to the baptism at the first time, or even the second. When this was the case the power of God, after dealing with a person, would simply lift from him. When He filled him and spoke in tongues He remained with him. This position, we held from the first, and we hold it today. All who are really baptized speak in tongues at the time.

One thing we have observed, and we have been careful to observe all that has happened in this glorious movement. Whenever they cease in any place to teach that the tongues are the evidence the power of God lifts and they have very few baptisms any more. Wherever they stand for this truth and really preach it, if they are straight, or reasonably straight, in other doctrines and are a clean people, the power never leaves them, and people continue to get the baptism. In a word, it is a truth that God has been pleased to honor from the first, and He is honoring it just as much today as ever. God always honors His own message.

CHAPTER SEVEN

Ambrose Jessup Tomlinson
(1865–1943)

Ambrose Jessup Tomlinson was born into a relatively secular family in central Indiana. One set of grandparents had been Quakers, but that faith never made its way down to Ambrose while he was a child. What Tomlinson did inherit from his grandparents on both sides of the family was a concern for politics. His maternal grandparents had been abolitionists, and his paternal grandfather was vocally opposed to both capitalism and war. Tomlinson himself said he was practically addicted to politics until, at the age of twenty-four, God literally knocked him for a loop with a bolt of lightning that struck the ground next to him.

Tomlinson did everything wholeheartedly, and, once he was converted, he pursued his new faith with vigor. He began teaching Sunday school at the local Quaker meetinghouse and soon became involved in a variety of other religious endeavors. Moving to North Carolina, he took work as a colporteur for the American Tract Society while simultaneously founding an orphanage and publishing his own monthly religious newspaper. His religious rhetoric sometimes still included a populist political dimension with a tone that irritated his wealthy neighbors, but Tomlinson was not one to back down, and he kept right on preaching.

By happenstance, Tomlinson had settled in the region of North Carolina where Richard Spurling and his little group of followers called the Christian Union were active. Tomlinson joined this group in 1903 and soon moved into a leadership role. During this time, the group also changed its name to the Church of God. Five years later, Tomlinson experienced the baptism of the

Holy Spirit while listening to a sermon by G. B. Cashwell (a revivalist who had just returned to the Carolinas from the Azusa Street Mission), and he subsequently led the rest of his church into the pentecostal fold.

From 1909 until 1923, Tomlinson was the undisputed head of the newly pentecostal Church of God, and in that role he became one of the most well-known and influential leaders of the movement. Carrying his business sense and organizational skills into the church with him, he devoted himself to founding new congregations, setting up a church hierarchy, and strengthening the financial base of the church. To some he seemed like a denominational autocrat, but to others Tomlinson was the essence of what a real church leader ought to be.

The selection here comes from his first book, *The Last Great Conflict*, published in 1913. In this volume, Tomlinson's energy and passion are clearly evident. He begins the work with a pentecostal call to arms, writing: "Satan is mustering his forces and drafting every man and woman into his service. . . . The smoke of an awful battle is already rising from the battle field . . . it is now high time for the regulars to advance with the full equipment of Pentecost, and to pour into the ranks of the enemy the shot and shell, grape and cannister of gospel truth and power until the roar of the cannons can be heard all over the world."

But while Tomlinson's rhetoric could be hot, his real genius and lasting contribution to the pentecostal movement was more ordinary and organizational than it was revolutionary, and that is what is highlighted here. The question he pondered repeatedly was: What is required for the church to be a well-run, well-financed theocracy? While institutional matters predominate in his writings, Tomlinson also believed that he himself had a special role to play in God's work in the world. At points, this more personal aspect of his leadership is also visible.[1]

The following selections are taken from *The Last Great Conflict* (Cleveland, Tenn.: Press of Walter E. Rodgers, 1913).

Chapter VI. Christ Our Law-Giver

There are a number of people who have enjoyed the "latter rain" showers that have been falling, and who have received the baptism with the Holy Ghost, but are floating around as a sailing vessel which has no chart or compass. Their sails are spread, and as the wind blows in a certain direction they move

---

[1] For more information, see R. G. Robins, *A. J. Tomlinson: Plainfolk Modernist* (New York: Oxford University Press, 2004).

off with great joy and liberty; but when that puff of wind ceases and another one comes from another direction, off they go again with that gust, though it may be driving them almost in an opposite course. Just so they are sailing, they seem to be satisfied.

Sailors with a chart and compass for a guide will hoist their sails and fly before the wind, provided it carries them the way they wish to travel, but when the wind comes that is contrary they either take down their sails and anchor or shift them and tack until a more favorable breeze comes again.

We should not be carried about by every wind of doctrine. It is very unsatisfactory to be unsettled. One who is unsettled is unsafe, and one who is settled on the wrong foundation is also dangerous. It is always good for a man to change from the wrong to the right, but it is very serious to change from the right to the wrong.

I have in mind a sweet Christian character who was very strong against a certain line of truth, but in a short time the tempest seemed to blow so hard in the right direction that the precious soul was driven by the tempest and accepted the truth, but he remains so unsettled, judging from his conversation, that there are some fears that if he was to get into a severe tempest beating against this same line of truth, he would fall in with that tempest and turn in the opposite direction again. We cannot trust such a person, neither can God depend upon him. Rooted and grounded in the truth is the only safe place.

The question is often asked, "What should the Pentecostal people do as pertaining to organization? Should they organize, or remain with no order or government?" There is only one way to settle these questions, and that is to examine the Scriptures unbiased and without prejudice. Not only should the whole "latter rain" affection be ONE in answer to the prayer of Jesus, but all real Christians ought to be joined together in one body. "Now I beseech you, brethren, by the name of our Lord Jesus Christ, that ye all speak the same thing, and that there be no divisions among you; but that ye be perfectly joined together in the same mind, and in the same judgment." (1 Cor. 1:10.) "Fulfill ye my joy, that ye may be like-minded, having the same love, being of one accord, of one mind." (Phil. 2:2.) Two or more minds might run together and they agree on something that was wrong, and for fear that this might be the case, and as if in order to cut off occasion for such a serious error, Paul adds, "Let this mind be in you, which was also in Christ Jesus." (Phil. 2:5.) This then is intended to put us in one accord with Christ, and if all the followers and disciples of Jesus Christ are in accord with Him they will be in one accord with each other as a whole.

What should the Christian people do? Get in perfect harmony and one accord with Christ in spirit, mind and teaching, and this will bring us together into one body, one organization, under one government, with one lawgiver—Christ—who is the head of the church. Jesus instituted His Church for government, and all the laws for government came from Him to us through His holy apostles.

I admit that we have those in our ranks who oppose government and any form of organization, but such are false teachers. They refuse to submit to government, and are holding themselves aloof and independent, every one for himself, even contending against any form of organization, and say they are members of Christ's church. It matters not how spiritual they may seem to be, or how honest they may be, they are dangerous characters, and enemies to Christ and His truth. "But there were false prophets also among the people, even as there shall be false teachers among you, who privily shall bring in damnable heresies, even denying the Lord . . . and despise government. Presumptuous are they, self-willed, they are not afraid to speak evil of dignities." (2 Peter 2:1, 10.) "Likewise also these filthy dreamers defile the flesh, despise dominion (government), and speak evil of dignities." (Jude 8.) No one can be a member of Christ's church and refuse government and hold themselves aloof from organization—His organization—His government—His laws.

His Church means government. It is not a legislative or law making body, but an executive body. It executes the laws already given. It is also a judicial body, because it applies the laws already enacted to particular cases. To object to dominion, to despise government, to refuse organization means opposition to the council at Jerusalem (Acts 15), and means opposition to Christ's church.

His church for the saints in this world is what His kingdom is to be universally in the millennium. If we prove ourselves to be good executives here, we will more likely receive a kingdom over which to reign there. If we prove ourselves obedient to His laws here and now, He will more likely trust us with the reins of government there and then.

In the teaching of the parable of the pounds given by our Lord (Luke 19:12–27), He shows the value of obedience and faithfulness to His government and laws, and in verse 27 He calls the people His enemies who refuse His reigning over them, commanding them to be brought and slain before Him. If I reject His government and disobey His laws, I make myself a disloyal subject, and according to this teaching I must be slain. . . .

Many people today who claim to be members of Christ's Church (government), remind me of people who come from foreign countries to the United States and fail to take the "oath of allegiance." They are on United States soil or territory, reaping the benefits there from, but not United States citizens. Israel was recognized by God as His children and chosen people, but not until they crossed the Red sea and accepted and covenanted to keep the laws of God given them through Moses were they recognized as, or called the "Church in the wilderness."

Church then means government—Christ's government: His Church. Here then is where women are to keep silence, that is, they are to have no active part in the governmental affairs. (1 Cor. 14:34.) Here, too, is where Paul said he would rather speak five words with his understanding that with his voice he might teach others, than ten thousand words with an unknown tongue. (1 Cor. 14:19.) Here, also, is where not over three at most, and they one at a time, may speak in tongues and let one interpret, and if there be no interpreter let him keep silent in the church. (1 Cor. 14:27, 28.) There were no women speaking in the council at Jerusalem: no one talking in tongues. They were a Judicial body, searching for and applying the laws to a particular case. When the law was found touching that particular case it was applied, and James, who seemed to be chairman or moderator, made the statement which settled all discussion and debate, and there were no votes taken because they only had to obey the law already given, and only added words of explanation.

His Church is not a government by the people, which is democratic form, neither is it government by the people by representatives, which is republican form; but "The government shall be upon his shoulder." (Isa. 9:6.) His church is a theocracy. God giving His laws through Moses is a type. God giving His laws through Christ is evidently the antitype and very image—the perfection for government. "For the law having a shadow of good things to come and not the very image of the things." (Heb. 10:1.) This signifies that Christ's is the real government of which Moses was only a shadow. The government through Moses has had an end, but the government under Christ is to continue— perpetuate. "Of the increase of His government . . . there shall be no end." (Isa. 9:7.)

He is to rule or govern His church in this world as Moses governed Israel in the wilderness. As Israel was a peculiar treasure unto God among thousands of inhabitants, but separate from them, so Christ "gave himself for us, that he might redeem us from all iniquity, and purify unto himself a peculiar people, zealous of good works." (Titus 2:14.)

We are in the world but not of the world. We are under Christ's government, but must be subject to "the powers that be" in whatever country we are placed, except [when] the world governments conflict with our obligations to Christ. Then Christ must be honored and obeyed rather than the world governments even at the peril of our lives. (Acts 4:19; 5:29.)

"Christ is the head of the church and he is the savior of the body." Therefore the church is to be subject to Him in everything. "Christ also loved the church, and gave himself for it; that he might sanctify and cleanse it with the washing of water by the word, that he might present it to himself a glorious church, not having spot, or wrinkle, or any such thing; but that it should be holy and without blemish." (Eph. 5:23–27.) Those then who have followed and obeyed Him faithfully here will constitute His great host of rulers and governors during His thousand years reign on earth, when He shall reign without a rival. All people and all nations will be subject onto Him. "And the Lord God shall give unto him the throne of his father David . . . and of his kingdom there shall be no end." (Luke 1:32, 33.)

Chapter XV. The Church of God, Continued

When Jesus was preaching to the people He very often used, for illustration, the common things around Him, and taught them largely by comparison.

He would sometimes use the sheep and the shepherd to make His teaching impressive, and would sometimes use the vines and branches. He took the penny at one time to teach the lesson. He used the rulers and laws of the country sometimes. He spake in parables and many ways to impress the truths on the minds of the people.

He would sometimes seem very humble and subdued in spirit, at others He would wax bold and speak as one having authority. He would at one time manifest the lamb like spirit, and at another the lion like spirit would prevail. He was fully able for every occasion, and could fill the requirements under all circumstances. There are still remaining signs and fruits of His life and ministry.

He said to His disciples, "I am the vine and ye are the branches." He also gave the thought that upon them the fruit would appear, because they were the branches.

As we study His teachings and instructions as well as the writings of the Apostles, we infer that He must have said something like this: "I am going away, and upon this rock I'm going to build my Church, which is to take my place when I am gone, and she shall be called my body, but I will still remain the head. She must always be subject to me, and I have left all the laws she needs, and she must not leave off any nor add any more."

We acknowledge that He really did establish His Church, and she showed herself in all her beauty and effulgent glory as she sprang fresh from His hands on the day of Pentecost. He had already said, "Greater works than these shall ye do because I go unto the Father," and sure enough, under the very first sermon after the Church really took His place, three thousand souls were added to the one hundred and twenty. And besides this great in-gathering, "The Lord added to the Church daily such as should be saved."

The work spread and grew, and "multitudes both of men and women were added unto the Lord." When the Church (His body) was really manifested and took His place the fruit was seen in abundance. From the Church went out the teaching of repentance, as a branch from a tree, and on this branch were people who repented. Another branch was extended from the same body named baptism, another sanctification, another baptism with the Holy Ghost, another feet-washing, etc., etc. From the body (the Church) extended every line of truth and teaching that He had given them. Although His disciples were the branches while He was with them, yet when He went away and the Holy Ghost came upon them they were all baptized into one, and became the body from which all the teachings or commands branched out, and then appeared the fruit. People were converted, sanctified, baptized with the Holy Ghost and healed.

Behold, there stands the full developed tree. First is the trunk, and from the trunk extends the branches, and upon the branches appears the leaves and luscious fruit hanging in great yellow or red clusters. The Church of God is to the gospel or doctrine taught in the Bible as the trunk—or body of the tree is to the branches, leaves and fruit.

Where did Martin Luther get the doctrine of justification by faith? From the Church of God as it was given by its members through the Bible. The branch had grown and grown and lengthened out through the "dark ages" until by and by Martin Luther appeared as a cluster of fruit away out on the end of the long branch.

Where did John Wesley get the doctrine of sanctification as a definite and instantaneous experience subsequent to justification? From the Church of God. This branch had also extended away out through the darkness, and finally blossomed with George Fox, and then fruited heavily in the time of the Wesleys. These two branches have grown and borne much precious fruit ever since.

Where did Dr. Simpson get the doctrine of divine healing? Where did this branch come from? The Church of God. Hundreds, yea thousands have given up physicians, thrown away remedies, wheel chairs and crutches, and have been suspended on this wonderful branch.

Where did Dr. Seamore [sic] get the doctrine that he preached in Los Angeles, Cal., a few years ago, that not only stirred that western city and our own beloved America, but also the countries across the deep blue sea, yea, and many parts of the world. Where did he get the doctrine—the baptism with the Holy Ghost and the speaking in other tongues as the Spirit gives utterance as the evidence? From the Church of God. This branch, also, had been reaching out and growing in length until it budded, blossomed, and is today filled with delicious fruit. The rich experiences, the shining faces, the good clean lives, the love for one another and the lost souls of earth, the "Go ye" spirit, tears and sacrifices, all tell the story of this special branch having life and fruitage, although thought to have died long ago and been buried with the Apostles. All these branches have been bearing fruit. Thank God.

But the wonder is that none of these men, who discovered these wonderful truths, ever crawled back down the branch to discover, if possible, where they started from, and locate the trunk of the tree. But no, they seem to have been so occupied with present surroundings and conditions, and the branches had grown so long, and through the long, long night of the "dark ages," that the darkness was too dense and the task too great. And thus instead of discovering the trunk of the tree, men went to work and got up articles of faith and creeds, and have tried to make out that these precious truths were doctrines of church so and so. For example: It has been said so often that "Sanctification is a doctrine of the Methodist Church," "Baptism by immersion is a doctrine of the Baptist church," etc., etc. None had been able to see just where the branches sprang from and to what body they were attached.

At last, after centuries of fruitage, the branch of sanctification put forth a little unassuming bud and other little buds made their appearance about the same time. Finally the fruit appeared, and, as if they wondered and consulted with each other as to where such delicious sap and nourishment could come from, finally this least of all, and the most insignificant and uncouth in appearance, disappeared in the darkness as it went rolling and tumbling and rattling down the bark of the branch, and although the way was lonely and dark, and the obstructions thick and hard to penetrate, yet as if determined to reach the trunk or die, it kept scrambling away until finally the discovery was made, and sure enough, not only that special branch was located, but also all the others, whose tip ends had been bearing fruit, were located, and found to be fastened to and held in place by the Church of God.

As the discovery was made a shout pierced through his soul, and almost before he was aware of it, he was back again at the end of the branch, shouting at the top of his voice, and leaping and clapping his hands as he cried, "The Church of God! The Church of God! From her extends all these precious truths! From her comes all the laws and government we need! Away with your articles of faith! Away with your creeds! Upon 'this rock' Jesus built His church, and there it is just like it was, only it has been hidden from view by the debris of the 'dark ages,' unbelief, and man made churches and organizations! Hallelujah! Hallelujah! Glory! Glory!" And the shouts and cries of joy were taken up by the other fruit, and echoed and re-echoed until dread consternation seized scores and hundreds of people who looked on with amazement and wonder.

As we trace every branch of truth it runs us right back to the Church of God—the body of Christ.

The Church is still rising, the light is still shining, and many are seeing the brightness of her rising, and gathering themselves together unto her. People are seeing and flowing together, their hearts are fearing and being enlarged. Prophecy is now being fulfilled, and the glory of God is already resting upon the Church of God in a measure. (Isa. 60:1, 5.)

In conclusion I wish to ask the following questions: If justification, sanctification, the baptism of the Spirit, etc., are really branches or teachings from the original Church, and dependent upon her for a foundation, does it not look like robbery for men to establish or make a church with articles of faith and creeds, and take these branches or teachings from the Church of God and put them in their churches? Does it not look like Nebuchadnezzer taking away the sacred vessels from the house of God at Jerusalem? Does it not look like Belshazzer and a thousand of his lords drinking out of these sacred vessels contrary to the will of God? And is there not already faintly, yea, plainly seen the form of a hand writing on the wall the doom of all those who have taken these sacred commands, branches or teachings that rightfully belong to the Church of God and made them principles or creeds in their own organizations? Is God's wrath going to be held back forever? . . .

Chapter XVIII. Money System

When He created this earth, God, with His infinite wisdom, placed the most precious metals and treasures in obscure places beneath the surface.

It has always been the duty of man to search for these hidden treasures. It is a fact, too, that the most costly treasures have always been the most difficult to locate and procure. It is true, also, that the scant supply and difficult task in securing such treasures is the cause for the high value placed upon them when they are found.

In God's economy He has made the spiritual blessings difficult to obtain in like proportion. Justification by faith is more easily seen and obtained than sanctification through the blood of Christ. In like manner is the baptism with the Holy Ghost a little deeper down and more difficult to obtain, and much more patience is required in seeking for it, as is the case with the search for gold and precious stones. And the result is, that many fail to find the precious experience because so much time, patience and perseverance is required.

The money system that God intends His Church to adopt has not been thrown down carelessly on the surface in His Word like sticks or dust on the surface of the ground, but like sanctification, the baptism with the Holy Ghost and the gifts, it requires toil, sacrifice, consecration and perfect submission to His divine will and plan to locate and unearth it and put it into practice.

People can see all these precious truths and obtain the experiences in proportion to their willingness to sacrifice their own ways and opinions, consecrate their lives to God for His service and submit to His divine will. Many are deprived of the rich blessings God has promised them in His Word, and He does not reveal to them the hidden treasures and costly gems of glory provided for them in the atonement, simply because of lack on their part of perfect submission to Him.

All governments have some kind of a money system. Some rude enough, while some have reached such a high state of perfection that all classes of people have ample opportunities granted them for the commodious use of money. All churches have adopted some plan for securing money to meet the expenses and for charity funds. All orders, political and fraternal, have more or less system for the proportionate collection and distribution of the necessary funds for running expenses, projects and investments. Railroad companies, express companies, banks and nations have plans for business intercourse, making their exchanges with system and order. . . .

Hundreds of thousands of honest souls are searching for the truths hidden away in the Bible and realizing great spiritual gain by the required sacrifice and toil. Not a few have accepted the tithing system, and some are advocating the practice of selling their possessions and laying the proceeds at the Apostles' feet, as was done by the early Church in Judea, while still others claim we should not have any special system, but everyone should give as he purposes in his own heart, much or little, and anywhere he wishes.

In the glaring light that beams upon the Bible when the Holy Ghost illuminates its pages, our ways have many times appeared very crude and immature. No doubt the time will come when we will see our imperfections in handling the Lord's money. The Bible teaches order and system about other things; why not about money matters? We have learned many things by types and shadows; it is surely not improbable that we can learn something about the money system in the same way. The Holy Scriptures surely teach a money system, so we would do well to search for it. True, it is not always called money, but generally its equivalent is the term used in its types and shadows.

The tithe is first mentioned in the Bible at Gen. 14:20, where the account is given of Abram returning from the slaughter of the kings and met Melchisedec, "the priest of the most high God," and Abram "gave him tithes of all" the spoil he had taken in battle, and Melchisedec blessed him. At Gen. 28:22 is the closing of the narrative of Jacob's vow to God about 153 years later, where he said, "If God will be with me, and keep me in this way that I go, and will give me bread to eat, and raiment to put on, so that I come again to my father's house in peace; then shall the Lord be my God: And this stone, which I have set for a pillar, shall be God's house: And of all that thou shalt give me I will surely give the tenth unto thee."

We do not read of God ever giving Abram and Jacob any command to pay tithes, but it seemed to be voluntary on their part, but in each case the giver received a blessing. While there is no history showing that God had commanded these, his servants, to pay tithes, yet 269 years after, when the law was given, the tithing system was instituted and placed in the law, as if it was something of importance. In the law is given the tithing system, and from that time tithing was practiced and mentioned by the prophets, and that subject is taken up in the New Testament and emphasized. . . .

Chapter XIX. Money System — Continued

. . . To whom did the members of the early church give their possessions? Was it to the poor, or to the missionaries, or evangelists, or orphanages, or charity homes? No, to none of these. If not to the poor, nor to missions, nor evangelists, nor homes for the widows and orphans, then to whom did they give their possessions?

Abraham gave to Melchisedec in person. In the time of the early church Jesus was high priest after the order of Melchisedec. Jesus Himself, the head of the church, had ascended to the Father, but the church, which is His body, was on earth, and the apostles were the officers of the church; then it is easily seen that all the offerings were laid at the apostles' feet, as that was the only way to give literally to the High Priest. The offerings must be made to the High Priest who was after the order of Melchisedec. The church, then, was His body. (Eph. 1:22, 23, and Col. 1:18.) All literal offerings were made to His body, the church, of which the apostles were chief. This was following the order in which Abraham gave a tenth of the spoils to Melchisedec. This was as though the law had never been. They were not under the law, but under grace. (Rom. 6:14.) Abraham was not under the law, for he was before the law, but he gave the tenth of all before the law came.

If Abraham gave a tenth of his spoils before the law came, would it be reason[able] to expect people to give any less after the law was ended? Remember the law was a schoolmaster, teaching in types and shadows and Abraham had no such training. The early Christians proved that no less than a tenth should be given, and also proved their willingness to give more than the tithe, and they gave directly to the church instead of scattering it around promiscuously, as is the case with people who give in these days.

The law, our schoolmaster, has taught us, then, that tithes and offerings should be made to our High Priest — Jesus, for whom His body, the church, stands in His place. The priests and Levites received the tithes and offerings from all Israel in the tabernacle service, and they were called "the church in the wilderness." The members of the early church made their offerings to the church in direct harmony with the type. After these offerings were placed in the treasury, then distribution was made proportionately as every one had need.

By this time surely every one who has followed us closely can see the mistakes of recent years by those who have been paying tithes and offerings. They have been throwing them out here and there as they felt led to do, and probably under the existing circumstances it has been the best that could have been done, but it is now evident that God has a wiser plan, a better way, a perfect money system to be put into practice for these last days. It is certainly plain that tithes and offerings should be placed or paid into the Church, His body, and distribution made to supply the demands in all places and for all purposes.

We are indeed in the last great conflict, and the money system is no little factor in it. It is on conditions that all tithes be brought into the storehouse until there is a surplus on hand that the windows of heaven are to be opened and blessings poured out to such an extent that there will not be room enough to receive them. The members of the early church made all their offerings to the church, His body, and what happened then? Read the first chapters of Acts, and you can see that the windows of heaven were wide open and multitudes were added to the Lord.

Christ's body, His church, has been ignored, and God is not well pleased with it, and thus leanness of soul and poverty among the members is the result. "Bring ye all the tithes into the storehouse, that there may be meat in mine house, and prove me now herewith, saith the Lord of hosts, if I will not open the windows of heaven, and pour you out a blessing, that there shall not be room enough to receive it." (Mal. 3:10.) Where are the tithes to be placed? "Oh, just anywhere," is the answer given by hundreds according to their weekly practice. "Just so I pay the tithes, it don't make any difference where or to whom I give them. I want some to go to foreign missions, and some to home missions, and some to the poor." Yes, and as you have been doing this, hasn't your soul become leaner and leaner, and are you not wondering what is the matter with you? The fact of the matter is that throwing your tithes out hither and thither out of God's plan closes the windows tighter and tighter, until you can scarcely breathe any spiritual atmosphere. "Where then should my tithes and offerings go?" I answer, by the authority of God's Word both in types and shadows and apostolic practices, they should be given into the church. . . .

CHAPTER EIGHT

Joseph Hillary King
(1869–1946)

J OSEPH HILLARY KING was the most gracious and judicious of all the pentecostal theologians of the first generation. Like most other theologians, he was convinced that his own views represented the best expression of Christian faith, but he always showed his opponents the respect of arguing with them. He never merely denounced those with whom he disagreed.

As a child, King grew up in a region of South Carolina that he later described as a spiritual wasteland. A few churches existed in the area, but "a high state of Christian experience was absolutely unknown," he later said. At the age of sixteen, he was converted at the meetings of a traveling evangelist, and this led him to join the Methodist Church. Sitting in church just a few months later, he had a mystical encounter with God that filled his heart with "light, love, and glory." He was convinced that in that moment he was fully sanctified and that God had taken away his penchant to sin. When he got home from church and told his mother what had happened, she replied in the skeptical tone only a parent can muster: "Oh, you know you are not sanctified." King trusted his own inner experience, however, so much that he would later proclaim "my experience is my creed."

While experience was always important for King, he was by no means an emotional thinker. Quite the contrary, every time he faced a significant theological decision, he rigorously examined all the evidence before making his choice. That is, in fact, how he decided to become a pentecostal. G. B. Cashwell, who had recently been to the Azusa Street Mission, was preaching in the area about the necessity of tongues as the evidence of the baptism of the

Spirit. When King first heard Cashwell, he contradicted him publicly. But the question gnawed at him. For the next day or two, King read and reread all the biblical passages that dealt with tongues. Finally, he became convinced that Cashwell was right. The next day he went back to Cashwell's services and received the baptism of the Spirit with the accompanying evidence of speaking in tongues.

King was a churchman. At age twenty-two he was licensed by the Southern Methodist Church and served for seven years as a "circuit walker" (his parishes being too poor to afford a horse) in the tristate region where Georgia, Tennessee, and North Carolina come together. By the late 1890s, however, he was beginning to feel restrained by the staid structures of the Methodist Church. In 1898, he joined the livelier Fire-Baptized Holiness Church (FBHC), and in 1900 he assumed the leadership of this small denomination when the founder was ousted for sexual improprieties. King later led the FBHC into the pentecostal fold and subsequently let his church be merged into the larger Pentecostal Holiness Church (PHC). After taking a short leave of absence from leadership, King would serve as general overseer of the PHC from 1917 until 1941.

The passages reproduced here are all taken from King's first book, entitled *From Passover to Pentecost* (1914). While King was a pentecostal believer, he was also a holiness Christian through and through, and he believed strongly in the doctrine of second-work sanctification. He was thus appalled by William Durham's new finished-work view of salvation, and he confronts those views in this excerpt. What is also evident is King's generous spirit. Among other things, this led him to suggest that people who have never heard of the "historical Christ" might still come to know the "essential Christ" and be redeemed. The last selection included here deals with King's understanding of tongues as a sign of the dawning of the "Pentecostal Dispensation" and not merely as the personal sign of one's baptism of the Spirit.[1]

The following selections are taken from *From Passover to Pentecost* (Senath, Mo.: F. E. Short, 1914).

Chapter IV. The Manner of Sin's Existence in the Unsaved

In every unsaved heart sin exists in a twofold manner. There are sins and sin. The former refers to acts, the latter to condition. Sins are actual, sin original. Sin is inherited, sins are committed. The former descends to us by transmission

---

[1] For more information, see Jacobsen, *Thinking in the Spirit*, 164–93.

from Adam's fall, the latter are acts of disobedience against God's law. Sin separated us from God; sins bring His condemnation upon us. Sin is a principle, sins are practical. Both are intimately related. Sin is the root, sins are the fruit. Sin is the fountain; sins the stream flowing from it. Sin is the lawless seed; sins are the lawless deeds. Sin is the parent; sins are the offspring. Sin is Adamic, sins are individual and personal. Sin is called the *Old Man*, sins are designated as transgressions.

In harmony with the foregoing we affirm that all who are born after the fall are born in sin, or with the principle of sin in them. We sinned in Adam in the Garden. We were in him potentially when he disobeyed. Every soul was in the first man germinally when he was made. God breathed a part of Himself into the body of clay, creating the man, and in that divine inbreathing the human race was germinally given birth. We being potentially in Adam the head of the race, we participated in his sin of disobedience. "Wherefore as by one man sin entered into the world, and death by sin; and so death passed upon all men, for that all have sinned." We being potentially in Adam the head of the race, we participated in his sin of disobedience. "Wherefore as by one man sin entered into the world, and death by sin; and so death passed upon all men, for that all have sinned." (Rom. 5:12.) "For that all have sinned," in the original is more *emphatic*: "In whom all have sinned," that is, in Adam the first. We sinned in him and we fell with him into death and ruin. God viewed the race in Adam when he sinned and looked upon that act as the act of the whole human family. Hence each one received the effect, and experienced the result of his and their disobedience. . . .

The condemnation of Adam's sin has not been imparted to every one born into the world, but only the effects of his transgression have been transmitted to us. The effect of his sin upon himself was the sense of guilt, and planting of the principle of sin in his nature, but the effect of his sin only has descended to every one born of him, planting in them the same principle. Why [would] not the guilt of his act be transmitted to all his vast offspring? Because of the atonement of Christ placed beneath man's feet the moment he sinned, securing him from instant death, and damnation in hell. The atonement, virtually offered from the foundation of the world, and including all in its provisions, was unconditionally applied to Adam at the moment of his sin, not in the removal of its guilt or effects, but in keeping him out of eternal punishment which he had merited, and granting him the privilege of living on earth and propagating his seed. The atonement at one stroke removed the guilt and condemnation of Adam's sin from the whole human race, so that not one is under obligation to go to hell for that sin. As Adam was exempted from instant eternal punishment for his first sin through the unconditional application of the atonement, so all his posterity was exempted from the like consequences by the same gracious means. No man has to go to hell because of Adam's transgression. Adam was given a second probation and permitted by the atonement to live and find the way back to God. All his posterity have the same opportunity through the same probation granted us (not in the next world) of escaping from sin's consequences through Christ, and obtaining the favor and peace of God.

This seed of sin inherited from the fall is the source of all sinning in our life. It is lawless in essence, and produces lawlessness in conduct. "Sin is lawlessness." (I John 3:4 Greek). Sinning is the outward manifestation of the lawless principle in the heart. Somewhere in childhood we yield to the movings of the unholy principle within and openly sin against law, and then we are sinners, rebels in God's sight. We are now under condemnation. Our conscience reproves us and we feel guilty. But do we immediately return to God? Nay. Satan prevents such by lying and deceiving us. We keep on sinning for years until we are loaded with guilt. Our sins reach unto heaven. Through much sinning the sin principle has grown rapidly in us in lust and deceit, so that our whole nature is depraved, and sold under sin. Thus sin in its twofold manner exists in us, and we are filled with its pollution.

From the foregoing it will be seen that sin is to be dealt with in a twofold manner, or in a way corresponding to its existence within us. Sin as a principle exists in us some time before sin as an act is committed by us. Sin in nature precedes sin in act, but the latter is the first that is dealt with by the Lord in His dealings with us. The Spirit convicts us of our sins and shows to us that we are guilty. He deals altogether with our sins and their consequences. If he shows us that we are corrupt, it is the effect and result of our sins. All is held up in the light of our own conduct, and all is entailed upon us because of our sins. Original sin is not in view. The sinner is not made to see original sin imbedded deep in his consciousness, but all is seen and shown up in the light of his own acts and doings. This department of sin is dealt with alone until it is removed. No one is able to go any further in the settling of the sin question, as it is very severe. We cannot stand any more than conviction for our own sins at the time. The being saved from our sins through grace is what we call conversion, with all its accompaniments, which we briefly described in the previous chapter.

Original sin is dealt with separately in God's economy. It is a distinct department of sin, as related to us, and its destruction demands a separate, distinct act on God's part. It is not removed in regeneration. It remains in us after that grace is received. It remains, but does not reign in the converted heart. It is held in check by the grace of regeneration. It disturbs, but does not control us. It exists in the saved, but its dominion is destroyed. There may be outbreakings at times, but not the recapturing of the soul by such momentary manifestations. Its removal is by a distinct act of grace. This is subsequent to regeneration. It is that which completes our justification from sin. The Old Man's death and removal is a distinct experience, different from conversion, and subsequent to it. It is death within its own character. Its removal must be by an apprehension of the provisions in the atonement for this purpose.

This removal is called by many the sanctification of the believer; by others full salvation; and by still others the second work of grace. We prefer the latter designation, as to our mind it is just as Scriptural as the others. Purity, or purification is more appropriate than either, but we shall not confine ourselves to any single designation of this great work or experience. . . .

Chapter XX. The Finished Work of Calvary

Romans is the atonement epistle. The fifth chapter is the greatest discussion of the atonement in the Bible. It requires study to understand, and understanding to appreciate it. What may we learn from this most profound discussion?

1. The Atonement is parallel to the Fall. The fall is universal. Sin touches every living being. Not one has escaped. Wherever man is found, sin is found. Wherever sin is found, there is some vague idea that there is some power that can remove it, or that there is some way to escape from its consequences. The atonement covers all the ground of sin. Millions know nothing of it, historically. Yet every one is mysteriously touched by the atonement in that aspect of it which is unconditionally applied. There may be those who have the essential Christ that know nothing of the historic Christ. They may have pressed, in heart, up through the mist of heathenism, and prayed to the God that made the heaven and earth, and in this way touched the Christ and found peace. We do not know this to be true, but we infer the same from certain statements in the Word. Christ "enlightens every man that cometh into the world," addressing them through creation, and through the written Word, to those who have it. "For the invisible things of him from the creation of the world are clearly seen, being understood by the things that are made, even his eternal power and Godhead, so that they are without excuse." "For when the Gentiles, which have not the law, do by nature the things contained in the law, these, having not the law, are a law unto themselves, which show the work of the law written in their hearts, their conscience also bearing witness, their thoughts the meanwhile accusing or else excusing one another."

All this shows, indirectly, the effect of atonement upon heathen hearts, preventing the absolute erasure of every trace of the divine image from their being, and opening a way whereby truth may find its way into their conscience and reason.

We all sinned in Adam and we are made righteous in Christ. This is in a representative sense. We were germinally in Adam when he sinned, and his sin was attributed to every soul in him. All were regarded as participating in his act.

The atonement, in its virtual institution, preceded the sin and fall of man. It was in this respect an accomplished fact in the mind of God. And every one in Adam was potentially in the atonement before the first sin, and because of this, Adam was prevented from dropping into the abyss of eternal night, the moment he sinned. And also those germinally in him, being potentially in Christ at the same time, were delivered from the guilt of the first sin and its obligatory punishable demerit. In this sense they are made righteous. All condemnation was removed as a result of their germinal participation in the Edenic transgression. The transmissible effects of the sin was not cut off; therefore its depraving influence flows on through the channel of human generation throughout the whole world. This will continue till the final removal from the world of all the effects of the Adamic sin in the Edenic restoration, through Christ's coming and reign. The atonement will erase every trace of the fall from the whole creation.

2. We all died in the first sin. This referred to death spiritual, and partly mental. Death is nothing more than separation from God. We were severed from him in Eden, and died. The death of the body is only an indirect result of the fall. It was not in an immortal non-perishable state before the entrance of death into the world. The tree of life was that which ministered to the non-perishable preservation of the body in Eden. When Adam sinned, God thrust him out of the Garden, and placed a flaming sword around the tree of life to keep man from eating of it and living forever, that is, preserving and perpetuating his physical existence upon earth forevermore, in the misery of sin in his soul and spirit. His body began to decay at once when he was driven from the Garden. The decaying would go on till the body would succumb, and this we call death. It is only the end of death's work. If man had not sinned, his body would have been lifted to the plane of absolute non-decayable existence when we should have been translated to a higher life. This would have been done when his Edenic probation ended.

The atonement will deliver, or has provided for deliverance from death, spiritual, mental and physical, and all decay in the world around us. All born of Adam will be raised from the dead, to die no more, in the sense of death in this sphere of existence. They shall be made alive physically in Christ in the resurrection. The spirits of the wicked will remain in death eternal, because they refused to let it be removed from them in this life. The saved chose to accept the atonement in its removal of sin here, and they will be placed beyond its possible recurrence in glorification. The bodies of the saints will also be glorified as a result of the provisions of the atonement for its being lifted to a state of eternal non-decaying existence before the fall—the same being applied to it in and after the resurrection, which will be its glorification.

3. The atonement exceeds the effects and limits of the fall. It was instituted before the fall, in anticipation of its full extent, and so the atonement must not only cover all the ground of the fall, but it must go beyond, and cover all the original infinite purpose of God in the creation of man and all things from eternity.

4. The one offense of one man brought condemnation but the free gift of justification is the pardon of multitudes of transgressions committed after the similitude of Adam's transgression.

As sin, the old man, abounded in us through daily transgressions, even so grace doth much more abound, not only in the removal of all sin, but in the continual increase of joy and peace in us as a consequence thereof.

5. As sin laid its curse upon all creation subject to man, so grace in the general regeneration of all things, and the final glorification will so abound as to place all creation in a far more glorious state than it would have been had sin never entered.

These general observations will serve to bring before us that phase of the subject that we wish to discuss in relation to the removal of sin from the heart through the atonement.

The Antinomians and Plymouth Brethren of England and America have for a long while discoursed and written upon what they are pleased to term the "finished work of Christ," or the "finished work of Calvary." Especially have the Plymouth Brethren emphasized this, and the phrase has become a pet one with them. They present the atonement as being objectively and subjectively finished at the same time, or rather that its subjective application in the first instance equals its objective completeness. And yet they are compelled to admit from experience and observation that atonement is not completed in us at its first application. What do they do to reconcile the inconsistency? They resort to this species of interpretation: The atonement, in its subjective application, is completed in us in the purpose and view of the mind of God. God makes our standing at the moment of our salvation in Christ as complete as it will ever be in the glorified state, and he refuses to view us in any other light but that of eternally saved beings glorified with Christ. What then? We are not glorified the moment we are saved. No, indeed. Our state of character is as imperfect before God as our standing is perfect in God's mind; according to the advocates of this theory. Perfection of standing in Christ is to them a most pleasing theme, while perfection of character in us is a most horrible doctrine. We are, according to this theory, as perfect as angels in our standing before God, in Christ, and as imperfect as constant necessitated sinning can make us in character, upon earth. What is to be done? The Holy Spirit has come to bring our state up to our standing before God. This is the way they so teach. How the Spirit is to accomplish this is difficult to see, as we are constantly sinning before God and cannot keep from it. But we are to rest in the "finished

work of Christ" imparted to us in the mind of God, and as we rest we are being
perfected in state, corresponding to our perfection in standing before God.
This perfection of state is going on in us though we are constantly sinning
against God. Sin cannot interfere, as it is put away in pardon, once for all,
both past and future. Christ took all our sins, past and future, upon Himself
and they are His, not ours, and we take His righteousness by faith, and God
never sees our sins, but upon Christ, and he never sees us but as in the perfect
righteousness of Christ, and hence sin has taken its eternal flight from us in
the mind of God, and he can never see them again. They are Christ's sins,
not ours, and as he put them all away, God sees no sin upon him, and so they
are gone eternally, even though we be sinning all the time. We object to this
(1) because there is no scripture that teaches perfection of standing, absolute,
before God, and imperfection of state at the same time; (2) it does away with
the necessity to prayer and faith, and all promises of reward for faithful service.
All law is abolished, as they teach, and consequently, all duty is abrogated, all
possibility of apostasy is annihilated, and so we can go to sleep in carnal security, till death, and wake up in the bliss of glory eternal. This comes as near
being a "damnable heresy" as anything we know.

But the thing that is surprising and painful to us almost beyond degree is
that this thing has found its way into the ranks of the Pentecostal people today.
We hear the cry of the "finished work" throughout the world, heralded most
ardently by many with an earnestness surpassing that of the first proclamation
of Pentecost by the same individuals. It is Antinomianism, Darbyism dressed
up in a Zinzindorfian garb and going through the land with all the intrepidity
of a new resurrection, doing its old destructive work among believers. To be
sure it has some new phases that did not belong to it originally, but nothing
surprising about this, as every resurrection ought to present some new aspect
to the thing raised.

What is the teaching of this theory as found among Pentecostal people? It
is this: When we are saved the atonement is applied to us with a "finishing
stroke," removing all sin of all kinds, so that we are sanctified wholly at the
moment of pardon. We are of necessity completely cleansed from inbred sin
at the moment of forgiveness and regeneration. We object to this theory for
the following reasons:

1. It makes no distinction between the objective completeness of the atonement on the cross, and its subjective completeness in the heart and life of
believers, here and hereafter. That the atonement was objectively completed
on the cross we gladly admit, and boldly teach. Christ saith, "It is finished,"
and His word is true. God, the Father, accepted it as finished, and also all
the host of Heaven. The Christian church has accepted, and taught it from
Pentecost to the present without exception. But that the atonement is subjectively finished in us at its first application we stoutly deny. The Bible, which is

the text book of the atonement, from Genesis to Revelation, does not so present the atonement as finished in us at the first application of its benefits. We
have studied diligently the history of the Christian church, and also the history
of its doctrines separately, from the days of Christ to the present, and we have
never seen anything that even intimated that the atonement was subjectively
finished in us upon the forgiveness of our sins. The finishing of the atonement
subjectively in us has never been defined by any theological system in the
Christian church for nineteen centuries except that which we have presented
of Antinomianism and Plymouth Brethrenism. And they do not teach it so,
absolutely.

2. It is a limitation put upon the atonement. If the atonement is finished
in the work of justification (for in that work we are sanctified, also, according
to this theory) then there is no more to be done in, or for, us in its provisions,
as they are all granted or bestowed in this first and only work of grace. To say
that it is finished in us in the removal of all sin is to affirm that all the provisions of the same are limited to the sin question, and can go no further. If the
complete removal of all sin of all kinds from the heart and life is the purpose
of the atonement, and that when this is done all is done that was provided for,
then there can be no further benefit bestowed upon us. If this is the finishing
of atonement, it is finished. If it is finished, nothing more remains to be done;
and if any more remains to be done, or given, then it is not finished. This
means that when one work is done all is done. One application is the completeness of the whole.

The advocates of the "finished work" do not thus believe, for they teach
that there are other experiences and blessings beyond justification. In this
they are inconsistent and illogical. The finished work of Christ is the removal
of all sin from the heart, and a finished work is complete. When God finished
the creative work it was complete, nothing more to be done. He rested at that
juncture, and did not keep on creating. When Jesus said, "It is finished," the
atonement was complete; he did not have to die any more. He gave himself
"once for all" and there could be no repetition. Justification, according to this
theory, necessarily embracing sanctification, both being one and the same
thing without distinction in nature and time of reception, and this one work of
grace being the "finished work of Christ," the whole atonement being applied
in all its provisions, therefore, nothing more can be done. It is finished, and a
finished work is a finished work; no more additions, or repetitions, the thing
is impossible.

3. We object to it because it places the greatest and most extensive work of
God outside and beyond the atonement. We mention a few:

(a) The baptism of the Holy Ghost. This is promised in the Word, and
we have always believed that it was provided in the atonement. We are mistaken, according to this theory, as the atonement is finished, and the whole of

its provisions applied in justification. There is no relation between the Spirit and the blood, the one did not purchase the other. The ground of the Spirit's reception must be sought for elsewhere.

(b) The healing of the body. Isaiah 53 is the prophetic atonement chapter, and in it the healing of bodily diseases is explicitly stated as one of provisions of his sufferings and death. Matt. 8:17 plainly states that Christ "took our infirmities and bore our sicknesses" to fulfill this statement in Isaiah 53. And we have always thought since we accepted this truth of healing, that it was in the atonement, but in this we are in error, as the whole atonement is finished in the one work of grace removing all sin.

4. The victory over the world and Satan is through the blood of Jesus, for "they overcame him by the Blood of the Lamb, and the word of their testimony." The victory is through Christ, but not by virtue of His death. Victory has nothing to do with the blood. We have always thought that Christ died to "deliver us out of this ungodly world," and have been simple enough to believe it, but in this we are wrong, as the atonement is entirely finished in the one work of grace, received in justification.

5. We have been taught that through the precious blood we would enter through the gates into the City of Light; for it is said that the saints in glory give all the praise of their eternal salvation to the Lamb whose blood secured it for them. "These are they who have come up through great tribulation, and have washed their robes and made them white in the Blood of the Lamb. Therefore are they before the throne of God." It is rather disturbing to find in this we have been mistaken also, and we are at a loss to know just how to get to Heaven since the blood can not avail to help us, as its whole benefit is entirely and completely applied in saving us from all sin in the one work of grace.

Do not all these blessings come to us through the atonement of Christ? Yes, yes, shout all the advocates of the "finished work of Christ" in justification. Then we inquire, soberly, what do you mean by the "finished work of Christ?" You use it constantly to set forth justification as that which delivers from all sin. In that you say the work of Calvary is finished. If it is, then you should never preach another blessing or benefit beyond, because it is not in Christ, as nothing can come from or through Christ except His blood. If it is not so, then candidly we say, be consistent, be honest, be sober, and quit using the phrase in relation to sin's destruction alone, as that is misleading, unscriptural and false.

In concluding this chapter we boldly assert that there can come no blessing, benefit, experience, or victory, in body, mind, or spirit, in time or eternity, except as it comes through the Blood of Jesus, and that alone. The blood purchased everything absolutely for us. The "finished work of Christ" subjectively does not end with this life. The resurrection and glorification comes through the Blood of Jesus, and so far as we know, everything in the eternal ages will come through the Blood of Jesus. We do not believe that the work of the atonement will ever be finished in and upon us in time and eternity, subjectively.

Chapter XXXII. The Sign and the Gift
(Mark 16:17–18; Heb. 2:4.)

Among the signs that shall follow faith in Christ as given in Mark 16:17–18 is the speaking in New Tongues. We must not think that this sign necessarily follows the first exercise of faith in Christ, for in that case every one believing in Christ to the forgiveness of sins would receive this sign and exercise it the moment that pardon was granted. Many believed in Christ in his day, but never spoke with new tongues; and in the book of Acts, the only book that presents Pentecost from an historic standpoint, we have no instance where any one ever spoke with new tongues the moment pardon was granted. None of these signs accompanied saving faith.

The faith by which we appropriate the baptism of the Holy Ghost does not necessarily belong to the order of the miraculous, but it touches the borders of it, and may eventually enter into it fully, by development through the Baptism of the Spirit. The full baptism is attended with miraculous manifestations, as the record in the book of Acts clearly shows. This manifestation is one of the signs mentioned in Mark 16:17–18, that is, "New Tongues." Are we to infer that the other signs mentioned there are associated with the Baptism of the Spirit? We think not. The signs of healing and the casting out of demons were exercised by the disciples even before the death of Jesus. As to any one taking up serpents purposely or even by Divine directions, we have no record in the Word. A viper accidentally took hold of Paul's hand at Melita, but he shook it off into the fire and experienced no harm. He did not take hold of it to demonstrate Divine power to the savagous inhabitants of the island. No instance is on record in the Word where any one drank deadly poison as an evidence of faith. None of these signs were ever produced as an evidence of salvation from sin. The witness of the Spirit to our spirit is the evidence of this fact.

New tongues denote more than a mere change in our speech from an unholy to a holy conversation. It signifies a language distinct from our mother tongue. Such language is not acquired by the study of some foreign tongue as some have affirmed. It is done by Divine power just as the other mentioned signs are exercised by Divine power solely. We may acquire a knowledge and use of a foreign language upon natural grounds, but we cannot speak with new tongues upon the basis of the natural [any] more than we could heal the sick or cast out demons by natural forces. Every sign is of supernatural origin, and is exercised upon this basis entirely.

New tongues accompanied the Pentecostal outpouring of the Spirit by Divine choice, as recorded in the Acts, and we infer that their connection possesses a significance worthy of note. It was not given as an idle attendant to excite morbid curiosity, or to create a sensation. In that case God would be acting in a manner inconsistent with the dignity of his person. God cannot debase himself, nor sacrifice his wisdom in such a trivial manner. There is a purpose, a significance, in the association of new tongues with the Pentecostal baptism; and it is our duty to ascertain this by study and experience. . . .

What is the significance of this miraculous phenomenon? It was one of the tokens given to distinguish the Pentecostal baptism of the Holy Spirit from previous outpourings in past ages. Many effusions of the Spirit had taken place with Holy Prophets and Special Messengers in the Old Testament days, and even in the New Testament previous to the death of Christ. But this beginning of the fulfillment of Joel's prophecy concerning the Spirit's outpouring in the last days must be distinguished from all previous effusions; and for this purpose the utterance of unknown languages by the Spirit was given. The Pentecostal Dispensation is a grander and loftier one, and its inauguration must be accompanied with miraculous phenomena hitherto unknown. Its internal aspects would be characterized by revelations of the Godhead in a manner unknown by holy men of past dispensation. The indwelling Messiah in glory transcending that of the Mosaic Age was a mystery hidden in ages past, but revealed to the saints of the Pentecostal Dispensation. The speaking in other tongues is the only outward aspect of Pentecost, the same being given as an evidence of its reception.

Peter and those brethren with him at Caesarea regarded the speaking in other tongues as an evidence that the Gentiles had received the gift of the Holy Ghost as they (the Jews) and if it was an evidence in relation to the Gentiles, it must be equally so in relation to the Jews. The Gentiles spake as the Jews, and hence this was evidence of the fact that a like baptism had been given them. The book of Acts is the only one in the Bible that presents to us the Pentecostal baptism from an historic standpoint; and it gives the standard by which to determine the reality and fullness of the Spirit's outpouring. Since in every instance where the Spirit was poured out for the first time this miraculous utterance accompanied the same, we infer that its connection with baptism is to be regarded as an evidence of its reception.

But what of those who have received great anointings of power by the Spirit and did not speak with other tongues? Must we infer that they did not receive the real gift of the Holy Spirit? That they received the Spirit can not be denied, but it was of the nature of the Spirit's outpouring such as men received previous to the glorification of Jesus Christ. Zacharias and Elizabeth, Mary, Simeon and Anna received the baptism of the Spirit in a wonderful manner, but it was not according to the measure of the Spirit's outpouring after the glorification of the risen Christ. The Spirit was given in all ages previous to Pentecost, but it was not the Pentecostal gift of the same Spirit. This could only be given as a result of the glorification of Jesus our Lord. Since this great event took place in Heaven it made possible the gift of the Spirit on a higher and loftier scale, and His coming must be far more glorious than in former dispensations. What should mark the distinct object of this greater gift of the Spirit but the "speaking in other tongues as he gave utterance"? Jesus received the baptism of the Spirit up to the highest degree in his day, and it was accompanied by a sign, "the Spirit in the form of a dove," and the disciples received the Spirit up to the highest degree in this day, and it was also accompanied by a sign, the new tongue speaking languages unknown to the speaker. . . .

CHAPTER NINE

Esek William Kenyon
(1867–1948)

Esek William Kenyon is one of the more enigmatic figures in early pentecostal history. In fact, there is some dispute about whether he should even be classified as a pentecostal. Kenyon was never formally a part of any pentecostal church, and his view of the Spirit's work in the world is different from many other early pentecostals. But Kenyon himself counted a number of important pentecostal leaders among his friends, and his publications were popular in many pentecostal circles. It is probably best to think of Kenyon as a borderline figure, sometimes a pentecostal associate and at other times an outsider. Regardless, the enormous continuing influence of his ideas requires his inclusion in this volume.

Kenyon hailed from the Northeast, spending the first fifty-five years of his life, with only a few trips elsewhere, in New England and New York state. But while his geographic roamings were relatively limited, his religious curiosity was wide-ranging. He had connections with the Methodist Church and with Dwight L. Moody and the YMCA, but he was also conversant with a number of leaders in the late-nineteenth-century healing movement, and he studied for a while at the Emerson School of Oratory in Boston, which would later become an early center for New Age–style spirituality.

Kenyon was an energetic entrepreneur. His many projects included starting up a publishing company, founding two Bible colleges, running a custom-made shirt business, launching at least two radio shows, organizing several new churches, and writing about his faith. Kenyon was sometimes almost manic in his pace of life. He was also generous with both his time and money—so much so that his first marriage failed partly because he was always bringing home needy guests and giving away his possessions. Because Kenyon was on the road most of the time, his wife had to cope with what Kenyon dumped in her lap, and eventually it was too much.

His first contact with pentecostalism proper likely came during a visit to Chicago, where he met William Durham. Rather than join the movement, however, Kenyon seems to have thought the movement ought to join him. At the very least, he believed his own vision of God and the world was broader and more inclusive than pentecostalism. He was willing to work with pentecostals, but was not willing to shrink his own views to a size that would fit within the confines of pentecostalism as he knew it.

The Father and His Family, written in 1916, was Kenyon's first book. His many later works tend merely to fill in the gaps and further develop the themes of this first volume. Kenyon's basic message is that Christianity includes both a vital and a legal relationship with God. The vital side has to do with new life in Christ; the legal side has to do with claiming all the rights and privileges available to people as children of God. Kenyon's emphasis was on claiming those rights, and because of that he is often seen as one of the founders of what is known as the "word of faith" movement (detractors sometimes call it the "name it and claim it" gospel) that is so popular in pentecostal circles in America and around the world.

Kenyon's prose style often mimics in print the breathy, punctuated style of revivalistic preaching. Short, one-sentence paragraphs drive home his points. The following selection, which comes from his first book, both illustrates that distinctive style of writing and nicely summarizes his message of living fully within the divine inheritance available to everyone who calls on Jesus' name.[1]

The following selections are taken from *The Father and His Family: A Restatement of the Plan of Redemption*, 1916 (Reprint, Seattle: Kenyon's Gospel Publishing Society, 1964.)

Chapter the Fifteenth: Claiming Our Rights

Christianity is a legal document. Most of our basic legal terminology comes from the Scripture. The very titles, Old Covenant and New Covenant, are legal terms.

Every step in the plan of Redemption, from the Fall of Man until Jesus Christ was seated at the right hand of the Majesty on High, having redeemed the

---

[1] For more information, see Jacobsen, *Thinking in the Spirit*, 313–52; and Dale H. Simmons, *E. W. Kenyon and the Postbellum Pursuit of Peace, Power, and Plenty* (Lanham, Md.: Scarecrow Press, 1997).

human race, is simply a series of legal steps perfecting the most remarkable Legal Document the human has in its possession.

The plan of Redemption cannot be understood unless one reads it from the legal point of view.

In this plan of Redemption there are three parties to the contract: God, Man, and Satan.

God must be just to Himself, just to Man, and just to the Devil.

We understand that God created man, placing him here on the earth, and that He conferred upon him certain legal rights. Legal rights that are conferred are more easily forfeited than those that come by nature. These rights man transferred to Satan, God's enemy.

This brings the Devil into the plan so that he must be dealt with, and the whole scheme of Redemption is God's seeking to redeem the human race from Adam's sin, and doing it upon such an equitable basis that it will perfectly satisfy the claims of Justice, meet the needs of man, and defeat Satan on legal grounds.

The Fall of Man was a lawful act; that is, Adam had a legal right to transfer the authority and dominion that God had placed in his hands into the hands of another.

This gives Satan a legal right to rule over man and over creation.

The plan of Redemption is one of the most ingenious, and most wonderful of all the many works of God.

Notice what He is obliged to do.

Man sold himself out to the Devil, making himself a bond slave, and that slavery will last until the lease or period of man's dominion expires.

God must in some way redeem fallen man from his sin, and Satan's dominion.

He must do it in such a way as not to be unjust to Satan, nor unjust to man.

God must recognize and hold inviolate man's treacherous act of transference of dominion.

It was a legal act, and God has no right to arbitrarily annul it.

He must show to Satan perfect justice at all points, and at the same time He must reach man in his helplessness and redeem him.

In order to do this, it is necessary that one come to the earth who is not a subject of Satan, and yet a man, and as a man meet every demand of justice against man.

In order to accomplish this, there must be an Incarnation.

This Incarnate one must not be a subject of Satan, nor a subject of death, and to this end God sends the Holy Spirit to a virgin in Judah, and she conceives and bears a son.

This son is born, not of natural generation but of supernatural.

The child is not a subject of death nor of Satan.

He has the same type of a body that the first man, Adam, had before he sinned.

Every step of the work that was accomplished by this Incarnate One was based upon perfectly legal grounds.

This Incarnate One met the demands, first, of the heart of Deity for a perfect human who would do His will; second, He met the demands of fallen man in that as a man He met the Devil and conquered him in honorable open combat.

"Being tempted in all points, yet without sin."

He goes on the Cross, and God lays upon him the iniquity of the human race.

He, then, with this burden upon Him and under Judgment of God, goes down into Hell and suffers the penalty demanded by Justice.

When He had paid this penalty, He arose from the dead.

He conquered Satan. He broke his dominion and took away his authority and power.

Then, with the trophies of His triumph, He ascended to the right hand of the Majesty on High and laid the tokens of His victory at the feet of His Great Father.

On the ground of this victory, the sinner has a legal right to accept Jesus Christ as a personal Savior.

He has a legal right to Eternal Life.

He has a legal right to Victory over sin and Satan.

He has a legal right to a home in Heaven.

He has a legal right to use the name of Jesus in prayer.

He has a legal right to his Father's protection and care.

He has a legal right to a son's place in the Family of God.

He has a legal right to the indwelling presence of the Holy Spirit, to the care and protection of the Spirit, and in the intercession and teaching of the Spirit.

He has a legal right to be translated at the Second Coming of the Lord Jesus.

He has a legal right to immortality for the body.

He has a legal right to an inheritance in the New Heavens and New Earth.

He has a legal right to live with his Father throughout Eternity.

Are We Claiming Our Rights?

There is no excuse for the spiritual weakness and poverty of the Family of God when the wealth of Grace and Love of our great Father with His power and wisdom are all at our disposal.

We are not coming to the Father as a tramp coming to the door begging for food; we come as sons not only claiming our legal rights but claiming the natural rights of a child that is begotten in love.

No one can hinder us or question our right of approach to our Father.

When we realize the great need of the unsaved world and know that need can only be met by the great heart of the Father operating through the Church, it stirs us to mighty intercession for a needy world.

God cannot touch the human today except through the Church. It is His only mediator, and if the Church fails to assume its obligation then the hand of God is powerless.

It staggers one to realize that God has limited Himself to our prayer life, and when we refuse to assume the obligations of prayer, God's hands are paralyzed.

Our Authority

"For sin shall not have dominion over you: for ye are not under law, but under grace." Rom. 6:14, or "Sin shall not Lord it over you."

Sin has lost its dominion or authority over us.

Satan has no legal authority over the New Creation, though he has over the old.

Satan has Legal Rights over the sinner that God can not dispute or challenge.

He can sell them as slaves; he owns them, body, soul and spirit.

But the moment we are born again, receive Eternal Life, the nature of God,—his legal dominion ends.

Christ is the Legal Head of the New Creation, or Family of God, and all the Authority that was given Him, He has given us: (Matt. 28:18), "All authority in heaven," the seat of authority, and "on earth," the place of execution of authority.

He is "head over all things," the highest authority in the Universe, for the benefit of the Church which is His body.

Eph. 1:20, "Which he wrought in Christ, when he raised him from the dead, and set him at his own right hand in the heavenly places."

Here He is at the "Right Hand of God."

"Far above," that is, His seat of authority transcends all other rulers.

Phil. 2:9–11, "Wherefore also God highly exalted him, and gave unto him the name which is above every name that in the name of Jesus every knee should bow, of things in heaven and things on earth and things under the earth, and that every tongue should confess that Jesus Christ is Lord, to the glory of God the Father."

He has the Name above every name in the three worlds: Heaven, Earth, and Hell.

Every demon and angel is subject to the Imperial Name of Jesus and, wonder of wonders, He gave us the Power of Attorney to use that Name of Might.

All our Authority is based on His Finished Work, but it is all enwrapped in His name.

By His giving us the Legal use of this name He has put omnipotence at our disposal in our combat with Satanic hosts.

Mark 16:17–20, "And these shall accompany them that believe: in my name shall they cast out demons; they shall speak with new tongues; they shall take up serpents, and if they drink any deadly thing, it shall in no wise hurt them; they shall lay hands on the sick, and they shall recover."

"So then the Lord Jesus, after he had spoken unto them, was received up into heaven and sat down at the right hand of God."

"And they went forth, and preached everywhere, the Lord working with them, and confirming the word by the signs that followed."

"In my name shall they cast out demons."

Here He defines our Legal Authority.

We shall cast out demons: (this means Authority over demons in their relation to men;) cast them out of peoples' bodies; break their power over those bodies, minds, and spirits; break their power over meetings, homes, and sometimes communities.

Our combat is not against flesh and blood but against the principalities and powers in heavenly places; or in other words, our war is against demons of all ranks, kinds, and authorities.

They are attacking the human everywhere, and especially the children of God.

How are we to defend ourselves against them, or lead an assault on their hosts, and deliver the captives?

The air is pregnant with evil spirits who seek to infest our bodies as bats do old buildings.

The awful power of evil in our land eloquently proves what we write.

"In my Name ye shall speak in new tongues."

This new and startling manifestation of the Spirit is our Legal Right in the Name, where all the mighty powers of God are kept for us.

"In my Name they shall take up serpents, and if they drink any deadly thing it shall not harm them."

"They shall lay hands on the sick, and they shall recover."

Here it is not sufferance or pity, but Legal Authority.

You have as much right to demand healing as you have to demand the cashing of a check at a bank where you have a deposit.

You have a Legal Right to deliverance from Satan.

If any one oppresses you or enslaves you in this country, you have a Legal Right to protection from the government to which you belong and pay taxes.

So you have Legal Rights in the Family of God.

No man has a right to hold a white slave today; neither has Satan a Legal Right to hold a child of God in bondage.

All disease is of the Devil.

How glad the Father would be, if we would arise and take our Legal Rights.

All bad habits are of the Devil.

John 14:13–14, 15:16, 16:23–24, "And whatsoever ye shall ask in my name, that will I do, that the Father may be glorified in the Son."

"If ye shall ask anything in my name, that will I do."

This scripture does not refer to prayer as do the others. It is not coming to the Father with a petition, but it is taking the Master's place. It is using His authority to cast out demons, to heal the sick.

A literal translation would read: "If ye shall demand anything in my name, that will I do." In His place we demand sickness and demons to leave in the authority of His Name, and He is there to confirm by His power the word that we speak.

This scripture refers to our using the authority that He gave us in Mark 16:17–18.

Now notice Jn. 16:23–24.

"That whatsoever ye shall ask of the Father in my name, he will give it to you."

"And in that day ye shall ask me nothing."

"Verily, verily, I say unto you, If ye ask anything of the Father, he will give it to you in my name."

"Hitherto have ye asked nothing in my name; ask, and ye shall receive, that your joy may be made full."

This is praying to the Father in Jesus' Name.

Here the Mighty Son of God who is now seated in the highest seat of Authority in the Universe gives us the Legal Power of Attorney to use the Might, Authority, and Power of His Name, in our earth[ly] struggles against Satan and demons.

In the face of this mighty Fact, poverty and weakness of spirit are criminal.

Here all Heaven with its might and Authority are at our disposal.

It is not trying to have Faith, but knowing the Legal Rights that are yours, as much yours as the clothes you wear—as the bed you sleep on,—the hat you wear, all yours, legally, blessedly yours.

Satan cannot stand before that Name now, any more than he could before the Man who gave you the right to use it, when He walked in Galilee.

Disease is as impotent before it now as it was when its owner, as the Son of Man, walked the earth.

Demons fear it today in the lips of a person who walks with God, as when they bowed before it in Jesus' Day.

All Hell knows the power of that Name; they know our Legal Rights and Authority.

So they are fighting to keep us in ignorance of our Legal Rights; or if we know them, to keep us under condemnation so we will not dare use them.

Matt. 18:18–20, "Verily I say unto you, what things soever ye shall bind on earth shall be bound in heaven; and what things soever ye shall loose on earth shall be loosed in heaven.

"Again I say unto you, that if two of you shall agree on earth as touching anything that they shall ask, it shall be done for them of my Father who is in Heaven.

"For where two or three are gathered together in my name, there am I in the midst of them."

Here the heart stands hushed at its power and God-delegated Authority.

"Whatsoever ye shall bind on earth shall be bound in heaven."

This is unexplored territory to most men today.

We can bind Demons, bind disease, and habits, and bind men so they can not go on in the will of Satan; or use fearsome power to deliver souls over to Satan for the destruction of the body.

"For I verily, being absent in body but present in spirit, have already as though I were present judged him that hath so wrought this thing, in the name of our Lord Jesus, we being gathered together, and my spirit, with [the] power of our Lord Jesus, to deliver such a one unto Satan for the destruction of the Flesh, that the spirit may be saved in the day of [the] Lord Jesus." 1 Cor. 5:3–5.

We may bind the power of Satan over a community, making it easy for men to accept Christ.

"Whatsoever ye shall loose on earth shall be loosed in heaven."

Whatsoever in Jesus' name we set free, God in Heaven will make good.

What power we have! Let's use it!

Will we arise to our mighty, heaven-given privileges?

Look at the bound men and women everywhere, and the Word challenges us to go out and set the prisoner free.

What does this mean?

All that it says, thank God.

You can set diseased men free. We are doing it daily in our work!

You can set demon-bound men free; you can break the chains that bind men, in that mighty Name.

Most Christians are bound in some manner, either in testimony or in prayer, by fear and devilish doubt; they can be set free by a word if [they] use that name and then take their privileges.

What bondage to the world and the binding, devilish spirit of the age we endure, that unseen bondage of the god of this age.

How he holds men in leash!

Yet every spirit may be free, yes, as free as Jesus.

What bondage to the fear of man; yet one authoritative word and the bond shall be broken.

What bondage to fear of want that makes men give pennies instead of dollars; yet there is freedom, glorious freedom for every bondaged soul.

Reader! the Spirit is challenging you to arise and live this Truth.

What prayer meetings we would have if the Christians were free in prayer and testimony!

God's hands are tied until He can use ours.

Angels are our servants.

They cannot do our work. God is limited to our Faith, our obedience.

God is as small in the world as we make Him.

God is big only where some man makes Him big, by using this divinely given authority.

We are the body of Christ; the Head is powerless without our hands and feet.

Oh, men, can't you see how helpless God is until we let Him live omnipotently in our acts?

A sin in the heart binds the arms of God that would embrace a multitude.

Our fear to be used binds God's omnipotence.

Men of God, be God's men and use the authority delegated to you.

Chapter the Twentieth: How to Become a Christian

. . . You have read this amazing message. What does it mean to you? What will be the aftermath?

You have been let into the heart secrets of the Father. You have seen the death agonies of the Son for you. It has been a personal affair, and you have been saying, "He died for me. He suffered for me. He fought that great battle before He arose from the dead for me."

"It was my fight. He conquered Satan for me. It is as though I had fought that battle, suffered all the agonies of it, and conquered the enemy alone. The enemy must forever be a conquered foe. He may be persistent. He may challenge me again and again, but I know I am his master."

"I know that in the Name of Jesus I can conquer demons and any affliction that they may bring upon the bodies and minds of men. I am, in that Name, God's instrument of healing and deliverance."

You have seen the reality of the New Creation, what it means to have Eternal Life, the nature of God.

You have seen that this New Creation heads up in Jesus; and when He said "I am the vine; ye are the branches," He was uttering a statement of the absolute truth of your union with Him.

You have His life and nature in you. He took your spiritual death and your old nature on the cross and He gives you His life and nature in His Resurrection.

You know that it is possible for you to let this Life dominate your spirit until it gains the ascendancy over your reasoning faculties, until really you have the mind of Christ.

You know that His Eternal Life coming into your spirit gives you a creative ability, that you belong to His class now.

Your faith becomes a dominating power, a creative energy.

His Life has become your life, your light, your wisdom, and your ability.

When He told the disciples to tarry in Jerusalem until they received power from on high, that meant that they were to receive God's ability from on High.

You have that ability in you now. It is the nature of God. You are going to let that nature loose.

You are going to learn the secret of freeing the ability of God in you.

You have not only a perfect New Creation, a perfect Redemption wrought by Him, but you have received from Him through this New Creation, His Righteousness.

Righteousness, you know, means the ability to stand in the Father's presence without the sense of guilt, weakness, or inferiority.

Isn't it a strange fact that we need Righteousness to stand in the presence of Satan, and of his works, in the presence of cancers and Tuberculosis with fearless faith?

Nothing will reveal man's utter helplessness and inability and force back upon his consciousness his inferiority like a body filled with cancer.

Yet this Righteousness that is imparted to us at the New Birth gives us a holy boldness in the presence of the works of the adversary.

We are his absolute masters and we know it.

Jesus said, "In my name ye shall cast out demons."

That means mastery over the adversary. This newly discovered Righteousness in Christ gives us courage to use the Name of Jesus in setting men and women free from disease and financial bondage, yes, and every other Satanic control.

It gives a fearlessness in the fact of overwhelming circumstances that ordinarily would drive us into defeat.

We have become masters where we served as slaves. We have become freemen where we were held in bondage.

We have become leaders where we did not have courage even to be led.

We have become the light-bearers. We recognize what He said, "Ye are the light of the world."

The Son has set us free. We know what it means to stand in the presence of impossibilities as conquerors.

We are not afraid to walk the sea with the Master. We are not afraid to face the "old serpent" in open combat to set men and women free.

We know we have the Sword of the Spirit that gives us absolute mastery.

We have seen the power and authority of the Word in human lips. The Word is a dead thing in the Bible, but it becomes impregnated with God Himself in the lips of faith.

When we dare say "In Jesus' Name, you are conquered. My Father laid that cancer upon Jesus, and He bore it away, and by His stripes healing belongs to this suffering one,"—the Word is as fresh in our lips as it was when Jesus gave it to the apostles.

The Word is a part of God Himself, just as our word is a part of us.

Creation came into being when faith said, "Let there be." That creative element is in that Word today.

"The Words that I speak unto you, they are spirit and they are life."

That means they are creative, they dominate, they bring into being whatever the will of the speaker demands.

How big Christianity becomes. It makes super-men out of slaves.

God takes the "nobodies" and makes "somebodies."

But greater than any of these is the reality of our fellowship with the Father. Fellowship means sharing together. As husband and wife enter into the fellowship of marriage, to share with each other, so we who have been born into the family become fellowsharers with Jesus and the Father.

The Holy Spirit is the One who enables us.

We have His ability, for He promised that when He came He would empower or give ability to the New Creation. We have that ability. We share with Him.

Our fellowship is the light and joy of this wonderful life.

We are walking in the light. There is no darkness in our spirit. Everything that was displeasing to Him has been put out of our life.

We are no longer consecrating, surrendering, and yielding; that belonged to the babyhood state of this marvelous life.

We have grown up into the full stature of the measure of the sons and daughters of God. We are getting under His burdens, we are carrying His loads.

We who are strong, are bearing the burdens of the weak. We are healing them with our faith. We have become the healers, the reconcilers, the helpers in the body of Christ.

We are taking Jesus' place. We have taken over His work. We hear Him say, "Greater things than these shall ye do because I go unto my Father."

We have a right to His Name, His wisdom, His Word, and all His ability. All He is in Himself, He is to us.

The Father gave Him to us. "God so loved the world that He gave His only begotten Son."

He has never taken the gift back. As our Lord, He is our caretaker, our preserver, the mainstay of our life.

"Greater is He that is in you than he that is in the world." We have become God-inside minded.

We remember the day He came into our life. He became our absolute, indwelling Lord.

We know what it means that he is greater than Satan.

He is the One who raised Jesus from the dead. He is the One who made the dead body of Jesus just as sweet and fresh as Heaven's fragrance. He is the One who touched the dead, decaying body of Lazarus and filled it with life and vigor and health.

He is the Renewer, the Healer, and the Sustainer of the church.

He has come into our life. He is to guide us into all reality. He is to take the things of the Father and the things of Jesus and unveil them to us.

This book we have read is the product of His going into the treasure house and bringing out the long-lost riches of Christ, and turning them over to us.

He is asking us today what we are going to do with them. Are we going to hide them in a napkin, or are we going to invest them?

It is our privilege and our responsibility.

CHAPTER TEN

Fred Francis Bosworth
(1877–1958)

A S A CHILD, Fred Francis Bosworth was an accident waiting to happen. He was a Nebraska farm kid, and on an almost regular basis he fell out of the barn, sliced himself up with scythes, ran pitchforks through his feet, and got attacked by bees. Writing years later, his biographer said this string of injuries was providentially provided so that Bosworth would later be able to sympathize with the suffering of others. Whatever the inspiration, it is true that Bosworth's adult ministry largely centered on healing and helping those in pain.

When Bosworth was growing up, few would have guessed that he would someday be a preacher and healer. He was a typical teenager. In an effort to make a little extra cash, he and his brother spent one summer wandering all over Kansas and Nebraska hawking stereoscopic picture viewers and skipping out on their rooming bills to save money. But Bosworth met God in a revival service in Omaha when he was seventeen and left his lust for lucre behind. Revivalistic services were often somber affairs, but Bosworth's encounter with God made him bubble over with joy. In fact, he was so overcome that he burst into laughter and only managed to get himself back under control when forced to by sheer embarrassment. From then on, joy was always at the center of his theology.

Finding God did not make Bosworth any healthier. Shortly after his conversion he acquired a serious lung ailment. Convinced that he was mortally ill, he took a train to Georgia, where his parents had recently moved, to visit them before he died. While there, he heard of a woman preacher who was running a series of Methodist healing meetings in town. He sought her out, went forward for prayer, and was soon back in good health. As a result, he became a believer in divine healing.

Few people in America had a greater reputation for healing than Alexander Dowie, and when Bosworth heard about him, he decided to relocate to Zion City, Illinois—Dowie's home base—hoping to get involved in the organization. Dowie recognized his abilities, and soon Bosworth was part of the leadership team, heading up the musical program. It was at Zion that Bosworth came in contact with pentecostalism. Charles Parham visited the city in 1906, and Bosworth heard him preach the first day he was in town. His response was immediate; before the night was over, he had received the baptism of the Spirit and spoken in tongues. The relationship between Parham and Dowie was tense—they were religious competitors—but Bosworth tried to stay on good terms with both. Eventually, however, he decided to leave Zion and move to Dallas to help the pentecostal churches Parham had planted there.

Bosworth proved himself a pentecostal's pentecostal. He was rock solid. The revival services he organized in Dallas in 1912 were seen by many as a continuation of the outpouring that had begun at the Azusa Street Mission. He was at the very center of things. Thus, when the Assemblies of God was organized in 1914, it is no surprise that he was among the sixteen members of the original governing board. But then he asked one awkward question and everything changed: Must all pentecostals speak in tongues? When Bosworth said "no," many of his closest friends turned their backs on him. While his healing ministry flourished in subsequent years, the Assemblies of God never welcomed him back. What Bosworth's writings reveal, however, is not a repudiation but a reformulation of pentecostal faith. For Bosworth, trust and joy were the core, not physical manifestations.

The following selection illustrates Bosworth's reformulated faith. It comes from his booklet, *Do All Speak in Tongues?* (New York: The Christian Alliance Publishing Company, [1917]).[1]

Was Speaking in Tongues at Pentecost the Gift of Tongues?

After eleven years in the work on Pentecostal lines, during which it has been my pleasure to see thousands receive the precious Baptism in the Holy Spirit, I am absolutely certain that many who receive the most powerful baptism for service do not receive the manifestation of speaking in tongues. And I am just as certain on the other hand, that many who SEEMINGLY speak in tongues,

---

[1] For more information, see Jacobsen, *Thinking in the Spirit*, 290–313.

are not, nor ever have been, baptized in the Spirit. Although I have in the past very tenaciously contended for it, as many of the brethren still do, I am absolutely certain that it is entirely wrong and UNSCRIPTURAL to teach that the miraculous speaking in tongues on the Day of Pentecost was not the gift of tongues God set in the church and which is so often mentioned in Paul's first letter to the Corinthians. Not only is there not a solitary passage of scripture upon which to base this doctrine, but on the other hand the Scriptures flatly deny it. That there is no Scripture for this distinction between speaking in tongues as the Spirit gave utterance at Jerusalem and the gift of tongues at Corinth, is being seen and admitted by many Bible students and teachers in the Pentecostal movement. In fact, some in the movement have never believed this distinction was Scriptural or true.

At a recent State Council of the Assemblies of God, when the chairman of the Council was asked by one of the young ministers if there was a passage or a number of passages upon which to base this distinction, he publicly admitted that there was not a single passage. Charles F. Parham, who came forward with this doctrine in the year 1900, is the first man in the history of the world to publicly teach it. He saw that it was not possible to teach that speaking in tongues will in every case accompany the Baptism in the Spirit, unless he could make it appear that the speaking in tongues on the Day of Pentecost was something separate and distinct from the gift of tongues at Corinth. He is also the first man in the history of the world to teach that none have ever been baptized in the Spirit except those who have spoken in tongues.

The facts are that hundreds of the greatest soul-winners of the whole Christian era, without the gift of tongues, have had a much greater enduement of power and have been used to accomplish a much greater and deeper work than Mr. Parham.

The argument that the miraculous manifestation of tongues on the Day of Pentecost is distinct from the gift of tongues, called, in the Scriptures "The manifestation of the Spirit," falls flat when we consider the seventh and eighth verses of the twelfth chapter of First Corinthians. In the seventh verse Paul says, "The manifestation of the Spirit is given to every man to profit withal." Some have taught and written that "The manifestation of the Spirit" here mentioned is always the speaking in tongues as the Spirit gives utterance, as on the Day of Pentecost. They claim that this is for all who receive the Baptism in the Spirit, but that it is not the gift of tongues later mentioned in the same chapter. But Paul in the next verse entirely demolishes this argument, by explaining what "The manifestation of the Spirit" is. "For to one," he says, "is given by the Spirit the word of wisdom; to another the word of knowledge by the same Spirit; to another faith by the same Spirit; to another gifts of healing by the same Spirit; to another working of miracles; to another prophecy; to another discerning of spirits; to another divers kinds of tongues; to another interpretation of tongues. But all of these worketh that one and the selfsame Spirit, dividing to every man severally as he wills." So you see that each one of these nine gifts is called "The manifestation of the Spirit." God's definition of a gift is "THE MANIFESTATION OF THE SPIRIT," and is therefore identical with the gift of tongues about which Paul writes to the Corinthians. These Galileans had no power in themselves, without the Spirit, to speak in these languages, but it was GIVEN them by the Spirit to utter words and form sentences not originating in their own minds. We therefore contend that this was the real gift of tongues that God set in the Church. The fact here mentioned that the gift of tongues is always "THE MANIFESTATION OF THE SPIRIT," refutes the theory held by many that the gift of tongues is the ability to speak in tongues at will. THE WORD OF GOD DISCOUNTENANCES ALL SPEAKING IN TONGUES EXCEPT THAT WHICH IS "THE MANIFESTATION OF THE SPIRIT." The eleventh verse makes this clear by saying that the Spirit works each of these manifestations, or as Weymouth translates it, "These results are brought about by . . . the Spirit." In other words, the Holy Spirit uses us instead of our using Him. God, we are told in this chapter, has set these gifts or manifestations in the church. Now, brother, if the speaking in tongues on the Day of Pentecost was not the GIFT of tongues, I ask you when did God set the gift of tongues in the church? Chapter and verse, please. The Scriptures tell us that when Christ ascended up on high He gave gifts unto men.

Another argument used to prove that the gift of tongues is not speaking as the Spirit gives utterance is based upon Paul's instructions to those with the gift of tongues to be silent in the church unless there is an interpreter. They argue that if Paul told them to keep silent, it is proof that it was not the Spirit's utterance, because that would be rebuking the Holy Ghost. This idea arises from the mistaken notion that the manifestation of the Spirit in tongues is always for the public, whereas Paul said where there is no interpreter, "Let him keep silence in the church SPEAKING UNTO HIMSELF AND TO GOD." It is a great mistake to think that the manifestation of tongues must always be spoken to the church, and that it will be quenching the Spirit to obey Paul's inspired instruction to speak "unto himself and to God." Ignorance here has made much confusion in Pentecostal assemblies. Many after disobeying these inspired directions say, "I could not help it." This is a mistake, for Paul commands silence unless there is an interpreter. Sometimes, when the church is being greatly edified by a sermon, there may be many at the same time who feel like worshipping God in tongues, but this may be controlled without quenching the Spirit, for even where there IS an interpreter Paul says for only one to speak at a time. Even the GREATER manifestation of prophecy, which is especially for the edification of the Church, is to be restrained, so that the "Prophets speak one at a time that all may learn and all may be comforted." The apostle evidently purposed to effectually heal the Corinthians of THE CAN'T HELP

IT idea that has caused so much confusion not only in the Corinthian church, but also in modern times. He tells them distinctly that God is not the author of this confusion, but that "The spirits of the prophets are subject to the prophets." Of course, we are always glad when God, in the middle of our sermon, saves and baptizes souls with the speaking of tongues, as He did while Peter preached to the household of Cornelius.

Doctrine Never Mentioned in Any Epistle

But once again as to the distinction, or supposed distinction, between tongues in the Acts and at Corinth, after which we will leave you to an impartial search-ing of the Scriptures touching this point. It is insisted that the speaking in tongues in the Acts was only temporary and that every Christian should speak in tongues as the initial sign of being baptized, while the gift of tongues dealt with in Paul's letter to the Corinthians implies permanence and that few have the permanent gift. If this theory is right, with its necessary distinction between tongues and tongues, then we agree that it is the most important doctrine of the New Testament, for what can be more important than for Christians to receive the enduement of power so absolutely necessary to accomplish the work that God wants done? Then is it not strange indeed that not one of the inspired writers of any of the epistles to any of the New Testament Churches, preachers and saints scattered abroad, ever made the slightest passing refer-ence to that kind of speaking in tongues which is the evidence of the baptism? Think of it, and then think again, all the New Testament epistles, and not a single mention of this doctrine. We hear in these letters of backsliding from most every other doctrine, even the truth of justification by faith, the resurrec-tion from the dead and the second coming of Christ. They backslid from the great truth of faith and love, and the apostles were careful to line them up and get them straight, but if they ever held the doctrine of tongues as the evidence, they never once deviated from it, but held it so tenaciously that not even a word of exhortation was deemed necessary to keep them from letting down on this point. Will any of the brethren make the charge that the writers of these epistles had let down and compromised on the question of the baptism before writing all these letters?

The doctrine that all are to speak in tongues when baptized in the Spirit is based entirely upon supposition without a solitary "Thus saith the Lord." It is nowhere taught in the Scriptures, but assumed from the fact that in three instances recorded in Acts they spoke in tongues as a result of the baptism. While this notable fact should serve as an eye-opener to all who contend against all speaking in tongues, it is by no means a conclusive proof that God gave the same gift to all the multiplied thousands added to the church during this most marvelous period of church history, extending over more than a quarter of a century.

God always has a definite purpose and an infinitely wise reason for everything He does. The Day of Pentecost witnessed the grandest and most effective display of the gift of tongues the world has ever seen. And God's purpose was that it should be a "sign," not to believers, but to the UNBELIEVING Jews dwelling at Jerusalem "Out of every nation under heaven." And God's purpose was most wonderfully realized, for three thousand unbelieving Jews were, by the fact that these Galileans spoke in their own languages, forced to believe that Jesus was actually the Messiah. Perhaps there was no other sign that God could have manifested so effectively under these circumstances, as the speaking in tongues. And then eight years later Peter and the six Jewish brethren who accompanied him to the household of Cornelius were, with all other Jews, unbelievers as to the Gentiles being included in the privileges of the Gospel. And so God made the gift of tongues a sign to them, thus convincing them to their astonishment that "God also to the Gentiles hath granted repentance unto life." Later when Peter returned to Jerusalem, the Apostles and brethren contended with him saying, "Thou wentest in to men uncircumcised and didst eat with them." So Peter rehearsed the matter from the beginning and closed his argument by saying, "As I began to speak, the Holy Ghost fell on them, AS on us AT THE BEGINNING." If all the multiplied thousands saved and baptized by the Spirit during that wonderful revival period of eight years between the second chapter and the tenth chapter of Acts, if they all spoke in tongues when baptized in the Spirit, why did Peter say, "AS on us AT THE BEGINNING?" He could just as well have said, "As He has been baptizing all since the beginning." If it was well known that all received the gift of tongues with the baptism during those eight years, why should he point back to the time they spoke in tongues on the day of Pentecost? Again, years later, when Paul met the brethren at Ephesus who had never heard that there was any Holy Ghost, God gave them both tongues and prophecy when they received the Spirit. And if Luke was so careful to record it when only these few spoke in tongues, why did he not record it when all the multiplied thousands since Pentecost spoke in tongues, if they all did?

If it be objected here that perhaps the multitudes added to the church during this unparalleled revival period did not receive the Holy Ghost, let it be remembered that in apostolic days converts were not left in the dark concerning the baptism in the Spirit as they are in modern revivals. Peter preached to the multitude on the Day of Pentecost that as many as would repent would receive the gift of the Holy Ghost; that THE PROMISE was unto them and to their children, etc., Acts 2:38, 39. And it is distinctly stated of the three thousand added to the church on that day, that "They all continued steadfastly in the apostle's doctrine and fellowship," proving that they all received the Holy Ghost. The baptism in the Holy Spirit held an important place in the apostles' doctrine and is clearly stated in Peter's first sermon. We read in the eighth chapter of Acts that as soon as the apostles at Jerusalem had heard about the revival at Samaria they sent unto them Peter and John, who prayed for them that they might receive the Holy Ghost. And when Paul met the brethren at Ephesus, his first question was "Have ye received the Holy Ghost since ye believed?" By reading the epistles, we find that all the churches had received the baptism in the Spirit.

Another argument most commonly used to prove that all will speak in tongues is based upon St. John 15:26, 27: "When the Comforter is come, he shall testify of me: And ye also shall bear witness." It is contended that because two testimonies are here spoken of, that one is the Holy Ghost speaking in tongues. But in Heb. 2:4 we are told how the Holy Ghost testifies, or bears witness. "God also BEARING THEM WITNESS both with signs and wonders, and with diverse miracles, and GIFTS [not the gift of tongues only] of the Holy Ghost, according to his own will."

The facts are that it is unscriptural to teach that they all received that one manifestation, and this is the force of all of Paul's argument to the Corinthians. For instance, from the twelfth verse to the close of the fourteenth chapter Paul teaches the exact opposite of what many today are teaching, endeavoring to show them that all are not to expect the same manifestation of the Spirit. He uses the illustration of the human body and its members and asks, "If the whole body were an eye, where were the hearing?" etc., and then to make it still more emphatic he asks, "Are all apostles? Are all prophets? are all teachers? are all workers of miracles? have all the gifts of healing? do all speak with tongues? do all interpret?" Of course the answer to each of these questions is NO. In other words, Paul is distinctly saying that all are NOT teachers, and all do NOT speak in tongues. We cannot dodge this question by saying that this is the gift and not the speaking in tongues as on the Day of Pentecost, because as already shown, Paul distinctly states that this is "The manifestation of the Spirit," making it identical with the manifestation of the Spirit that came on the Day of Pentecost.

Gifts Not for Evidence but for Service

Teaching that tongues is THE evidence of the baptism in the Spirit, makes it a sign to believers, whereas Paul distinctly says that it is not a sign to the believer, but to the unbeliever. If made a sign to the seeker for the baptism, it not only leaves no place for faith, but on the other hand destroys faith already divinely given. After God has most powerfully baptized the seeker, and with perfect faith

divinely inwrought, he is rejoicing with joy unspeakable and full of glory with
every ounce of his flesh quivering under the power of the indwelling Spirit,
some one will tell him that he has not yet received the Holy Ghost because he
did not speak in tongues. This destroys his faith which Paul says is both "THE
EVIDENCE" and "THE SUBSTANCE," Heb. 11:1, and sends him home discouraged, to continue his seeking as some have for several years. Everywhere
I have gone I have met hungry souls who seemingly speak in tongues, but
who have not this assuring faith that they are baptized in the Spirit. Nothing
short of the real faith can satisfy the heart and put the soul at rest. The word
"EVIDENCE" in the Scriptures is never used in connection with a spiritual
gift, or manifestation, making faith to depend upon any sign or physical manifestation, but the Apostle distinctly states that "FAITH is the evidence." Anything
that is to be received in answer to prayer is to be received by faith, even the great
miracle of the new birth, and Paul expressly states that we are to "Receive the
promise of the Spirit through faith," Gal. 3:14. Nothing short of faith can satisfy
the heart and give us power. Paul said, "Let everything be done with a view to
building up faith," but the tongues evidence teaching reverses this, not only
destroying faith, but making it impossible until the gift of tongues is received.
This teaching causes people to reject the mightiest baptism in the Spirit, disre-
garding the personal Holy Spirit within, and puts them from that time on seeking for years in many instances for a physical manifestation that Paul plainly
teaches all are not to expect, for the Spirit is to divide the manifestations "As
HE will."

This teaching, besides destroying faith, puts some to seeking a hundred
times after God has baptized them, in many instances much more powerfully
than others who spoke in tongues. It is absurd that Jesus must pour out the
Spirit upon the same person a hundred times before He succeeds in getting
him baptized. There is not a single instance like this in all the Scriptures. John
the Baptist completed the work the first time he undertook to baptize those
who came to him. And so with Jesus, according to the Scriptures, He never
had to make two attempts to administer HIS baptism. Jesus taught that the first
time the Spirit comes upon a consecrated seeker he was to "Abide forever."
And I insist that when a consecrated seeker has been correctly instructed, he
should receive the Holy Ghost the first time the Spirit falls upon him.

Again, this telling those who have been baptized that they have not been
because they did not get the gift of tongues also robs them of a testimony for
months and even years, and puts them to seeking for a physical manifestation when they ought to be witnessing and laboring for souls. Jesus said, "Ye
shall receive the power of the Holy Ghost coming upon you: and ye shall be
my witnesses." If allowed to believe, their testimony under the power of the
Spirit would have led others into the baptism. Instead of this those who might
have been led into the baptism by their testimony have watched them seek

for hours after the Holy Spirit had fallen upon them, and this has discouraged many, delaying the revival that much, besides denying Christ's encouraging words, "How much MORE will your heavenly Father give the Holy Ghost to them that ask him."

It is a notable fact that many of the deepest and best teachers and preachers in the Pentecostal movement have the poorest success in getting the seekers through to speaking in tongues. The reason is they are too conscientious to use the "Glory-glory-glory-say-it-a-little-faster" and other similar methods, which have made some of the shallowest and most fanatical workers apparently the most successful. Proper instruction, followed by consecration and prayer, will in every instance bring down the baptism in the Holy Spirit, but it will not always bring down the manifestation of tongues. Repeated seeking and methods never used in the Scriptures have been employed to get all the seekers through to the "Bible evidence," and then I am certain that many who really have the baptism and seemingly speak in tongues, do not really do it, although they are sincere in the matter. This over-emphasis in teaching tongues and unscriptural methods is responsible for this. I recently heard a prominent preacher in the Pentecostal movement preach from the tenth chapter of Acts. He preached for nearly an hour insisting that unless we press the tongues evidence teaching the people will not receive the Holy Ghost. He overlooked the fact that Peter, in this chapter, had better success in getting his audience through to the baptism without even mentioning the subject, than any preacher in modern times by preaching that tongues is the Bible evidence. While Peter was preaching about Jesus unto them, they all received the baptism, even to the astonishment of Peter himself.

Personally, I am determined never to try to get any seekers to speak in tongues until after I see God tries to get them to, and then if they are not yielding or co-operating properly, I will instruct them to yield and obey the Spirit. This will leave the proper place for faith, and I have found that it will bring the real speaking in tongues much quicker, for where any sign is placed before faith, it always hinders the Spirit, and lessens the power. Jesus taught that "These signs shall FOLLOW" faith, and not "Faith shall follow these signs."

No "Thus Saith the Lord"

We have no "Thus saith the Lord" in the Scriptures that all are to speak in tongues, but the very opposite, as above shown, but we have many "THUS SAITH the LORDs" as to other Bible evidences, or rather results of the baptism in the Spirit. For instance: "They SHALL prophesy," "He WILL convict the world of sin," "He WILL guide you into all truth," "He WILL take the things of mine and show them unto you," "He WILL glorify me," "Ye SHALL receive the power of the Holy Ghost coming upon you," "He WILL make intercessions through the saints with groanings that cannot be uttered," "Ye SHALL be endued with power from on high," etc.

The Scriptures tell us that "Jesus is the author and the finisher of our faith," and He never taught the doctrine that all would speak in tongues. Then why should we? Not one of the inspired apostles or prophets ever taught it, and not one of the world's great soul winners ever taught it, so it is clear that this doctrine is not essential to the greatest success. On the other hand, it greatly circumscribes our usefulness by shutting out those who are so well versed in the Scriptures that we can not convince them of our unscriptural theory. It will split any church on earth wide open, separating equally devout Christians, unless we can make them all believe it. Even those who speak in tongues, equally devout among the Pentecostal ministry, can not possibly agree on this point. For God does not want them to agree upon a theory for which there is not a solitary passage of Scripture, making it a test of fellowship and a basis upon which to build a new church. When we, as a movement, will confine ourselves to what the Scriptures plainly teach upon this important subject of the baptism and ALL the manifestations of the Spirit, and preach to the world the great things about the baptism in the Holy Ghost, our usefulness will be enhanced many fold. . . .

The Greatest Phase of the Baptism

I am determined that those converted in my meetings shall expect and receive a real baptism of power that will put them under the real sway of the Spirit and into loving sympathy with Christ in His great work of saving a lost world. To me the greatest phase of the baptism in the Spirit is the spontaneous life of intercession. Paul said that the Spirit Himself would make intercession through the saints with groanings that cannot be uttered, and I have seen Spirit-baptized souls, some with, and others without, the manifestation of tongues, carried clear out and beyond themselves into the ever flowing stream of Christ's intercessions for a lost world, experiencing that exquisite love that enabled them to "offer up prayers and supplications with strong crying and tears" until they were heard. I believe there is no manifestation of the Spirit that means so much to God and to the church and to a lost world, for it is in this intercession that both the Christian and the Church are to find and wield their highest power. In this way each Christian, as the Prophet Isaiah said, can "Make his voice to be heard on high to loose the bands of wickedness, to undo the heavy burdens, and to let the oppressed go free." One of the names given to the Holy Ghost is "The Spirit of Grace and Supplication," and one of the great marks of the baptism is a power in prayer hitherto unknown. In this phase of the baptism there are possibilities whose limits never have been found. It was this power working in Spirit-baptized saints at Rochester, N.Y., under the ministry of Charles G. Finney, that brought about EIGHTY THOUSAND CONVERSIONS IN SIX MONTHS. Finney, himself, said: "I would not give my Spirit of prayer for the intellectual endowments of an Archangel." One man in Finney's day, while on a sick bed dying with tuberculosis, noted in his little memorandum book the dates when he was enabled to pray the prayer of faith for revivals in thirty different localities. And after the man died God poured His Spirit in a gracious revival upon each of these places. I have seen many who were the deepest in intercession and soul travail who have never spoken in tongues, and among those who professed the baptism under the tongues evidence teaching I have met hundreds who have never been full of the Spirit enough to be carried out of themselves into the intercessions of Christ. It is recorded of the three thousand converted on the Day of Pentecost that "they all continued steadfastly in prayer." Surely, those who have the greatest love and compassion for souls and the greatest spirit of prayer have the most of the Holy Ghost, whether they speak in tongues or not. I have told the young converts at every place I have been that unless they got a baptism that gave them the Spirit of prayer, I would consider my ministry, as far as they were concerned, a failure. We have a positive "Thus saith the Lord" that the Spirit will make intercessions through the saints, and if this had been preached as "The Bible evidence of the baptism" the work as a whole would be deeper.

Teaching the people that speaking in tongues is to be the evidence to them that they are baptized in the Spirit stands in the way of faith—destroys faith already divinely given—robs the baptized child of a testimony until he receives the manifestation of tongues—puts them again to seeking, while already baptized, for a physical manifestation perhaps less in value to the one already received—wears out the workers at the altar praying for weeks and even months for those upon whom the Lord has poured His Spirit many times—delays the revival just that much—discourages others from seeking, and denies Christ's encouraging words, "How much more will your heavenly Father give the Holy Ghost to them that ask Him?"

I find that by standing right with the Scriptures with regard to all these manifestations of the Spirit, our revivals will be deeper and quicker, and it will free us of many of the irregularities and much of the fanaticism that has so torn up the work and hurt the cause of God in so many localities. I have been waiting for some of the other Pentecostal brethren to come out with some literature on this line, but I guess they have been a little timid like myself, so I have felt it my plain duty to my brethren to write the above for their perusal. I know I will lose the friendship of some who may not be able to see the truth herein contained, but if I can be a help to others, opening the way for their greater usefulness, I will feel well repaid. I am sure if this movement could be free from this one error in teaching and would preach the greater things about the baptism our opportunities for usefulness would be increased many fold. The way would then be opened for more of the manifestations or gifts of the Spirit, and consequently the revivals would be greater and deeper. May God speed this day is my prayer.

CHAPTER ELEVEN

Andrew David Urshan
(1884–1967)

Andrew David Urshan was born in Persia (Iran) into that country's Nestorian community. The Nestorians are a remnant of a once-flourishing Christian community in Iran that has slowly dwindled during the centuries of Islamic rule. Being a Nestorian in the late 1800s was as much a matter of ethnic identity as it was religious, and it is thus not surprising that Urshan still considered himself a Nestorian even though his father had become a Presbyterian minister.

Urshan's parents were intensely religious, and concerned about their son's unruliness and seeming lack of faith, they sent him, at the age of fifteen, to the American Presbyterian Training College in the neighboring city of Urmiah. Their strategy seemed to work, for a year later he returned home as a devout believer and budding young minister. His work with youth sparked a religious awakening in the town. But it was not just fervor that Urshan acquired at college. He also learned the importance of religious self-discipline, and that discipline became a permanent aspect of his faith.

Urshan enjoyed his town and family, but he also had a case of wanderlust. In the early 1900s he emigrated to the United States. Settling in Chicago, where a number of his cousins lived, he took work as a waiter. As a Nestorian-Presbyterian, Urshan had been baptized in his infancy, but one of his cousins, who had become a member of the Brethren Church, which baptized adults, eventually convinced him that infant baptism was meaningless. Urshan was rebaptized as an adult, and this was a turning point. He later explained that his rebaptism was the result of "new light" received from God, not simply human insight. For the rest of his life, Urshan tried assiduously to follow whatever other new light God sent his way.

In Chicago Urshan attended the Moody Church, pastored by the popular fundamentalist preacher A. C. Dixon. At first, he and Dixon got along quite well. Dixon even allowed Urshan to use the church building to run afternoon services for Persians living in the city. But tensions developed when God's new light led Urshan, first, into a holiness view of faith, and then into pentecostalism. Once Dixon learned that Urshan had become one of "the tongues folks," he barred the doors against him. In response, Urshan opened his own Persian Pentecostal Mission on North Clark Street.

Urshan and his pentecostal colleagues were known for their spiritual dedication. They sometimes spent the entire night in prayer seeking God's guidance and searching for more light. Then, in 1910, they received a significant new revelation. Baptism was not supposed to be performed "in the name of the Father and the Son and the Holy Ghost," but it was instead to be administered simply "in the name of Jesus." At first, Urshan and his friends did not know what to make of this new revelation, but as time progressed and as other pentecostal leaders received the same revelation, they became convinced that baptism in Jesus' name was the only valid form of baptism. Urshan was re-baptized once again and soon rose to prominence within the ranks of "Jesus-only" pentecostalism.

While the issue of what words to use in baptism may seem minor, it raised the much deeper question of how to understand the nature of God. The new movement seemed to claim that "Jesus" was the name of the entire Godhead, and that raised questions about the traditional Christian vision of God as Trinity. Eventually most Jesus-only groups rejected traditional trinitarianism, opting for a "oneness" view of God.

The following selection, taken from Urshan's *The Almighty God in the Lord Jesus Christ* (Los Angeles: Andrew D. Urshan, 1919), reflects his thinking on this complex issue.[1]

Chapter IV. The Great Christian Commission and The Name of God in Jesus Christ

Beloved, we wish thankfully to testify of the great blessing for the upbuilding of our faith in Christ with which the gracious God has favored us by flashing the glorious light of His Spirit upon the scriptures which specifically speak of

---

[1] For more information, see Jacobsen, *Thinking in the Spirit*, 232–59.

what is termed "The Great Christian Commission" as recorded in Matthew 28:17–19; Mark 16:14–19, and Luke 24:45–49.

The Commission

A commission is generally a band of specially chosen and appointed capable men, being authorized and supplied by the highest office and set forth to perform their demanded and specified duties according to the law and requirements of their commissioners. So is the Great Christian Commission.

The Christian Commission, religiously speaking, is called "A Mission or a band of Missionaries to the home land and foreign countries," but the Bible name and language for missionaries and divinely commissioned men is "witnesses," as we read in Acts 1:8, "But ye shall receive power after that the Holy Ghost is come upon you and ye shall be witnesses unto me both in Jerusalem, and in all Judea, and in Samaria, and unto the uttermost parts of the world." Here is the great Commissioner, The Lord Jesus, sending forth His chosen and appointed commission—commanding them that they should wait until they are fully supplied and empowered from on high (Luke 24:48–49), then go forth to do only one thing, and that specific duty is applied unto His own Person; as He said "ye shall be witnesses unto me." Thus, we see the definite and positive purpose and service of the Great Christian Commission, viz.: "Go ye therefore and teach all nations, baptizing them IN THE NAME"; notice, please, it is not written in the names, but IN THE NAME. Just as commercial and political commissions are sent forth in the name of the highest office of the government, exactly so the divine commission from the beginning has been sent forth in the one great NAME of the Almighty God. The interesting question is then whose name is this mentioned "NAME" in Matthew 28:19, in which the great Christian commission should go forth. The following sentences answer the question. It is the one name of the T-H-R-E-E—O-N-E God (1 John 5:7), yea the NAME of the Father, of the Son and of the Holy Ghost.

The infallible record, therefore, clearly states and concludes that God the Father has a NAME and that this very name of the Father is the name of the Son and of the Spirit also; thus, whatsoever NAME the son has, the Father has. Then the other important query is "What is the NAME of the Father?" It is the same name that the Son has. What is the name of the Son? The answer is that it is the VERY name that the Father bears. Then the anxious heart will cry out, "Tell me, please, this one great NAME of the Father, of the Son and of the Holy Ghost, which is called 'THE NAME' in Matthew 28:19?"

Beloved Saints, when Jacob met the Lord he anxiously asked Him what was His name, (Gen. 32:29) and when Moses met God he also asked Him His name, by which he desired to go forth (Exodus 3:13). And the wisdom of God also in the Book of Proverbs (30:4) inquires the name of God and His

Son. Dearly beloved, have we stopped prayerfully and diligently searching, long enough to find out the name of our great God, like the old Saints of the Almighty, for this Gospel dispensation? If you have, please tell the world what is His NAME; by what name you and I should go forth as God's delegates and His ambassadors before all nations.

Have you found out that one hallowed NAME of God, the Father, the Son and the Holy Ghost before you baptize people into it? You may say, "I baptize them in the name of the Father, of the Son and of the Holy Ghost." Please permit us to ask you again, "What is that one NAME?" Now, let us tell you frankly and lovingly, that you have never baptized converts absolutely according to the commandments of our Lord if you have not found out first what that one NAME of God and the Lord of the Apostles is.

Many of us, through ignorance, have unconsciously misread and misinterpreted the plain commandment of our Lord and have given a wrong impression and interpretation to the new converts for Matthew 28:19, as if it read, "Go ye therefore and teach all nations and baptize them in the name—"Father"—"Son" and "Holy Ghost." We have paid no attention to the two most important written words, "OF THE." These words "of the" should make us understand that Father is not a proper noun, but a common noun, and that the Heavenly Father has a name which makes Him properly to be known, just as your father has a name. That is why we are taught to pray "OUR FATHER who are in Heaven, Hallowed be Thy Name." We should not baptize in the name "Father," etc., but in the NAME of the Father, of the Son and of the Holy Ghost. Please let us come back to the important question again, and ask you "What is that one great, glorious and highest NAME of our T-H-R-E-E—O-N-E God for this dispensation?"

Important Question Answered

Well, Beloved, the answer to the important query may upset the theology and the interpretation of many preachers and Christian workers, and put a ban of humility upon our boasting, for we have given the impression of having suffered for our loyal obedience to the commandment of our Lord and Savior as recorded in Matthew 28:19, and of having practiced the same faithfully; yet when we soberly study in the light and interpretation of the Holy Ghost the Christian Commission as described in Matthew 28:19, we find we have withstood, opposed and misjudged those who have actually obeyed and practiced the command of our Lord up to the last letter, just as the anointed and appointed apostles of our Lord Jesus Christ taught and practiced. Read, please, Acts 2:38; 8:12; 10:47–48 and 19:5; Gal. 3:27, etc., etc.

You may ask us to tell you the one NAME of the Father, of the Son and of the Holy Ghost. We will point you to the record of Mark and Luke, which is a part of the very same conversation of our Saviour on this great Christian Commission which Matthew wrote of. Please read carefully Mark 16:14–19; Luke 24:45–49, with Matthew 28:19. You will clearly see, if you wish honestly to see, that Jesus Christ is that one NAME of the T-H-R-E-E—O-N-E God, in which we are called and sent forth to preach repentance and remission of sins, to cast out devils and to lay hands on the sick and on the seekers to receive the healing and the baptism of the Holy Ghost. Yes, in this very NAME, the one, the single name of the Father which is also the name of the Son and the name of the Holy Ghost. If you do not accept this God-given light and testimony of this blessed commandment of our Lord in Matthew 28:19, please read the apostolic record and practice, and the Holy Ghost-given exhortation through the Great Apostle Paul and for the Gentile Believers, who commands us that whatsoever we do in word and deed that we should do it all in the name of the Lord Jesus Christ, giving thanks to the Father. Amen. Col. 3:17 and etc.

The Old Dispensations and Commissions

Beloved, God has been graciously taking us through the whole Bible and showed us His leadings and His great Commissions to His chosen people of old and that when He commissioned them or when He sent them forth He not only told them to go at His command but He gave them His great and mighty NAME to be their shield, buckler, hiding place and fortress. He taught them to lift up their banners and their swords and their voices against their enemies and that in His single and mighty NAME, by which He appeared unto them. So we read that when He commissioned our Father Abraham He appeared unto Him by His singular name "the Almighty God" and said unto Him that he should walk before Him and be perfect, and gave him also the great promise for himself and his generation. Gen. 17:1–8. So our Father Abraham went forth and conquered all his foes, prospered above all his fellowmen and became the Father of many nations and the friend of God, the Almighty.

Then we see God appearing to His servant Moses also to deliver his people from their bondage and ushering in another new dispensation and that with His new Name. So we read, "and God spake unto Moses, and said unto him, 'I am the Lord: and I appeared unto Abraham and to Isaac, and unto Jacob, by the Name of God Almighty, but by [the] name Jehovah was I not known to them, and God said unto Moses, I am that I am: thus shalt thou say unto the children of Israel, I am hath sent me unto you." Exodus 6:1–3 and Exodus 3:13–14.

Moses did not stagger at the new name of the Almighty T-H-R-E-E—O-N-E God; he did not go around and teach the people of God that this new name Jehovah was the second name and that he and the people of God should go forth in the first and the second names of their God as we are teaching and doing in these days; but he simply obeyed the voice of his God and went forth in the name Jehovah — Lord God — before the Pharaoh King, and before Israel. Therefore, he prospered and prevailed and conquered all his foes, and finally he triumphed over death itself, and arising from his sleep he ascended into the very Heavens.

Now the vital question is: Has the Almighty God of Abraham and of Moses ushered forth this gospel dispensation? You and all must agree with us and say yes. Has He appeared unto us with a new name or not? You again must say yes with us. Then the important question is the same question that the wisdom of God inquired in Proverbs, 30th chapter and the 4th verse, "What is His name, and what is His son's name, if thou canst tell?"

Now, dear friends, we humbly confess and testify to you and to all who may hear us that the same God of our Fathers, the Ancient of Days, hath appeared unto many saints and unworthy us also and hath told us that His proper NAME is not Father, nor Son, neither Holy Ghost, but the Lord Jesus Christ. That does not do away with the loving Fatherhood of the Almighty, nor with the gracious Sonship of the Lord, and neither does it do away with the blessed existence of the excellent Spirit of God, but it makes clear and harmonizes all the scriptures with all the fullness of this T-H-R-E-E — O-N-E Godhead summed up in this dispensation for all the human race in that sweetest of all names, JESUS, the anointed Jehovah Lord. Oh, let us use all the tongue, and voice, and the speech that we ever have by the Holy Ghost and confess and proclaim that Jesus is the Lord, bowing on bended knees with a humble, contrite and obedient heart and worship God, the Father, the Son, and the Holy Ghost in His new revealed NAME for this dispensation, of which the heavenly race and family is thereby named "Christians" or the Christ-ones. Hallelujah! God was in Christ reconciling the world unto Himself! Oh glory! He is yet with all His greatness, power and glory dwelling and manifesting Himself before the angels in that lovely Person of His Christ, the Son (see Col. 2:1–9).

The Apostolic Commission

Beloved, this scriptural revelation makes Matthew 28:19 and Acts 2:38 equivalent, not two separate verses contradicting each other, but a blessed prophecy and command and its sure fulfillment in the power and revelation of the Holy Ghost through the teaching and practice of the chosen appointed and anointed apostles of our Lord and Saviour; thus we can with gladness read the Christian commission with one singular name of our God, viz.: "Go ye therefore, and teach all nations, baptizing them In the NAME of the Father, and of the Son and of the Holy Ghost." Amen!!! . . .

It is no wonder then that all the prophets and apostles give Jesus Christ the name and all the titles of the Almighty God of Abraham, Isaac and Jacob; no wonder our Saviour Himself could boldly say "Before Abraham was, I AM, and I am the First and the last, the beginning and the end, and the Almighty." And His loving exhortation for us all, over and over is to abide in Him, which means that we should not get our heart, our mind, our spiritual vision and all we are and ever will be, out of Him, and look away from Him to see the triune God.

We gospel ministers preach and exhort the people that everything spiritual and eternal, which includes our blessed and adorable T-H-R-E-E — O-N-E God, is all in the written word and that we should prayerfully and carefully study it and hide it in our hearts and bring our lives and experiences into subjection to it, for it is the only sure way of life. Then a question arises: What is all this infallible and Holy Word of God, if it is not Jesus Christ the Lord? Can a human being find a triune God out of the written word? If not, then why should we think, or try, to find God our Father apart from His Son, who is the Alpha and Omega or the whole written Word of the Almighty God!! Brethren, let us not be too proud or imagine we can see and think beyond Jesus Christ. Let Christ, the Lord, fill our vision and be satisfied with Him.

Abraham, Isaac and Jacob, Moses and all the prophets of the Bible went forth living and proclaiming their message to the people of God, the Jews, and to the Gentiles in the NAME that was revealed unto them for their dispensation. Why should we stagger at the name of God in His Son which has been given unto us to live and to proclaim in the whole world? "GO ye therefore and teach all Nations, baptizing them in the Name," etc. There lies the whole secret and the power and the message of the apostles "in the NAME."

Confusion Over Subject Defeated

A few days ago a lady came to our meetings, an earnest child of God. She could not grasp the spirit and the motive of the message: "the Godhead in Jesus Christ." She went home disgusted, thinking we were misleading people. But in the silence of the night the blessed Spirit spoke to her saying, "Have you a father and a son?" She said, "Yes." Then the Spirit asked her, "Is your father's name Father?" She said, "No, my father's name is Brown." "Is your son's name son?" She said, "No, it is Clarence." Then God asked her, "What is the name of your Heavenly Father?" She honestly and prayerfully thought and thought, but she could answer nothing. Then the Spirit proceeded, "What is the name of the Son of the Father?" She said, "Jesus Christ." Then the Spirit proceeded, "Has your Heavenly Father a name; if so, what is it; don't you want to know it?" and He graciously showed her that Jesus was the name of our God, our Saviour, and Christ was the anointed One which stands for the Name and the fullness of the Holy Ghost in Him, and the Lord was the name of the Father and all the Deity.

The Name of the Holy Ghost in Jesus Christ

In the Syriac translation and also in the Greek the Holy Ghost is not called "the Comforter," as in the English version (John 14:26), but is called "the Parakleta." Jesus Christ bears this very name of the Spirit in 1 John 2:1. (See the Scofield Bible, page 1136.) The Holy Ghost is called "the quickening Spirit," so is the Lord Jesus called "the quickening Spirit." Compare John 6:63 with 1 Cor. 15:45. The Holy Ghost also is called "the Lord." Thank God, Jesus Christ is "the Lord" also. The Holy Spirit is called "the Spirit of the Lord" and "the Spirit of Christ."

Just as your spirit has not a separate name from the name you bear, but your name is the name of all that is in you, just so the Spirit of Christ bears the name of Christ, for he dwelleth in Christ (Col. 2:9) and is given to us by Christ (John 7:37), and comes forth from Christ (Acts 2:33).

The Holy Spirit is called also "the anointing," 1 John 2:27. So Jesus Christ is "the Anointed One." Hallelujah!

There have been mighty revivals and reformations by chosen men of God in the past, over some part of the truth which they declared boldly; like Luther and John Knox over their message of Justification by Faith, like Wesley and other Holiness Reformers over their teaching on holiness, like the Christian Alliance and others on divine healing in the atonement and the pre-millennial message, and like Pentecostal people over the baptism of the Holy Ghost with speaking in tongues as the Bible evidence, etc., etc., etc. Although these movements and the Reformers faced great difficulties and suffered great persecution, and many were confused and stumbled over them, nevertheless the truth that was revealed unto them prevailed, and today there are thousands who have been justified, sanctified, baptized, and healed and are rejoicing in the blessed hope and the appearing of our Great God and Saviour Jesus Christ. Now this message on the name of God revealed by the power of the Holy Ghost in Jesus Christ contains more scriptures than any of the above mentioned messages. Will God let hundreds of scriptures in which His name is mentioned be obscured and not emphasized? No, he will not, and He is now putting it in our hearts with the greatest fire and zeal that we ever felt to declare, proclaim, and make mention of His name among all nations, as Moses did. Read Deut. 32:1–3. As David did. Read Psalm 22:22, 34:3, 102:21, 145:1, 148:13. As Isaiah, the prophet did. Isa. 12:4, and as the Apostles did. Read Acts 4:15–20, 5:27–32 and 42.

Loss and Suffering for His Name

When our Lord commissioned His apostles to go forth in His name (which is the name of all Deity for this dispensation), He told them that they would suffer greatly for His name and that they would be hated by all men, not for their spiritual experiences or gift of Tongues, but for His Name. Why for His Name? Because that was to be their message to the world, yea, the message that stirs up not only Hell but the religious world also. Read, please, Matthew 10:20–22, Acts 5:41, 9:14–16, John 16:20, Luke 21:17, etc., etc. We are glad we had the privilege in Persia, before those Mohammedans, of testifying to our Lord and God, Jesus; although being surrounded to be butchered for His Matchless Name, yet there was such an unspeakable glory possessing our whole being that it made us more than glad to be tortured and die for His worthy Name. And now it is a very small thing to us to be slandered and misunderstood and misjudged for The Name of the Father, of the Son, and of the Holy Ghost, which is the Lord Jesus Christ.

CHAPTER TWELVE

Richard G. Spurling
(1857–1935)

R ICHARD G. SPURLING grew up in the tristate region where Tennessee, Georgia, and North Carolina come together. His family was Baptist,
and at some point Spurling was ordained by the Missionary Baptist Church.
We know relatively little of his early years, but by the time he was an adult
he seems to have developed a strongly restorationist view of what the church
ought to be. Restorationists wanted to reconnect the church with its first-
century roots, ignoring all the years of history between Christ and themselves. In essence, they wanted to start the church all over again, trying this time
to get it right.

In the mid-1880s, Spurling, along with a small group of other restorationists, began to pray that a revival of primitive, first-century Christianity would
come to the hills of Appalachia. After being banned from his own Baptist
church for his views—or perhaps having just left, the feelings no doubt being
mutual—Spurling decided to take a more active role in trying to re-establish
the simple church of the New Testament. On August 19, 1886, Spurling and
nine other men, his own father included, covenanted together to start a new
church called the Christian Union. During the next ten years, at least three
other Christian Union congregations were formed.

We know almost nothing about the early years of Spurling's church.
Clearly, his fledgling organization had troubles, and the movement did not
grow quickly. His former Baptist friends most likely saw him as a cranky sec-
tarian, and his leave-me-alone mountain neighbors probably viewed him as a
troublesome fanatic who was always trying to tell them how God wanted them

to live. In turn-of-the-century Appalachia, that kind of meddling could get you shot. But Spurling and his colleagues held on, and their situation began to improve.

A key turning point came in the mid-1890s when Spurling joined arms with a Baptist deacon named William F. Bryant who was preaching in the area. Around this same time some members of Benjamin Hardin Irwin's Fire Baptized Holiness Church also became active in the region. Then a revival took place near Camp Creek, North Carolina, which included a range of powerful physical manifestations of the Spirit's presence, including speaking in tongues. Spurling and many others thought a new day was dawning and a wave of holiness was about to break over the land.

It was shortly after these events that Spurling penned the first draft of what would eventually become his one and only book, a short volume entitled *The Lost Link*. Spurling's *Lost Link* bemoans the degeneration of the church from its original state as a fellowship of love into its later existence as a tightly controlled, hierarchical organization that censured anyone who dared deviate from its teaching on any little point of doctrine or belief. He calls instead for a restoration of the law of love within the church. That love is the link that has been lost, and Spurling's hope was that God was in the process of restoring that love in his own day.

Spurling's group later became the nub around which A. J. Tomlinson built the Church of God, and Spurling's distinctive voice became harder to hear as a result. No doubt that was part of the reason that Spurling finally decided to publish this work in 1920, nearly a quarter-century after it was originally composed.[1]

The following selection is from *The Lost Link* (Turtletown, Tenn.: R. G. Spurling, 1920).

Chapter I

. . . I have said many times that love is the law on which Christ built the church. To make this clear in your mind I will use a figure like that of building and operating a railroad. Spiritually speaking this world is a wilderness full of reptiles and so sickly that all of its inhabitants die. And there was also a fair and happy land, almost in sight, where no serpents ever marked the elision plain [*sic*], where no death bells ring, no funeral nor sad good-bye, but so deep were the chasms and so huge were the bluffs that they never could reach that healthful shore. There was a great King in that good land who loved these

---

[1] For more information, see Jacobsen, *Thinking in the Spirit*, 50–56.

poor dying people in this wilderness so he sent His Son to make a railroad to carry these poor dying people to that better country where no sin nor death could ever mar their happiness. He first started His civil engineer to survey out and locate the best route. This was John the Baptist, who located the route by repentance and faith. He met the King's Son at the Jordan, who made known Himself and received all necessary preparations for making said railroad.

He began to select men suitable to help make this road. Then he began to blow down the bluffs of Judaism and to fill the valleys of idolatry and to bridge the rivers of infidelity. When this was done, hear Him saying, "Upon this rock I will build my church." The foundation is ready, the great underlying principle of the road is next, the rails the great law of love that reaches all the way to heaven. Yes, and upon it every wheel that rolls heavenward must roll. As we behold the mighty Christ laying down these golden rails, He thunders again the first and second commandment of God with double force, "Thou shalt love the Lord thy God with all thy soul, mind and strength." The second is like unto it, "Thou shalt love thy neighbor as thyself." Upon these two commandments hang all the law and the prophets. These are the golden rails that reach all the way to heaven and on which every wheel must roll.

Next comes the great drive wheels, the law of liberty and equality. Hear Him saying, "Whatsoever ye would that men should do to you, do ye even so to them: for this is the law and the prophets." The commandment of God has been so abused that no sect on earth is willing to let their brother read, believe and practice for themselves. Read it like we see it and do as our doctrine says or we will exclude you from our church. Here is where the side track is set in. But see the mighty Christ as all things were ready for His glorious church. The engine [is] on the track ready to roll but just then old grim death steps up and says, This land and all its inhabitants are mine. Your Father gave it to me to reign over and unless you can pay for it not one that has lived or will live shall escape by eternal vengeance. The King's Son turns to His chosen ones and says, Will you help Me to pay the debt, will you take up your cross and follow Me? That is, walk in this world as I have walked, denying yourself of the lusts and pleasures of this world, and not you only, but all that will may help Me redeem the world and share in the glory that shall be revealed? Oh, poor Christians, are you helping Christ redeem the world? Are you drinking of the cup that He drank of? Are you baptized with the baptism that He was baptized with? Are you filling the measure of the affliction of Christ which is behind? We see Christ in the garden sending a message to His Father asking Him if it were His will for Him to pay the debt. He assured Him to pay the debt and redeem the world and all should be His. Hear Him saying, You shall not take My life as you take the lives of these poor people. My life will I give for the life of the world. I lay My life down and I take it again. So He paid the debt, and after His resurrection, He came to His chosen ones and told them to wait for the Guide who would show them how to operate this heavenly engine, and to carry these people through to a better land. After ten days the Guide which is the Holy Ghost came from heaven with the fire that makes the power and so the steam was raised in the heavenly engine. The porters cried "All Aboard" and three thousand boarded the train the first day. On and on went the heavenly engine until Satan saw that the world would be saved if he could not wreck the train and get the heavenly engine off of those golden rails. One day in absence of the Guide, there being several engineers, firemen and porters (officers of the church), Satan tells them that the other fire will run this engine as well as the fire from heaven, and that other rails would be lighter and easier managed than the golden rails. So they hewed out wooden rails (men-made creeds); they took out the golden link of God's law and set in the wooden rails. Then they tried to roll ahead, but alas, their new track was narrow gauged. So on to the wooden rails goes the heavenly engine and a great crash followed. For 1500 years this golden link has been lost and denominations have been on men-made creeds. This occurred about the year 325 A.D.

Chapter II

Now standing on the verge of the twentieth century looking back through the history of the various churches or sects, back past the great reformers such as Luther, Wesley, Campbell, Calvin, Wyckliffe and Huss, back to popery's bloody history to the apostolic church as she stood on God's blessed law and ruled by His government only through persecution with blood-stained garments.

> Through blood and through strife
> They hazarded their life,
> They were hunted and killed
> Over mountain and hill.
>
> Through prisons and fires,
> And beasts from the lyres,
> Though much trouble they saw,
> They clung to God's law.

Thus three centuries passed while the one Church of God was building on the foundations of the apostles and prophets, Jesus Christ being the chief corner stone, but in the fourth century we behold the beast that was and is not and yet is, ascending into his political ecclesiasticism, that is, state and church united, compelling God's people to worship idols.

This same power or beast was in Nebuchadnezzar's reign in Babylon while God's people were in captivity under him. Down, down the history of time four centuries or more we call for God's church again. No answer comes, but from proud Rome comes the answer, saying she is the church which the gates of hell shall not prevail against. Sick with her foul breath and blood-stained hands we call to the valley of Piedmont, then we ascend the Alps again, call for God's Church and only an imaginary answer comes. At this many go over to ride on the beast and share in the Babylonian captivity, under Rome or some one of her daughters. Oh, that through all these years God's people had known what Jesus meant when He said, "Upon this rock I will build my church, and the gates of hell shall not prevail against it."

If Christ built a church, when did He finish the building? Not yet, I assure you, or He would come and receive it. Like the temple of old it was not built in a day or a year. So is the heavenly Jerusalem, the bride, every saint is a stone in the temple of God. Rev. 3:12. Thank God that you and I may be a part of God's church. Built by Christ—yes, here on earth is God's quarry, and every stone that does not spoil in dressing in the quarry (visible church) will, when perfected through suffering like Jesus was, fit perfectly in the church triumphant—the temple of God. So the church is being built. Persecutions may hinder some.

It may build fast or it may build slow,
But, glory to God, Christ will build it I know.

When complete in Him without wrinkle or spot,
With trials all past and troubles forgot,

When the fires are all built and the fagots applied,
When the last saint on earth for Jesus has died.

All crowned with glory by Jesus' side,
Not earth-worn pilgrims, but Jesus' bride.

Against her hell's gate shall never prevail,
[Nor] the powers of darkness ever assail.

But where, oh, where is the visible church that once kept God's law and government? Is it Rome or is it one of the many Protestant churches? They may all answer yes, or at least a branch of the church, and no doubt all will claim that their doctrines and articles of faith are in harmony with the Bible, but all cannot be in harmony with God's Word. They may believe they are, but we know that no uninspired man or men can make an infallible creed. We admit some truth in all, but will some truth justify the false? Nay, a little leaven leaveneth the whole lump. Then the leaven of false doctrine is in the entire group of sects. If one is excusable for false doctrine, all are, and if one is rejected, then all are, unless their creed is infallible.

Oh, what a confusion reigns in the various sects of earth today. It could not have been worse on the top of the tower of Babel when God came down and confounded the language of the people. It seems that our tower of Babylon is built and our spiritual language confounded. Above all this din of strife and confusion I hear Christ praying in John 17:21, that they may all be one. Would He have thus prayed for unity and given a law that would bring discord? Nay, never. But, say some, there is no division of God's people, but our reason says not so. Christ said the world might believe, but there is not a unity that the world can see. No, it is not the unity which Christ wanted by any means but a confusion that He does not want. Therefore we are driven to the wall and stand aghast and cry, "Where is the lost link of the golden chain of God's law? Oh, where did the Church sidetrack? Oh, where did they leave the golden rail and set in the wooden rails of creedism? Where did the builders fail to build with gold, silver and precious stones and commence building with wood, hay and stubble?" Some will ask, Did not one of the reformers, Luther, Wesley or Campbell find the lost link? No, they did not try to reform from creeds to God's law but tried to reform the creeds to a purer standard of faith like thousands today who fail to see that God's law wasn't a creed system. Then if we fail to find the disease we cannot give the remedy, so we will show the difference in God's law and the creeds of today in the following poem:

> The Lord of life from glory came,
> To make our minds and hearts the same;
> His gospel, law and government
> Unto His children he has sent.
>
> No more the Gentile and the Jew,
> But one new man made of the two;
> The lines of strife no more to lay,
> But walk in love from day to day.
>
> The law of love He did command,
> That by it we should understand,
> And by it all His children know,
> For out of it no strife can grow.
>
> Alas, where is this law today,
> From which the Church has gone astray?
> The law of Christ they have denied,
> By human laws they are supplied.
>
> Will Christians close their eyes and ears,
> Against the light that now appears.
> Yet still to bow to human laws,
> Which God will burn like useless straws?

O, brethren, for the sake of Christ,
Leave off these laws that gender strife,
Be by His Spirit ever led,
He is the church's only Head.

Oh, yes, it is the great law of love on which Christ founded His Church. Hear Him saying, "This is my commandment, That ye love one another; as I have loved you, that ye also love one another." John 13:34, 35. This great law of love stands out in God's Word with preeminence over all other laws as the law by which to know and fellowship each other. "He that loveth not his brother abideth in death." He shows that we should believe on Jesus Christ and love one another as he gave us commandments. In 1 John 4:7, 8 He shows the absolute certainty of the religion of man who loves his brother. Verses 20, 21 forever settle the fact that love is the infallible rule to know a man's true religion. St. Paul says though I have the gift of tongues, even to speak the language of angels, and have not charity, it is a failure. Neither is the gift of prophecy or knowledge or faith without charity sufficient to know God's people. God's Word puts it beyond all dispute as to the apostolic church being established on the law of love. Therefore fellowshipping each other by the law of love is the lost link. If this be so, we do not doubt it in the least. When and how did the church leave the law of love and take up the law of faith as a discerning law by which to fellowship each other? We find that about the year 325 A.D. when Constantine was emperor there arose a man by the name of Arius who differed in doctrine from the majority of the church or the preachers of the church, so Constantine ordered a council of 380 elders to convene at Constantinople. This council condemned Arius' doctrine as unsound. Arius thought [that] back before God made the world or anything else that He made Christ the first and noblest creature He ever made. The others claimed that Christ was ever with God and not made by Him at all. Constantine caused them to make the Nicene creed by which Arius was condemned as a heretic, and expelled him and his followers from their fellowship and communion regardless of their love for God and one another. One party became the Catholic church and the other the Arian church, each following their creed instead of God's law. This change gave birth to creeds, and every creed has made a sect or denomination. Oh, how glad we are that we have found the lost link. The next step Pope Sylvester was made head of the church, and the next thing, church and state were united. Thus the church and pope ruled the nations. Here came up the beast on which the woman sat, the mystery, Babylon the great. The mother of harlots, an abomination to the earth. Rev. 17:5. This corresponds with Paul's mystery of iniquity or man of sin. See him exalted as God to be head of the Church instead of Christ, girded with the sword and crowned as king, universal over all nations.

Come, children of the Lord of light,
Leave off your Babylonish strife,
Her merchandise no longer buy,
Nor heed the Babylonish cry.

The creeds of men her towers have built,
The blood of saints they sure have spilt,
The guilt the various sects shall share,
If now this voice you fail to hear.

This mystery is the man of sin,
In the Apostles' day it did begin,
To diminish each other's faith,
With days and years it kept apace.

Until the days of Constantine,
It then the church and state combined.
Dominion to the state did give,
And caused that horned beast to live.

Against its powers reformers strove,
Which caused them in strange lands to rove.
Though many of them their blood have shed,
Its lasso rests upon our head.

Like the souls of the saints under the altar we cry, How long, oh, Lord, holy and true, dost thou suffer this mystery of iniquity to sit in the temple of God (place of worship)? Surely the time of His destruction is at hand, for Paul says the Lord will consume him with the spirit of His mouth and destroy him with the brightness of His coming. Is not the Lord sending forth the spirit of His mouth or the Word of God accompanied with an outpouring of the Holy Ghost as never before since the apostolic days? Surely the brightness of the Son of righteousness is appearing in the spiritual skies. Surely the stars have been falling from the heavens. Here stars mean ministers of the gospel. It is true they have not all fallen during the dark age of 1500 years, but many are fading from before the light of latter rain or the evening light. Oh that I could speak in thunder tones, I would proclaim to every saint on earth and urge them to shake off the bonds of false doctrines of men as imposed on them by the tradition of their elders who make void the law of God as Christ told the Jews. It is impossible to set up a creed for a man to preach and the Holy Ghost to guide into all truth. Where can you lead an ox that is tied to a stake? It is impossible to teach the doctrines and commandments of men and not insult the Holy Ghost.

It is no wonder the once powerful Methodist Church has lost so much power with God and man. Her twenty-nine articles are enough to drive the

Spirit filled saints from her fold. Why are they not drawn from the Bible? Whether they be truth or error it differs not. If every article were as pure as gold it would break God's law as Moses broke the table of God's law.

For centuries we have been under creeds or doctrines, and instead of unity it makes division; instead of peace they make strife; instead of unity they bring discord; instead of love they bring hatred. The infernal regions never won a greater victory than when Satan gets a band of pious saints assembled together and some "smart elek [sic]" with self assumed infallibility gets up and says they won't ordain any man to preach unless he can teach their doctrine as they have it set up, and then they shout like Israel shouted when they saw Aaron's golden calf, thinking God is pleased with it. So on goes all the creed systems, the blind leading the blind and falling into the ditch of the apostasy. . . .

Chapter III

Shall I be as one calling unto a deaf man or one that waveth a signal to the blind? Oh, my brethren, can you not see and do you not know the awful state of the churches? Who can imagine for a moment that all this discord, confusion and strife is the will of God? It is a slanderous falsehood to say that Christ gave a law that caused confusion, malice and strife. Do you know that they are the cunning works of men and have proved destructive to all the true elements of religion, love, liberty, equality, being led of the Spirit and sanctification? Without these you have a dead mass of confusion. Even now when a man departs from iniquity he becomes an object of persecution. The spirit of persecution is awakened and aroused from its slumber when we begin to draw the line between the law of Christ and the laws of men, between holiness and sin, between a gluttonous and a self-denying ministry; when we begin to hew down the walls of prejudice and cut asunder the line of separation, to shake off the bonds of men-made creeds and laws, [and to] come into the unity of the Spirit in the bonds of peace unto the faith that sweetly works by love unto the charity which is the bond of perfectness. As we return from our captivity in Babylon to rebuild the temple of God, to crown it with the chief cornerstone of Christ and His law, they will persecute us, they will mock and say that we are a band of cranks and are fanatic, and say all manner of evil against us falsely for Christ's sake. Not because they love God or holiness or the church but because they love honor, money, division, a great name and greeting in the markets, chief seats in the council, conferences and associations; but some will persecute us because of their honest zeal, believing they are right. But I trust the Lord will give all my brethren spirit and light to see the truth and enough love for God to accept it, at any cost. Moses like, Christ like, Paul like, Luther like, in fact, like every one who would do God's holy will and not the will of man.

A land of gospel light have we,
How thankful then ought we to be;
What profit is that light to us,
If now that light we fail to see?

How shall we that light discern,
Which only in Thy Spirit burns?
O, Lord, each heart from darkness free,
That it may borrow light of Thee.

Send forth Thy law in every heart,
The law of God to us impart,
Like Thee, dear Father, and Thy Son
May we Thy children join in one.

May now the holy law of love,
Which cometh only from above,
In strongest ties our hearts unite,
That we may walk in gospel light.

CHAPTER THIRTEEN

Garfield Thomas Haywood
(1880–1931)

Garfield Thomas Haywood was the most intellectually wide-ranging of all early pentecostal theologians. In his various publications, he discussed theories of the atonement, the nature of the Godhead, the history of the world (including geologic developments and dinosaurs as well as the human saga), the resurrection of the dead, and the experience of conversion. In addition, he was a song composer and poet. Haywood was a proponent of Oneness (unitarian) pentecostalism, but his reputation was such that even convinced trinitarians sang his songs and read his books.

Haywood was born in Greencastle, Indiana, but his family moved to Indianapolis when he was three, and he spent virtually all the rest of his life in that one city. He was middle class. His father worked at the foundry, and his mother was a teacher. As a young person in high school, Haywood added his own income to the family coffers, working as a cartoonist for the city's two African American newspapers. His family was strongly Christian but ecumenical in spirit, exposing Haywood to both Baptist and Methodist influences in his youth. In 1902, he married Ida Howard from Owensboro, Kentucky (located about 150 miles south of Indianapolis), and the couple had one child, a daughter named Fannie Ann. All in all, Haywood seemed set to become a relatively prosperous, happy, ordinary member of the Indianapolis community.

Then he met Glenn Cook and Henry Prentiss. Both men had been at the Azusa revival, and they came to Indianapolis to spread the new pentecostal message. Somehow Haywood heard about them, and somehow he was converted to the cause. The details are now lost in history. What we do know is that when Cook and Prentiss exited town, Haywood was left in charge of the small pentecostal congregation that had been started. Still unordained at the time, he quickly sought and obtained ministerial credentials from a group called the Pentecostal Assemblies of the World (PAW).

Haywood must have been a good preacher because when Cook returned to the city in 1915, the congregation had grown to more than 450 members. The reason Cook returned, however, was not merely to see how things were going; he had another new message to share with Indianapolis. Cook had become one of the most vocal promoters of the new "Jesus-only" theology that was sweeping through the pentecostal movement, and he wanted to make sure Haywood's congregation had the chance to get on board. He shared his views with Haywood, who responded enthusiastically. Later the entire church membership was re-baptized in Jesus' name.

On the surface, the Jesus-only movement seemed simple, focusing on a new formula for baptism that referred to Jesus only and not to God the Father or the Holy Spirit. But that simple change had radical consequences. Most Jesus-only pentecostals eventually adopted a Oneness or unitarian view of the Godhead. They believed Jesus was the name of the one God, and the Father and the Spirit were merely other ways in which this one God could appear. Many Jesus-only pentecostals also adopted a new streamlined way of understanding the relationship between conversion, sanctification, and the baptism of the Spirit. Rather than envisioning them as separate experiences, they combined the three into a single mega-experience where everything happened at once. Haywood was one of the chief proponents of this position, and he called that single experience "the birth of the Spirit." In the selection that follows, Haywood explains this birth of the Spirit and then goes on to examine how the birth of the Spirit is related to speaking in tongues and other spiritual gifts.[1]

The following selection is taken from *The Birth of the Spirit in the Days of the Apostles* (Indianapolis, Ind.: Christ Temple Book Store, [1922?]).

Chapter I: The Birth of the Spirit in the Days of the Apostles

From the beginning of the Reformation even down to the days in which we now live, the cry of the hearts of the people of God has been incessantly, "Back

---

[1] For more information, see David Bundy, "G. T. Haywood: Religion for Urban Realities," in *Portraits of a Generation: Early Pentecostal Leaders*, ed. James R. Groff and Grant Wacker (Fayetteville: University of Arkansas Press, 2002), 237–54; and Jacobsen, *Thinking in the Spirit*, 197–232.

to Pentecost." Every advance truth that forged its way to the front, throwing light on the "path of the just," has always met with a storm of opposition from those who are supposed to be seeking for a closer walk with God.

The Jews were [so] set in their doctrines that the Lord Himself found it a difficult proposition to lead them into the way of life for which they had sought so long. "No man also having drunk old wine straightway desireth the new: for he saith the old is better" (Luke 5:39), is the manner in which He summed up the situation in His day. They were so imbibed [sic] in their traditional doctrine that they laid aside and rejected the commandments of God and made "the word of God of none effect" through their traditions which had been delivered unto them. (Mar. 7:5–13.) Even so it is today. We have been so absorbed in our ancestral views concerning the new birth that the Holy Spirit's work in bringing the people to the knowledge of the truth seems to be a difficult task.

Very few will agree with us on this subject at the first, but if they will lay aside the doctrine of men, and for a moment remove their thoughts from the abnormal state of the present day Christianity, they will find no trouble in grasping the truth as it is now revealed to many of the children of God in these closing days of the Gospel dispensation.

It is our purpose to take up the subject from a Bible point of view to see whether there is an experience in the New Testament scriptures, called the birth of the Spirit, aside from the baptism of the Holy Ghost, according to the second chapter of the Acts of the Apostles. If we cleave to the Word of God we cannot fail. Neither should we be afraid to declare what the Lord has revealed to us on this matter.

The Rest

The first scripture that we wish to bring to notice is that of Matt. 11:28. "Come unto Me all ye that labour and are heavy laden, and I will give you rest," is one of the most favored texts used in inviting the lost sinner to seek the way of Salvation. No one has ever been known to interpret the "rest" that Jesus offers here to be anything short of the new birth, or full salvation. With this we must all agree, and that that "rest" comes in being born again. But the question arises, what has that to do with the baptism of the Holy Ghost?

In turning to Isa. 28:11, 12 we find these words: "For with stammering lips and another tongue will he speak to this people. To whom he said, This is the rest wherewith ye may cause the weary to rest." It was on the day of Pentecost that God spake unto the people "with stammering lips and another tongue." (Acts 2:4.) From these scriptures it can be plainly seen that the "rest" and the baptism of the Holy Ghost are one and the same thing. Those who have really experienced the full baptism of the Holy Ghost and walked uncompromisingly before God can truly testify to these things, that they have in truth "found rest for their souls."

Born of Water and the Spirit

To Nicodemus Jesus said, "Verily, verily, I say unto you, except a man be born of water and the Spirit, he cannot enter into the kingdom of god." Nicodemus was a Jew and a Pharisee. His morals were perfect; he was a master of Israel. To him, to be born a Jew was a great favor of God, but his pride was humbled, and he was filled with astonishment when Jesus said unto him, "Ye must be born again." To be born into the kingdom of the Jews was one thing, but to enter into the kingdom of God was another. In reply to his question, "How can a man be born when he is old?" Jesus answers, "Except a man be born of water and the Spirit, he can not enter into the kingdom of God." In these words He set about to explain to him what He meant by being born again. Not that it was any different from the salvation that was offered, or to be offered, to the Gentile, but the illustration of a birth would best convey it to the minds of those who boasted in the fact that they were people of God through being born a Jew.

In fact, it was another way of saying, "He that believeth and is baptized, shall be saved." The statement was most astonishing to that stalwart Pharisee, but Jesus, knowing his thoughts, proceeded to further explain the manner of this new birth by saying, "The wind bloweth where it listeth, and thou hearest the sound thereof, but cannot tell whence it cometh, and whither it goes. So is everyone that is born of the Spirit." The fact that on the day of Pentecost there came a "sound" from heaven as of a rushing, mighty "wind," undisputedly links the baptism of the Holy Ghost with the experience of "everyone that is born of the Spirit."

St. John is the only writer in the New Testament who likens salvation unto a birth. St. Peter only mentions it slightly in one place. St. Paul, the apostle to the Gentiles, never used such a term in his writings to those whom he had brought "out of darkness into light." But instead, he used the word "baptize" or its equivalent, more than any other writer. While Jesus spake to Nicodemus concerning being "born of water and the Spirit," yet there is no record in the Acts of the Apostles that will indicate that his instructions were ever carried out, except by being baptized in water and the Holy Ghost. Not one place in the book of Acts can we find the words "born of water and the Spirit," or "born again," but we can find the words relating to "baptism" twenty-seven times. If to be "born of water and the Spirit" is not the baptism of "water and the Spirit," where is there any record of anyone ever being "born again?"

One dear brother, in his efforts to show that a man is born again without the baptism of the Holy Spirit stated that all the Jews had to be baptized for the remission of their sins before they could be born again, and that that was the reason Peter told them to "Repent and be baptized for the remission of their sins," but if we take our brother's word in this matter, it will strengthen the fact that the birth of the Spirit is the baptism of the Holy Ghost, because what they were to receive after being "baptized in the name of Jesus for the remission of sins" was "the gift of the Holy Ghost." (See Acts 2:38.)

Synonymous Terms

Scripture will interpret scripture if we seek to rightly divide the word of truth. To be born of "water and the Spirit," and "believe and is baptized" (John 3:5 and Mar. 16:16), are proven to be synonymous terms expressing the one and the self-same thing, by reading, or comparing the words of Jesus in John 10:9. All three of these expressions are spoken by the same Person. In the first mentioned scripture He says that if a man is not born of water and the Spirit he cannot enter into the Kingdom of God, while in the second, He says that he that believeth and is baptized shall be saved. But in the third, He combines the thoughts of the first and second by saying, "I am the door, by ME if any man *enter in* he *shall be saved*." A man that *enters in* [through him] is certain that he *shall be saved*; and no man shall be saved unless he enters in.

The Household of Cornelius

We take [the] record [of] the household of Cornelius as a proof that the birth of the Spirit, or full salvation, in the days of the Apostles, was the baptism of water and the Holy Ghost. Cornelius was not saved! (Acts 11:14.) He was a devout man and feared God with all his house, but he was not "born again." And as Peter began to tell him words whereby he should be saved, the Holy Ghost fell upon them and they spake with tongues and magnified God. And Peter later declared that the Spirit fell upon them as it did upon the Jews "at the beginning." (Acts 10:44, 46; 11:15.) Then answered Peter, "Can any man forbid water that these should not be baptized who have received the Holy Ghost as well as we? And he commanded them to be baptized in the name of the Lord."

It was God's plan that they be "born of water and the spirit," but because of the doubts in the minds of the six men that were with Peter as to the Gentiles being accepted, God, being sovereign, baptized them before they were baptized in water, in order to convince the Jews of their acceptance. The apostle, recognizing this to be a fact, remembered the words of the Lord, how that He said, "John truly baptized with water; but ye shall be baptized with the Holy Ghost," and immediately commanded them to be baptized in water in the name of the Lord. From the foregoing facts it can be clearly seen that it is utterly impossible for one to conceive the idea that the birth of the Spirit is separate and distinct from the baptism of the Holy Ghost. . . .

The Church and the Kingdom of God

A strong point to consider is that the church, which is the body of Christ, and the Kingdom of God are synonymous. A man must be born of water and Spirit in order to enter into the Kingdom of God, and he must be baptized into Christ in order to put on Christ. Upon first reading this it may sound somewhat foreign to some, but if it will be prayerfully considered, I am sure that all will agree that these things are so. The Church is the body of believers baptized in the Holy Ghost. The Kingdom of God is in righteousness and peace, and joy in the Holy Ghost. (Rom. 14:17.) When the Pharisee desired to know when the Kingdom of God should come Jesus answered, "the Kingdom of God is within . . . you," that is, in their midst. (Luke 17:20, 21.) It was Christ who was "among" or in the midst of them, but they could not see it (John 3:3), because it came "not with observation." To enter into the Kingdom of God one must be born of water and the Spirit, or, to enter in Christ, the Church, one must be baptized in water and the Holy Spirit.

What the Bible Teaches

In reading the Bible carefully it will be seen that its principal mission is to restore man to his Maker, and that this can only be done by the "washing of regeneration and the renewing of the Holy Ghost." (Titus 3:5). The foregoing scripture, or expression, is merely another way of expressing the thoughts conveyed in John 3:5; Mar. 16:1; John 10:9; Acts 2:38; Gal. 3:27.

No man who really reads the Bible will ever say that a man can be born of God without being baptized with the Holy Ghost. The Methodist, Baptist, Presbyterian, Christian, Episcopalian, Adventist and all others know that the Bible teaches this beyond dispute. If you confront them about the baptism of the Holy Ghost they will not hesitate to tell you that they have it, and that they received it when they were born of the Spirit. Furthermore, they will tell you that a man could not be born of the Spirit without being baptized with the Holy Ghost. And that is just what the Bible teaches.

The question may arise, "What is the difference between the view we take and that of these denominations above mentioned?" Let us say right here that there is as much difference between our views as there is between a millionaire and a pauper. The pauper talks about wealth, but the millionaire possesses it. The other denominations talk about the baptism of the Holy Ghost, but we believe in possessing it as they did at Pentecost. If everyone who called themselves Christians possessed the baptism of the Holy Spirit as they did in the days of the Apostles there would be no argument at all over the matter of the birth of the Spirit. . . .

Begotten and Born

Everyone with ordinary understanding knows that there is a difference between "begettal" and "birth." The begettal is from the father side while conception and birth is from the mother side. (Matt. 1:1–16, also note verses 16, 20, 25.) In those scriptures it will be seen that the father "begat" the child, while the mother "conceive[d]" and "bor[e]." A child of God is first "begotten" by the Word (I Cor. 4:15) of the Gospel before he can be born of the Spirit. The disciples were "begotten" unto a lively hope by the resurrection, but they were "born of the Spirit," on the day of Pentecost (I Pet. 1:3.).

No child can ever be born until it is first begotten, but there are many who have been begotten, but were never born into the world. So it is in the Spirit. Many may have been begotten by the word but have never been born of the Spirit. There are multitudes who are in that state today. They have been begotten, but the church has had no "strength" to bring them forth. (Isa. 37:3; 52:1.) In the fifty-second chapter of Isaiah the church is exhorted to awake and put on her "strength." Because of the lack of "strength," many had come into her "uncircumcised and unclean." But when she would put on her "strength" (see Isa. 28:5, 6; Gal. 3:27; Rom. 14:17; Neh. 8:10) no more would there come into her the "uncircumcised and the unclean." No congregation can bring the people to the "birth of the Spirit" except it is itself a congregation of Spirit-baptized believers. And when such a congregation enters into soul-travail, she will surely bring forth, for God will send forth the Spirit of His Son into their hearts, crying "Abba," (interpreted "Father" Rom. 8:15; Gal. 4:6.). Thus was the birth of the Spirit manifested in the days of the Apostles. . . .

Are the Unborn Lost?

The one question that is so often asked is, "Are all those people who thought they were born of the spirit, and were not, lost?" No, not by any means. They shall be given eternal life in the resurrection if they walked in all the light that was given them while they lived. God is a just Judge, and there is no unrighteousness in Him. But those who refuse to walk in the light shall be overtaken with darkness. (John 13:35, 36; see also John 15:22–24.)

It is often asked whether Wesley, Luther, Whitefield and other mighty men of God were baptized in the Holy Ghost according to the Acts of the Apostles. That is more than we can say. They may have been, and they may not. They lived up to the light of their day. We must live up to the light of our day. Their light will not do for us today, neither could they have walked in the light that we now embrace. The evening time has come, and the true light now shineth. If we compromise, God will raise up another people who will carry His word.

Many other words could be written upon this subject but time and space will not permit. Yet if any man will follow these lines with an open heart and Bible in hand, he will be made to see that the birth of the Spirit, in the days of the apostles, was a baptism of water and the Holy Ghost. If it were so then, why is it not so today? When, where and by whom was the change authorized? We await the answer.

Chapter II: The Gift vs. Gifts of the Spirit

. . . Many of today, although they acknowledge that the birth of the Spirit and the baptism of the Spirit are synonymous, yet they disagree on the point as to whether speaking in other tongues accompanies the "birth of the Spirit." As long as we were taught that the birth of the Spirit was one thing, and the baptism of the Spirit was another, practically all of those who received this miraculous experience as it is recorded in the second chapter of Acts, stood firm and proclaimed far and wide that, according to the apostolic record, all who were baptized with the Holy Spirit spoke with other languages as the Spirit gave them utterance. Wherever this was preached all who received the baptism of the Spirit spake with other languages as they did at Pentecost.

As time rolled on the illumination of the Holy Spirit began to reveal to the church more truth. (John 14:26, 16:12–15.) And many of those who saw the light began at once to walk therein (John 12:35, 36.) while others faltered, and began to draw back. Because of this some have attempted to prove that the "birth of the Spirit" and the "baptism of the spirit" are two different experiences, while others hold that the two are synonymous, but that all who receive it do not speak with tongues. It is the latter view that we especially wish to dwell upon.

The Controversy

The argument used is strengthened by this passage of scripture, "Do all speak with tongues?" (I Cor. 12:30.) We do not take this up for mere argument's sake, strife nor controversy, but that by this we may arrive at just what the word of God teaches on this matter. If we are wrong, it is our desire to be set right by the Word. The time is too short for us to seek honor, or applause. The church of God is at stake. If we err, many souls will be required at our hands. There is but one thing upon which we can rely to judge between us in this matter, and that is the infallible Word of God, "which liveth and abideth forever."

There Is a Difference

In the first place, the Bible teaches that there is a difference between the "gift" of the Holy Spirit, and the "gifts" of the Holy Spirit. The second chapter of

Acts records the reception of the "gift (singular) of the Holy Ghost," while the twelfth chapter of I Corinthians deals with the operation of the "gifts (plural) of the Holy Ghost." If we consider this, the rest will be clearly understood. The speaking with other tongues as the Spirit gives utterance accompanied the "gift" of the Holy Ghost; but the "divers kind of tongues" is one of the "gifts" of the Holy Spirit, which He divides severally as He wills.

At Caesarea the Apostle knew that the Gentiles had received the "gift of the Holy Ghost" (not one of the gifts), "For they heard them speak with tongues, and magnify God." (Acts 10:45, 46.) When Peter rehearsed the incident that transpired at the house of Cornelius, he declared that God gave them the "like gift" as He did unto them at Jerusalem on the day of Pentecost.

The Gift of God a Sacrifice

That we might note that there is a distinction between the "gift" of the Holy Ghost and the "gifts" of the Holy Ghost, we will refer you to the original Greek wording of the same. We do not do this to make a display of knowledge, but since some have resorted to this method to strengthen their points, or overthrow the truth, we feel that we have an equal liberty to use the same methods. We do not profess to be a Greek student, but we desire to use a little Greek at this point, as we believe it will help some. In the New Testament there are fourteen places where the word "gift" is used in reference to the Holy Spirit, directly or indirectly (note the following places: John 4:10; Acts 2:38, 8:20, 10:45, 11:17; Rom. 5:15, 16, 17, 18; II Cor. 9:15; Eph. 2:8, 3:7, 4:7; Heb. 6:4); and the word in each instance is taken from the word *doron*, which means, a sacrifice, while the word used for "gifts" is *charisma*, which means a spiritual endowment, that is, a religious qualification, or a miraculous faculty.

By this one can clearly see that the "gift" of the Holy Ghost refers to the life which was *sacrificed* and given unto us. The "gift" of the Holy Spirit is the life of Christ Himself. The gift (*doron*) which God has given us is eternal life. But the gifts are spiritual endowment, religious qualifications, or miraculous faculties, given for the edifying of the Church. (I Cor. 12:1–11.) In Eph. 4:8, the original word for "gifts" is *doma*, which means "presents." In Heb. 2:4, the original word used for "gifts" is *merismo*, which means "distribution." In none of these latter cases is the same word used as that which is used with reference to the Holy Spirit, thereby making a clear distinction between the "gift" (*doron*) of the Holy Ghost and the "gifts" (*charisma, doma*) of the Holy Ghost.

A More Simple Explanation

We trust that none of the children of God will stumble over these Greek words, for it is written to meet the oppositions of the learned ones. But we have a more simple manner of conveying the truth of this matter to those who love the Word of God.

"To speak as the Spirit gives utterance" is the thing that accompanies the "gift" of the Holy Ghost, but the gift of "divers kinds of tongues" is distributed among the members of the body as the Spirit wills. (I Cor. 12:11; Heb. 2:4.) Though every man "speaks as the Spirit gives utterance" when he receives the "gift" of the Holy Ghost (which is the manifestation of the Spirit, I Cor. 12:7), yet all are not given the gift of "divers kinds of tongues." It is this gift of "divers kinds of tongues" that the Apostle refers to when he says, "Do all speak with tongues?" By reading the entire chapter, it will be seen that he is dealing with all the gifts and not with speaking in tongues only.

The Gift of Tongues

It was this gift that was most particularly dealt with in the fourteenth chapter of his first epistle to the Corinthians. Those having the gift of tongues, and not knowing how to control it, were causing much trouble in the church at that time, and his instructions to those was "to keep silent in the church, and speak to himself and to God," if there was no interpreter present. If they were all "speaking as the Spirit gave utterance," would there be any confusion there? The Spirit of God is not the author of confusion (ver. 33). If they were "speaking as the Spirit gives utterance" would the Apostle give orders for the Spirit not to speak through them? Would he be so foolish as to dictate to the Spirit of God in such a manner, and then at the same time tell the saints "quench not the Spirit," and "grieve not the Holy Spirit"? God forbid. There must be a distinction between "gifts or divers kinds of tongues" and "speaking as the Spirit gives utterance."

Concerning the gift of tongues, the Apostle says, "If I pray in an unknown tongue MY spirit (not the Holy Spirit) prayeth" (ver. 14.) If it is his spirit praying in an unknown tongue, then there must be a difference between his Spirit operating the "gift of tongues" and the "Holy Spirit giving utterance." Hence, when he saith, "Do all speak with tongues?" he has no reference to the spirit's utterance when one receives the gift of the Holy Ghost, but to the "gift of tongues" which is among the gifts that are given to the members of the Church as He wills.

Tongues Are for a Sign

Tongues were a sign on the day of Pentecost that the Comforter had come. They were a sign to the saints at Damascus that Paul was one of them. They were a sign to Peter and the six Jews that God had accepted the Gentiles, and that they had received the Holy Ghost. They were a sign to Paul at Ephesus that the disciples had the real thing and were sealed to the day of their redemption. They were a sign that the Corinthians were baptized into the body. They were a sign that Isaiah's prophecy was true. They were signs to Apostolic Fathers that a man received the Holy Ghost. They are a sign that modern Christendom has not received the Holy Ghost. They are a sign that the time of refreshing has come from the presence of the Lord (Isa. 28:11, 12; Acts 3:19–21), and Jesus is soon to come. And we cannot believe that man has received the Holy Ghost until we see the signs as were manifested in Apostolic days, therefore tongues are for a sign.

CHAPTER FOURTEEN

Aimee Semple McPherson
(1890–1944)

Aimee Semple McPherson was in a class by herself. She was winsome, flamboyant, theatrical, sincere, practical, generous, embracing, and opinionated all at the same time. Sister Aimee, as she was often called (sometimes shortened to just "Sister"), was by far the most visible of all first-generation pentecostal leaders. No one else even came close. She was an American celebrity, reported on in the mainstream press alongside Hollywood stars and business tycoons, but she was also the genuine article: a pentecostal believer through and through.

Born Aimee Elizabeth Kennedy, she was a Canadian, raised in the town of Ingersoll in southwestern Ontario. Her family was religious. On her father's side, the lineage was Methodist, and on her mother's side, the Salvation Army. In Canada, however, denominations never meant as much as they did in the United States. Instead, almost all the churches shared a healthy sense of "just being Christian." She imbibed that attitude from her crib; it was part of the religious air she breathed, and it served her well her entire life.

In the winter of 1907–1908, a young evangelist named Robert James Semple passed through town and swept Aimee off her feet. They were married in August and moved to Chicago the next year—where William Durham ordained both of them—and then headed to China in 1910. Just a few weeks after their arrival, Semple contracted malaria and died. Aimee was left widowed, pregnant, and far from home. After her first child was born, she took a ship to New York City, where she hooked up with the Salvation Army. In New York, she met the man who would become her second husband, Harold McPherson. They married in October 1911.

Harold McPherson seems to have thought his new wife would become a typical woman, staying at home, raising children, and doing whatever religious good works could be squeezed in on the side. But he was mistaken. Aimee was called to preach—she had to preach—and when Harold proved unsympathetic, she packed her bags, took her children, and headed home to Canada. Harold joined her for a while and tried to be helpful, but Aimee's time and energy was now being funneled almost entirely into her itinerant evangelistic work. They eventually divorced in 1921.

Throughout the late 1910s and into the early 1920s, Sister Aimee was on the road constantly, driving her "gospel car" anywhere there was a road to take her. In 1918, she made a stop in California and fell in love with the place. While she never stopped traveling, Los Angeles became her permanent home and the headquarters for her Church of the Foursquare Gospel. Angelus Temple was her base of operations, opening its doors for the first time in January 1923. Its more than 5,000 seats were soon full every Sunday. McPherson often preached in costume, acting out her message as well as preaching it. The aura was theatrical, but it was still clearly church, and McPherson never forgot her help-the-poor Salvation Army roots. During the years of the Depression, her church served hundreds of thousands of meals to people in need with no regard to their race, faith, or ethnicity.

While McPherson was a pentecostal preacher, she rarely described herself that way. Instead, she saw herself merely as a Christian. Her message was the gospel—the "full gospel" of Christ–and that message didn't belong to any one group or denomination. During a time when many pentecostal leaders were vigorously staking out their own territory and denouncing everyone who disagreed with them, McPherson sought to draw people together. The sermon reproduced below, taken from her book *This Is That* (1923), illustrates both her theatrical prowess and her inclusivity of spirit.[1]

The following selection is taken from *This Is That: Personal Experiences, Sermons and Writings* (Los Angeles: Echo Park Evangelistic Association, 1923).

"Death in the Pot"

During the former rain outpouring of the Holy Spirit, which began on the day of Pentecost (Acts 2:4), the ark containing the glory of the Lord (spiritually

---

[1] For more information, see Edith Blumhofer, *Aimee Semple McPherson: Everybody's Sister* (Grand Rapids, Mich.: Eerdmans, 1993).

speaking), rested in Jerusalem as in Gilgal of old. Even as Saul had been sent to Gilgal to tarry till the Spirit of the Lord was come upon him and till the signs came to pass, so the hundred and twenty had been commanded to tarry in Jerusalem until the Holy Spirit should come upon them with signs following.

The long-looked-for, long-prophesied (Isaiah 28:11, 2:13; Joel 2:23 and 28; Zech. 10:1; Matt. 3:11; Luke 24:49; John 14, 15, 16; Acts 1:5 and 8) promised land had been reached. True, God had kept them whilst in the wilderness, and manna had come upon them, as the inspired words fell from the mouths of the holy prophets of old as they were moved by the Holy Spirit—true, the words of Jesus had been as manna from heaven, whilst He walked this earth in the fleshly body, but now—now—the Holy Spirit had come—N-O-W—they had entered Canaan's land, and instead of the manna which had been taken away, and fell no more upon them (Jesus being returned to the Father and His voice being heard no more), they had corn and oil and wine (Joel 2:19), as the Spirit spoke through them of Jesus and His coming kingdom. "*And they did eat the old CORN of the land*" (Josh. 5:11, 12) "*neither had they manna any more, but they did eat the fruit of the land of Canaan.*" (See fruits of the Spirit, Gal. 5:22.)

Jerusalem (as Gilgal of old) rang with the praises of the Lord, and with the marching feet of new converts, new men of war, who went forth to follow the Captain of the host. On the day of Pentecost three thousand souls were added to the church; with pure hearts o'erflowing with joy, and with unshod feet, His people walked softly before Him and fell upon their faces in adoration. Just as the twelve tribes erected their monument of twelve stones, so the twelve disciples stood as a monument of the mighty power of the great and holy One who had parted the waters of the Red Sea—"*Salvation*"—and parted the waters of Jordan to bring them to Canaan's land—"*The Baptism of the Holy Ghost.*" Each time did the Lord Himself have to part the waters before His children could cross over into the new experience.

Humanity could neither swim nor ford *the Red Sea*—The Lord Himself miraculously *opened*, through His blood, a path—salvation—which meant at once deliverance and *Life* to repentant believers—and *Death* to unrepentant unbelievers.

Mankind could not cross the judgment of *old Jordan's* waves, nor make themselves worthy to enter Canaan and, again through *parted* waters (His grace and His worthiness, which towered on either side), He led His people forth to the promised land, and filled them with the Spirit. Here are two experiences—Salvation and the Baptism of the Holy Spirit—which we could not have brought ourselves into, therefore did He part the waters each time. Bless His name.

"Elisha Came Again to Gilgal"

After the disciples and apostles had fallen asleep in the Lord, and the many years of blessing wherein the power and glory of the Holy Spirit had been manifested, came the gradual falling away of the spirituality of the church. The apostasy and dark ages followed, but holy, inspired prophecy had said:

"He who sent the former rain moderately shall send you the rain, both the former and the latter rain together in one month," and "It shall come to pass in the last days, saith God, I will pour out My Spirit upon all flesh," etc.

"AND ELISHA CAME AGAIN TO GILGAL," Hallelujah! The time for the latter rain outpouring of the Spirit which was to take place in the last days had come, and Elisha (who stands for the visual manifestation of the power of God in signs and wonders) came A-G-A-I-N to Gilgal.

And when he came he found that "THERE WAS A GREAT DEARTH IN THE LAND."

Ah, yes! What a dearth there was in the land! What a crying out for food, and pottage, and bread and lentils in and just prior to the years 1905 and 1906.

How many churches and saints cried to Heaven:

"Oh, for the old-time power! Oh, for another Pentecost!" The Methodist church, the Salvation Army, the Holiness church, and many others sang and prayed these words over and over (but Oh, how few really recognized the answer when it came, "wrapped in swaddling clothes and in a manger"). Nevertheless the Word of God said:

When you call upon Me I will answer, and in the day that you seek Me with your whole heart I will be found of you; turn unto the Lord with weeping and mourning, and . . . "He will return and repent and leave a blessing behind Him, even a meat offering and a drink offering."

"Set on the Great Pot"

Therefore, when Elisha came again to Gilgal, that is when the Holy Spirit, at the specified time for the latter rain, found the hungry saints sitting before Him with one accord and one desire, even as the hundred and twenty had sat in waiting expectation of old, "He said unto his servant":

"Set on the great pot and seethe the pottage for the sons of the prophets." "Blessed are they that do hunger and thirst, for they shall be filled."

Oh, glory to Jesus! I can just close my eyes as I write, here before my open Bible tonight, and see the great Pentecostal pot (the entire Pentecostal movement), being brought out and set upon the fire—the Holy Spirit is, of course, the fire—our prayer and praises are the WOOD (and Oh, it takes good dry wood, full of pitch, to make a real red hot fire—water-soaked, rotten wood of worldliness and unbelief will only smoke and smudge and hinder).

Once suspended over the fire of the Holy Spirit, the Pentecostal pot soon began to boil and simmer, as hungry saints came together, each bringing a contribution of carefully tilled vegetables in their hands as an offering.

What a mixture, what a conglomeration came together in that pot!

Perhaps there is not another movement on earth made up of such a varied assortment of teachings, creeds and organizations yet all melt and blend into one when put into the WATER of the Word, and boiled over the fire of the Holy Spirit.

It was as though myriad streams, coming from myriad fountain-heads, had met and mingled together, and NOW flowed on in ONE great stream as though they had never been divided.

Its fire was as that of a great burning pile of WOOD, hewn and gathered from many sources—from varied kinds of trees—from widely separated forests, *now* leaping heavenward in one great flame of love and devotion.

It was as many VEGETABLES, planted, watered, cultivated, tilled and brought from many fields, put into one pot, and now forming, with the strong meat of the Word, and the WATER of the Spirit of life, a rich, nourishing food, whose appetizing and inviting fragrance was wafted to all about upon the vapor of praise and testimony which arises from the dancing, joyful mixture within.

With lightning rapidity the Pentecostal revival has encircled the world: thousands and thousands of hungry souls have been filled with the Spirit.

Wait a moment! You who are investigating, or gazing curiously into the lively, bubbling, dancing Pentecostal pot. Let us halt and examine some of the people—the endless procession of people who are coming to contribute some edible to the movement. Let us begin with this man hurrying along toward the pot, laden with vegetables and bread of the first fruits, and see what he has to say.

The Methodist.

Q. "Halt! *Who* goes there? From whence do you come?"

A. "I am a METHODIST. I come from a church founded upon the sound doctrines of Justification and Faith in the present Power of God, as revealed to John Wesley—a church where the power of the Holy Spirit used to fall in bygone years, until *saints shouted,* and *sinners wept,* and the *joyful* danced before the Lord."

Q. "Oh? And what bring you in your hand?"

A. "I bring with me carefully tilled vegetables and bread of the first fruits, from a grand old field—a little sparsely '*sprinkled,*' and—well, a little '*short of water*'— nevertheless, diligently cultivated by watchfulness and the Word of God."

"Our harvests come from various gardens and are tilled by different gardeners, some of which are known as 'The Epworth League,' 'The Free Methodists,'

'The Ranters,' 'The Shaking Methodists,' etc., yet 'tis the same sun of righteousness which, from the lofty heavens, shines upon one and all."

"Coming out from the parent field I bring with me an appetite whetted by the cherished memories of how God once did work in the old-time Methodist church: for, alas! Dearth and formality came into our field, and many therein were an hungered."

"Kindly excuse me, and allow me to pass, for in these last days (Acts 2:17) the great pot of blessing has been set upon the fire of the Spirit, and thither do I hasten that I may find this old-time power increased an hundred fold."

(There! He is gone! I would that I could have detained and conversed with him a little longer. Let not our hearts be troubled, however, for lo, one goeth, and behold, another cometh.)

The Baptist.

Q. "Halt! Who goes there? And whence come you?"

A. "I am a BAPTIST. I come from a garden whose original plan of gardening (as recorded in our book of instructions) was patterned by the Word of God, the planning and springing up of the seeds required Justification and a Change of Heart. The young plants were well watered, too—in fact, 'completely immersed' in the beginning of their growth, but as the plants grew and developed, they had need of the wind of the Spirit and the falling of the latter rain for developing the harvest. Alas! between the high, well-guarded fence of 'close communion' and the heavy overhead trellis of theology and forms and ceremonies, neither wind nor rain could reach the garden."

"Consequently, many of our gardeners, realizing that the fruit of their labors was exceedingly 'hard shelled,' and that some life and breaking of the dry stiffness was needed, tried an artificial irrigation process of worldliness and structural magnificence. Lectures, concerts and amusements were recommended and tried as fertilizers. The spiritual life of the plants, however, did not thrive well under this method, and many withered and pined away, and there was a dearth in the land."

"Coming forth from behind our 'close communion' fence, I am hastening toward yonder brightly burning fire, for I do both 'see and hear' that the great pot has been set upon the flame. Hark! Can you not hear its dancing and bubbling, and see the vapors of praise rising, even from here?"

Q. "And what bring you in your hand to contribute to the Pentecostal pot?"

A. "I bring with me, as bread of the first fruits, the knowledge of the scriptures, sound doctrine, and a firm stand on Water Baptism as set forth by our forefathers. I bring with me a hunger for the real, tangible power of God."

"But, Ah! I catch the fragrant odors rising from yonder steaming caldron."

"Please allow me to pass, that I may receive my portion from the great pot."

The Salvationist.

Q. "Halt! Who goes there? From *whence* come you, and *why* do you come?"

A. "I come from the SALVATION ARMY, that, in obedience to the call of God, marched fearlessly beneath their banner of 'Blood and Fire,' into the very heart of the enemy's territory, taking captives and making love-prisoners for King Jesus."

"I come from a people who in their extensive gardening found labor for both the 'servant and the maid,' a body of people who were once deeply spiritual and prayerful, and entirely separated from the world and its earthly lore."

"True, amidst persecution and trial, they sowed the seed and gathered the harvest—not behind fenced enclosures, but in the streets and market-place, the slums and the hovels."

"I come from a people that used to stand for the manifestation of the Spirit, and many there were among them who shouted and danced, and fell prostrate under the power, and saw visions of the glory of God."

"Why do I leave? Why, because *there is a dearth in our land*—the old-time power is sadly lacking today, times and business are so pressing, popularity—our war work in the great world contest—never-ending financial needs—new barns for the extended harvest fields—have been as quick-growing weeds that have sadly choked and crowded out the old spirituality and whole-hearted abandonment and humble dependence upon God."

"Seeking and hungry for the old-time power, I come for food to the great pot which has been set over the fire of this Holy Ghost movement."

Q. "And what bring you in your hand?"

A. "I bring with me the first fruits of our labors. Our field of vegetables had a wonderful beginning; the planting was beyond criticism, and if our field had been watered according to the instructions of Chief Gardener Jesus, none should have excelled it. Our under gardeners, however, felt neither the pre-scribed water baptism nor the latter rain outpouring (The Baptism of the Holy Spirit, as recorded in Acts 2:4) to be necessary."

"Our vegetables were not even sprinkled. Nevertheless they contain a real zeal for souls and a courage to go after them. I bring in my hands the old 'Amen Corner' and the ringing Hallelujahs, singing and music, and a faith and perseverance that sow beside all waters."

On and on they come!

They are flocking in from every direction, each bringing some contribution to the Pentecostal Pot. Here comes the staunch PRESBYTERIAN—the old Scotch COVENANTER—the HUGUENOT, and the staid EPISCOPALIAN follows after—pride and formality forgotten.

One breath from the fragrant, boiling Revival on the fire brings back a rush of memories that recall the Faith and Power which rested in *their* midst in days of yore, when steadfast, persecuted forefathers fell upon their knees in caves and dens and dungeons, where plush and padded prayer-cushions were unknown—memories of old-time power and glorious blessing that followed in the days when "they who lived godly suffered persecution"—memories of long nights spent in prayer—the sincere unaffected heart's devotion of the Saviour and His love.

Ah, no! Neither gilded dome, nor frescoed arch, nor rolling tones that throb and thunder in the organ loft, nor surpliced choir, nor e'en the college-moulded, eloquent "divine" who speaks in modulated tones from flower-embowered canopy, can still the longing for the old-time power that glorified the sacrifice, surrender, prayer and faith of the Pilgrim Fathers' day.

Devoted saints come from the HOLINESS church, bringing the message of *Heart-Purity* and the *Coming of the Lord*, and wonderfully blessed of God, as fruitage needing but one thing—the latter rain.

The ADVENTIST adds his teachings on the *Coming of the Lord*, deep study of the *Prophetic Word*, teachings of *Holiness* and *Freedom from Worldliness.*

The QUAKER hastens up—deep wells of joyous recollections rising in his soul—eyes alight, beneath his broad-brimmed hat, with the memories of how HIS church, once shaken and controlled by the Spirit's power (before the dearth), had walked so close to God. Glowing coals within his heart, long banked and smouldering, now burst forth in flames again as he hastens to the Holy Spirit's fire and the great Pentecostal pot suspended thereupon. He adds the fruitage from his field—*"sterling qualities of truth," "unswerving faith,"* and *"yieldedness to the movings of the Spirit."*

And, would you believe it, here comes the ROMAN CATHOLIC—not one, but many of them leaving the old church, many have come to the Saviour, have been redeemed, filled with the Spirit, and bring with them a *Holy Reverence* and *Obedience* and *deep appreciation of this new-found reality* and *life in Jesus* to add to the happy mixture bubbling in the pot.

So many come from every quarter that it is impossible to halt and question them all. Then comes THE SINNER—Yes, what lines and lines of them. Attracted by the reality and the mighty moving of the Spirit, they bring with them the Fruits of Repentance and First Love.

"And Elisha said: SET ON THE GREAT POT, AND SEETHE POT-TAGE FOR THE SONS OF THE PROPHETS."

Oh, what a glorious feast we are going to have! What wonderful pottage!

Lift up the cover and peep in at the dancing, joyous mixture. See how, when boiled over the great *FIRE OF THE SPIRIT* and with the *WATER OF LIFE*, with the *MEAT OF THE WORD* and the *SALT* which has never lost its savor, a great change comes to all the viands within the pot; the fruits of the fields, the vegetables and the barley, lose their "hard shells," slip out of their walls of *differences, creeds,* and *forms*—forget they came from widely separated gardens and were tilled by gardeners who never could agree as to methods, and soon they burst with praise as their innermost hearts flow forth in love.

Then, as the fire burns on, they melt—and melt—and M-E-L-T until the pottage is but one united, savory mixture. Outside walls crumble and fall away, for vegetables must be peeled before entering the pot (that is, barriers of organizations and differences must be left outside; peelings do not make good pottage). Then, as the fire still continues to burn and the pot to boil, each vegetable and fruit, in melting, has lost its own identity and has so united and merged itself into the other broken, melting hearts round about it, that 'tis hard to realize they ever were divided.

The Man with the Lapful of Gourds

Many eyes and many footsteps were turned eagerly toward this Pentecostal movement; brethren patted each other on the back and said: "No more need of hunger or separation or dearth. Here is unity everlasting with nothing to mar."

Hungrily, servants and handmaidens alike drew near with clean plates and shining spoons. "What a wonderful feast we are going to have," they said.

But stop! Who is that man slipping in so stealthily behind the others, carrying something in his garment. Let us question him.

Q. Halt! *Who* goes there? From whence do Y-O-U come?

A. "Me? Oh, I come from no particular garden. I am the 'ONE WHO WENT OUT IN THE FIELD TO GATHER HERBS.'"

Q. "And what sort of vegetables do you bring in your lap?"

A. "Why—er—that is, I—It is not vegetables I bring. Vegetables must be most carefully planted in prepared ground, tilled and cultivated (study to show thyself approved unto God, a workman that needeth not to be ashamed). Whilst wandering yonder I found a wild vine full of nice, fat *gourds*, no trouble to till them at all. They were there already, and all I had to do was to pluck the wild gourds in passing. See? I have a good big lapful here. Fine looking specimens, are they not?"

Q. "Good specimens of 'gourds,' yes, but I am not so sure of their being good to eat, or being a desirable addition to yonder feast. I fear that they are poisonous?"

A. "Oh, no, they are not poisonous, I assure you."

Q. "Well, what are the names of these different gourds?"

A. "Why—a—This one is called '*False Teaching,*' this one is called '*Error,*' whilst this prickly one is known as '*Doctrinal Issues.*' This puffy fat one is '*Lover of Power and Recognition.*' Then there is '*Self-Righteousness,*' '*Formality,*' '*Pre-conceived Ideas and Teaching,*' '*Fear of Manifestations,*' '*Flesh*' and '*Fanaticism.*' There are many other gourds, and amongst their number are '*Lack of Brotherly Love,*' '*False Reports,*' '*Harsh Criticism*' and '*Tale Bearing.*'

Q. "Why, Man! You would never think of bringing such things into the midst of a Pentecostal gathering!"

"You are wrong, and the gourds are poisonous. They will destroy unity and curdle love and make endless confusion and trouble."

"Surely you do not realize what you are doing?"

A. "Oh, yes I do. The Lord (?) revealed this thing to me and I know this new idea is the only right one. I know these gourds are perfectly all right and you can't teach me anything about them. Kindly allow me to pass."

Q. "Wait, wait, come back!"

There, he is gone—he worms his way into the inner circle, gets close to the pot, lifts his lapful of gourds, and in they go, the whole lot of them, into the pottage. On-lookers innocently allowed the gourds at first to pass them, and even—Shred them into the pot of pottage, *"for they knew them not."* So they poured out for men to eat; and it came to pass as they were eating of the pottage that they cried out and said: OH, THOU MAN OF GOD, THERE IS DEATH IN THE POT, and they could not eat thereof.

Amidst the many who came with good contributions to the pot, here and there steals up a man or woman with a lapful of gourds, which they have plucked from some wild vine as they journeyed, and they are thrown, sometimes ignorantly, sometimes knowingly, into the great pot upon the fire.

"Oh what a distressingly large lapful of poisonous gourds!" exclaims the on-looker who had been approaching with his empty dish and spoon, ready to dine, and who now draws back in fear.

"Horrors—the whole thing is spoiled!"

There is false teaching and error in that movement, and I am afraid to have anything to do with it.

There is "So and So," who did "such and such" a thing, and if *that's Pentecost,* or if *that's the Baptism of the Holy Ghost,* I for one, don't want it. There's Mr. "So and So" in our assembly, and there's that one who professed to be a Holy Ghost preacher—did you hear what he did?

Did you hear of the gourd that he brought and dumped into this movement?

No, Sir! The whole pot is contaminated and poisoned. I tell you there's DEATH in the pot. And they are in a straight between two, whether to try to overturn the whole pot or to walk away and leave it, warning others as they go.

Some say, "Come on, let's fight this movement. Let's write some tracts against it and do what we can to overturn the whole thing." Others who walk away, warn everyone they meet by saying:

"Did you hear the news about that Pentecostal movement down there? Why, 'So and So' has just brought the most distressing lapful of gourds and dropped them into Pentecost; unity is disrupted; love is curdled, the people are made sick at their very hearts. Don't you go near that place."

Perplexity and confusion falls upon many an on-looker, some stay to criticize; others to wring their hands and weep.

What shall YOU and I do? We know that the movement is ninety-nine per cent pure, but Oh, that lapful of gourds has brought so much trouble! Of course we know that "WHEN THE SONS OF GOD CAME TOGETHER THE DEVIL CAME ALSO," and that there never was a movement but where some one came in to bring reproach, and that even amongst the twelve disciples one was a Judas. We also know how one who does not measure up to the standard is singled out from the ninety-nine others and enlarged upon until the "ninety and nine just ones" are forgotten in pointing to and discussing him who went astray.

"Well, we know the thing is not right anyway, as it is, and I guess we better go away. Too bad, isn't it?"

"But wait a moment—

Who is this so swiftly approaching with a well-filled sack clasped tightly in his arms?"

Q. "Who goes there, and what do you bring in your hands?"

A. "I am the man with the sack of meal. The meal is the Word of God. I go to cast it into the pot. This meal will simmer down to the bottom of the whole affair and settle all disturbances. It shall cry aloud:

What saith the scriptures? Bring forth the plumb line. Let God be true and every man a liar. Prove all things. Abhor that which is evil; cleave to that which is good. Be not overcome of evil, but overcome evil with good."

This word is quick and power[ful] and shall not fail, if cast into the pot, to purify and bring order out of confusion.

"And Elisha said, bring meal, and he cast it into the pot; and he said, pour out for the people that they may eat, and there was no harm in the pot."

Oh, hallelujah! The Word of God is being poured into this movement, and His Word is accomplishing that whereunto it has been sent. The Holy Spirit today is calling as did Elisha of old: "POUR OUT FOR THE PEOPLE THAT THEY MAY EAT."

I can seem to see the surrounding circle of empty plates and see the hungry faces of the dear ones as they are partaking themselves and calling to others to come, "taste and see that the Lord is good."

"POUR OUT TO THE PEOPLE THAT THEY MAY EAT." Oh, yes, that is the greatest mission of the hour. Give unto the people that they may eat.

If you have discovered something somewhere in your vicinity or in the movement at large which looks to you like a gourd, instead of turning your back and your judgment and wholesale condemnation upon the whole thing, go bring the meal (II Kings 4:41), get the Word of God and find out what saith the scriptures. "If this work be of men it will come to naught; but if it be of God, ye cannot overthrow it, lest haply ye be found even to fight against God." (Acts 5:38–39.)

Get out the meal—if you see this Baptism of the Holy Spirit with the Bible evidence, speaking in tongues, in the WORD, with the accompanying gifts and fruits of the Spirit, believe God and come boldly to receive this Bible experience even though every one round about you seems to be in error or falls below the standard.

INSTEAD OF BEING THE ONE WHO CRIES "THERE IS DEATH IN THE POT," BE AN ELISHA WITH A SACK OF MEAL; receive YE the Holy Ghost; let God make YOU to measure up to the Word. All your criticizing or scolding or telling where the trouble is, even trying to fix it, can never help. The Meal of the Word will alone avail.

Pour out for the people that they may eat. Dear worker, what are you feeding your hungry people on? Are you telling them and repeating over, meeting after meeting, every story and incident that has come to your knowledge where gourds have been put into the pot? If so, you are guilty and putting gourds of doubts and discouragement in the pot yourself.

When you set the table for your guests that hunger all about you, do not frighten people away by bringing up from your cellar the poorest potatoes or the moldy preserves, or the mildewed bread from your larder—*THEY DO NOT WANT TO HEAR ABOUT MAN'S WORST; THEY WANT TO HEAR ABOUT GOD'S BEST.* What are you feeding your people on? Relating the worst things you ever heard of man doing or the best things you ever heard of God doing? The former makes poor fighting food—the latter makes firm spiritual muscles and makes strong, developed, matured men and women who grow quickly under such teaching *"unto a perfect man, unto the measure of the stature of the fullness of Christ."* (Eph. 4:13.)

Remember that by relating past wrongs, etc., you are as guilty as those who committed them, and are only frightening people away by crying: "There's death in the pot." Go bring the meal: preach the Word. Lift up the pure standard and God will vindicate and honor His Word.

CHAPTER FIFTEEN

Robert Clarence Lawson
(1883–1961)

R OBERT CLARENCE LAWSON spent his childhood in New Iberia, Louisiana, about a hundred miles west of New Orleans, where he was raised by his aunt. We know almost nothing about the details of his youth, but he became a relatively successful singer in his adult years, first as a performer in the taverns of southern Louisiana and then further afield.

It was a singing tour that took him to Indianapolis in 1913, where he fell seriously ill and had to be hospitalized. His nurse was a member of G. T. Haywood's pentecostal congregation, and she introduced the men to each other. Lawson was impressed by Haywood. He listened to his message and was converted. Haywood must have been similarly impressed with Lawson, because he soon sent Lawson out as a "church planter," establishing new congregations in the Midwest as far south as Texas.

Tiring of life on the road, Lawson decided Columbus, Ohio, was a good place to stop and rest for a while, and he pastored a church there for three years. During this time, his relationship with Haywood took a turn for the worse. The two men ran into conflict on a number of issues, mostly concerning social mores related to family, gender, and sexuality. The conflicts were severe enough that Lawson finally split with Haywood and his denomination, the Pentecostal Assemblies of the World, and moved east to New York City.

In New York, Lawson found an environment where he could truly blossom and be appreciated for his ministerial skills. He organized a congregation known as the Refuge Church of Christ and helped found a new denomination called the Church of Our Lord Jesus Christ. He wrote a variety of hymns and

popular gospel songs, started a radio program, and later helped found a Bible
school in North Carolina.

Lawson also thought deeply about his faith. He had settled in northern
Manhattan, in Harlem, near Columbia University. This was the time of the
Harlem Renaissance—artists, writers, and musicians were everywhere—and
creativity was in the air. This was also the time when a number of professors
at Columbia, especially Franz Boas, were just beginning to move the study of
anthropology away from its racist roots toward a race-neutral study of human
cultures in all their diversity. Lawson breathed in both of these developments
as he rethought his pentecostal faith in the urban context of New York.

What Lawson found especially disturbing about pentecostalism was the
easy way in which racism had reinserted itself into the movement. At the
Azusa revival of 1906–1907, and during the years immediately following, many
believed racism had been washed out of the movement by the power of the
Spirit. By the 1920s, however, it was clear this was no longer the case. Racism
was rampant in the movement, but no one seemed to be addressing that issue
theologically.

By the mid-1920s, Lawson decided that silence had lasted long enough, and
he published his short book, *The Anthropology of Jesus Christ Our Kinsman*
(1925), which addresses the issue of racism head-on. Drawing on new developments in the field of anthropology and his own knowledge of world history and
the Bible, Lawson outlined an Afrocentric critique of Western culture and a
theological critique of racist Christianity. He then developed his own multi-
racial theology of Christ and the atonement. To his pentecostal friends, he
added a warning: overcome your racism or God will pass you by. Nothing like
this had been written before, and nothing like it would be written again for
several decades to come. The following excerpt comes from the second part of
this work where he develops his new anti-racist doctrine of the atonement.[1]

This selection is taken from *The Anthropology of Jesus Christ Our Kinsman*
(New York: R. C. Lawson, [1925]).[2]

Japhethitic Contribution to the Anthropology of Jesus Christ

You may ask, "Why are you so concerned to prove that Jesus Christ had Negro
blood in him?" It is vitally necessary and helpful, especially when the wave of
prejudice is causing so many to sin through the egotism of race-pride, thinking

---

[1] For more information, see Jacobsen, *Thinking in the Spirit*, 263–85.
[2] I am thankful to David Daniels of McCormick Theological Seminary for calling my attention to
Lawson's work and for sharing his copy of Lawson's book with me.

themselves better than other people because of race, and separating themselves in the body of Christ through shame of their brethren of the colored
races, bringing upon themselves spiritual leprosy as typified by that which
came upon Miriam who murmured against Moses because of his Ethiopian
wife. There are many of them murmuring today, especially among our white
brethren of the South, because of colored brethren occupying prominent posi-
tions in the church of Christ. Some even go so far as refusing to take credentials
signed by a Negro. What a shame! It seems that this issue has arisen time and
again in the history of the church in America, and all have failed lamentably to
measure up to the high Christian idealism of the "Fatherhood of God and the
brotherhood of all men." They did run well at first, but when this issue came
up between the black and the white races, they were hindered because of not
accepting their colored brethren upon absolute equality. The Baptists have
failed in this issue, therefore, we have black and white Baptist. The Methodists
likewise have let this issue separate them from the love of God, therefore, we
have white and colored Methodists, etc. This is something that Paul knew not
when he said, "Nothing shall separate us from the love of God." But today we
find that this color proposition is the one thing that is separating many from
the love of God. Whenever a people or a movement have come up to this
proposition and have failed to walk according to the truth of the gospel, they
have lost power with God, and have failed as an instrument in his hands, in
saving the world for Christ. How can we love and abide in God whom we have
not seen if we love not without respect of persons our brethren, and be with
them, not separating on any grounds, or reasons. All of these various churches
have failed on this issue of color, misrepresenting the spirit of Christ, but
when God poured out his spirit here some fifteen years ago, culminating the
movement called "The Apostolic Faith," we thought surely if ever there were a
people of God that would love one another, regardless of race, color or nationality, these were the people, namely, The Pentecostal People, possessors of the
faith of the Apostles. We thought surely that now had come upon the stage of
action a people who would rise above prejudice, and measure up to the high
ideals of the "Fatherhood of God and the brotherhood of man," regardless of
color, or race. We thought sure that wherein the other churches had failed
upon the issue of "color line" and had divided into race and national groups,
for instance, colored and white Baptist and Methodist churches, etc. Welsh
Presbyterian Church, German Lutheran Church, etc., that the Pentecostal
people would teach to these a wonderful lesson by example in showing that
the true people of God are one regardless of what nationality or race they may
belong: by abiding together in the bonds of fellowship, love, and organization,
thus bringing upon them the blessings recorded in the 133rd Psalm, "Behold
how good and pleasant it is for brethren to dwell together in unity! It is like the
precious ointment upon the head, that ran down upon the beard, even Aaron's

beard: that went down to the skirts of his garments: as the dew of Herman, and as the dew that descended upon the mountains of Zion: for there the Lord commanded the blessing, even life for evermore."

The terrible scourge of race prejudice, like a disease, has afflicted the nations, like a mighty monster holds them in captivity. It is the cause of war, famine: in fact every other ill that afflicts humanity, comes out of this evil in the heart, and nothing but the love of God through his people and the preaching of the Word of love can deliver and cleanse their hearts and minds. We trusted that the Pentecostal people would rise to redeem man by example and precept. It is all right to sing and shout and pray and preach loud, but what this poor world is longing for is the real love of God, lived. For, after all, the greatest badge of discipleship of the Master, is love. "For by this shall all men know . . . that ye are my disciples, if you have love one to another."

The thing that engages my earnest effort in proving that Jesus had Negro blood in Him, is even more vital than the fore-going. The fact that Christ had Negro blood in him is vitally connected with our redemption through Calvary. In the book of Ruth, that wonderful gospel romance, is illustrated the principle of redemption. You will recall how that a man, by the name of Elimelech, and his wife, Naomi, who with their two sons, left Bethlehem-Judah, because there was a famine in Palestine. They went to the plains of Moab and remained there for ten years, during which time Elimelech died and his two sons, who had married Moabite wives. Their names were Orpah and Ruth. Naomi, being deprived of her two sons and husband, consequently arose with her daughters-in-law and left the plains of Moab, for she heard that the Everliving God had visited his people and given them bread. She entreated her daughters-in-law to return to their people and not to follow her back to Bethlehem, but Ruth would not leave her, but declared her faith in the God of Israel, which promised so little for them or her. As Dr. Simpson wrote: Orpah, the more demonstrative of the two, expressed great affection, and went home; but Ruth clung to Naomi with those ever memorable and noble words which have been inscribed with the point of a diamond as the loftiest expression of loyal affection and devotion: "Entreat me not to leave thee, or return from following after thee; for whither thou goest I will go; and where thou lodgest, I will lodge; thy people shall be my people, and thy God my God; where thou diest will I die, and there will I be buried: The Lord to do so to me, and more also, if aught but death part thee and me." And so two lone widows came back to Bethlehem and began to seek a livelihood in the humblest way. Ruth took upon herself, as a loving daughter, the support of the home and went out, like Jewish maidens, to glean in the wheat and barley fields. It was there that she met Boaz, the rich farmer, who had heard of her kindness to her mother and her maidenly modesty and who became attracted to her, and showed her special kindness without sacrificing in any way her own womanly independence. Naomi, meanwhile, kept watching with motherly intuition the whole situation, looking constantly to God, in whose wings they had come to trust. At length, Naomi found that Boaz sustained to her and Ruth the peculiar relation of the Goel, or nearest of kin, whose duty it was to redeem her husband's inheritance and take his widow to be his wife. Naomi advised Ruth to take the bold, yet modest step by which she could claim her rights. Boaz was a relative of the family of Elimelech and was wealthy. He treated her kindly by letting her glean among the sheaves, and by giving her of the food and water to drink like those of his other servants. She was mindful of her mother-in-law and saved some of her food for Naomi and told Naomi, when she returned home of Boaz's kindness to her. Naomi inform[ed] her that Boaz was a near relative and that he could redeem their mortgaged property: for so it was a custom in Israel—Deut. 25, when brothers resided together and one of them died and left not a son, that the wife of the dead man should not be a wife to a stranger. Her brother-in-law or the next kin should marry her and the first son that she bears, he should bring up with his brother's name so that his name might not be wiped out from Israel.

But, if the man refuse[s] or is unable, he should pull off his shoes from his feet, thus signifying his inability, giving it to the next in kin who is able to redeem the property, and marry his relative's wife. So it was that Ruth was instructed by Naomi about this ancient custom. During the winnowing of the harvest, after Boaz had ate and drank and rejoiced in heart and had lain down to sleep, Ruth came quietly and uncovered his feet and laid down. It happened at midnight that the man was startled and turned over and found a woman lying at his feet. He inquired, "Who are you?" She replied, "I am Ruth, your servant. Therefore, spread your cloak over your servant, for you are a restorer." Then Boaz replied to her, "The Lord bless you, my girl. You have given more kindness at the last than at the first, for you have not gone after the young men whether poor or rich, therefore, my people know that you are a virtuous woman, and I am a near relative, yet there is a nearer redeemer than I. Stay here tonight and when morning comes, if he redeems for you, good, but if he is not pleased to redeem your property, then I will." Boaz that next day went up to the gates and sat. When the near relative of whom he had spoken of passed, he exclaimed, "Come here, sit down," so he turned and sat down. Then he summoned ten of the Elders of the village. When they had come, he addressed him in the presence of the Elders, saying, "Where is that part of our estate, which belongs to Elimelech? Naomi, who has resided in the plains of Moab wishes to sell it, so I have spoken it open[ly] to your ears to advise you to buy, in the presence of these men, the Elders of my people. If you wish to redeem it, redeem it, but if you will not redeem it inform me, for there is no one to redeem it except yourself, and I am after you." And he replied, "I will redeem it." But Boaz answered: "On the day that you purchase the estate from the hands of Naomi, you must buy it also from Ruth, the Moabitess, the wife of the dead man to raise up a name for the dead on the property." Then the next of kin said: "I am not able to purchase it of myself lest I should injure my own property. You can purchase my right for yourself, for I am unable to redeem it." Now this was a custom in Israel, that a man took off his shoes and gave it to his next of kin, this was an attestation that he was unable to redeem the lost inheritance of his next of kin. When the next of kin said to Boaz, "buy it for yourself," he slipped off his shoe. Boaz said to the Elders and all the people, "You are witnesses today, that I have redeemed all in Elimelech, also Ruth, the Moabitess, the wife of Mahlon, from the hands of Naomi, I have bought for myself to raise up a name for the dead so that his name might not be cut off from the gates of Israel." The Elders and people said, "We are witnesses, may the Everliving bless you and may your wife be like Rachel and Leah who built up the home of Israel." Thus did Boaz the next of kin redeem the lost inheritance. Above all is the piety of Ruth. It was not merely the love of her mother that made her true; but it was the love of her mother's God. Very finely Boaz alludes to it when he speaks of "the wings of the Almighty under which she had come to trust."

In this wonderful romance and in the laws of Moses are imbedded and interwoven a wonderful mystery of the principal of our redemption through Christ. Hallelujah! God created Adam, the progenitor of the human race and gave him lordship over this world. He shared with God innocency and purity. God delighted in the fellowship of man. Coming down often on the wind of the day, he instructed man in the way he should go, giving him the laws of faith and obedience: saying, "Thou shalt eat of all the trees of the garden, save the tree of knowledge of good and evil, and the day wherein thou eatest of it thou shalt surely die." It is implied in the scripture that this world was formerly inhabited by angelical beings who through disobedience were cast down from their holy state. Disembodied, they became wicked spirits under the leadership of Lucifer, the son of the morning, a former covering cherub, who essayed to become God. They sought the down-fall of man through the subtlety of the serpent. This was brought about through unbelief and disobedience of Eve, who told her transgression to Adam, the Lord of this earth, who willingly, willfully, sold his inheritance. The Lord in anguish, aware of the transaction, came down on the wind of the day broken-hearted: He sought man in the garden of Eden, crying "Adam where art thou." Adam, having sold himself for naught, was a slave to Satan. He feared God and hid himself in the under-bush when he heard the voice of God. With a broken heart Jehovah-Saviour continued to seek him until he found him trembling in the inner-recess of the garden. He elicited out of him his confession of guilt, the horrible transaction that lost for him the lordship of the world, fellowship of God, and purity of heart. The Lord in mercy, knowing that the adversary, Satan, was back of all this miserable deed, purposed in his heart to redeem man, saying unto the serpent "because thou hast done this, thou art cursed above all cattle, and above every beast of the field; upon thy belly shalt thou go, and dust shalt thou eat all the days of thy life; And I will put enmity between thy seed and her seed; it shall bruise thy head, and thou shalt bruise his heel."

Note, the promise of the seed of the woman was not simply the seed of Eve, but the Woman here is to be understood in a larger sense, that is, the Seed of the Human race. Therefore, the mixing of the blood of the three branches of the human race had a deeper significance than it is commonly thought. The very phrase "the seed of the woman" has no basis in the biological philosophy of man. Woman hath not seed, man is the progenitor, therefore we must look to a higher law than Nature for the production of this seed of woman. This is a revelation. In the hoary ages of time, God, foreseeing that to redeem man justly, according to his own principles of righteousness, it was necessary that he should become man's kinsman. Being higher than man, it was not possible to be begotten of man. He therefore conceived the mystery of the miraculous conception and virgin birth, saying, "The seed of the woman shall bruise the serpent's head." After the separation of the races at the tower of Babel, the Lord began to build up the medium through which this seed should come, having purposed to become our near kinsman because of our inability to redeem ourselves, even though there would be born unto us wise men, scribes and prophets. The hope was kindled in the breast of the human race at the birth of [Eve's] first child, Abel, that he would be the promised seed, and of every man child thereafter that was born, this hope increased as a fire. It blazed brighter and brighter and at times, after a great man arose, the question would be asked, "Is this he?" And sometimes the great men like Moses would be imbued with patriarchic zeal that they indeed were the deliverer. But as they began their career of deliverance, there came an inner revelation or a divine apparition that they were unable to redeem. Sometimes, as in the days of Moses, the divine voice would speak upon the threshold of their career, "Take off thy shoe, for the place whereon thou standest is holy ground," or in so many words, saying unto them, "Thou art unable to redeem, though thou art next in kin." Like Joshua, on entering the land of Canaan near Jericho, encountered a strange personage who had a drawn sword. Approaching in the audacity of self-confidence in his own ability to accomplish the task of destruction of the people of Canaan, and dividing the land to the people of Israel, he was quickly informed that this strange personage, and not he, was the captain of the Lord's host, and he only could redeem the land and accomplish the task. He said unto Joshua, as an acknowledgement of his inability to redeem, "Take off thy shoe, the place whereon thou standest is holy ground." So on through the ages though there arose David, he could only sing of redemption, but could not redeem, saying, "Over Edom have I kicked my shoe." And Solomon the wise, wrote, "I have put off my coat, and how shall I put it on? I have washed my feet, how shall I defile them?" But with all of his wisdom he could not redeem. Not until was heard the voice of one crying in the wilderness, the man whose meat was locust and wild honey. [He] openly declared, upon being questioned, was he the Messiah: He answered, "No, I am the voice of one crying in the wilderness, make straight the way of the Lord. I baptize with water, but there stands one among you whom you know not, He it is who is coming after me, is preferred before me whose shoe latchet I am not worthy to unloose." John realized that Jesus was indeed the seed of the woman and that he was fully able to redeem and had no need to take off his shoes, not even to have them unloosed. The sum total of what has been written is this, that Christ, in order to be a redeemer of man from sin, became a near kinsman when he looked and saw that there was none to help and that no eye pitied, and there was no arm to save. God disrobed himself of his glory, overshadowed the Virgin Mary, a prepared vessel, a woman in whose veins flowed the blood of Japheth and of Shem, and of Ham, for so had been the purpose and work of God in mixing the bloods of all three branches of the human race, that upon the basis of kinship, He might have [the] right—so to speak—to redeem all men. Therefore, when this miscegenation had been thoroughly fulfilled in the woman, Mary was found the fit vessel and medium through which the seed of the woman—that is, of the human race, would come into the world to bruise the head of the serpent. So spake the prophet of him, "Lo I come in the volume of the book to do thy will, O God, a body hast thou prepared me." Through the phenomena of the overshadowing by the Spirit, the Virgin Mary was found with child of the Holy Ghost, the only begotten of the Father, our near kinsman. Bless God. Job, looking down the highway of the ages, saw and cried in faith, "I know that my redeemer lives, and that he shall stand upon the earth in the latter day and mine eyes shall behold him and not another. Though after my skin worms destroy this body, yet in my flesh I shall see God." When Christ was born in Bethlehem, the Angels standing in the cloisters of invisibility stepped forth and sang over the fields of Boaz, "Glory to God in the Highest and Peace on Earth, Good will to all men." Then there was suddenly with the shepherds the Angel of the Lord which said, "Behold I bring you good news of great joy, for there is born, this day, in the city of David, a Saviour, which is Christ, the Redeemer." At last the seed of the woman, our kinsman to us all, had come. Straightway, the devil, the seed of the serpent began to bruise his heel. Our blessed Redeemer was born in such poverty that he had not means to procure a place for his birth. As there was no room in the Inn, his mother resorted to a stable. There under the golden glow of his own star, that shone through the window, he was born—he who became poor that through his redemption he might make many rich. The seed of the serpent bruised his heel by forcing his mother to flee from the face of Herod who had designed upon his life, [and] sought to accomplish it by having all the children under two years of age put to death. But deep in [the] unfathomable mind of never failing skill, he treasures up his bright designs and works his sovereign will. It was determined that the land of Ham should be the Asylum for the refugee, as it had been prophesied, "Out of Egypt, have I called forth my son." After Herod's death the Angel of the Lord directed Mary to return to Bethlehem. Later in the city of Nazareth, was the seed of the woman nurtured. All of this was done that it might be fulfilled that which was spoken by the prophet Esias concerning our Lord, "Behold a virgin shall be with child and shall call his name Emmanuel which interpreted is God with us." "For as much as the brethren were partakers of flesh and blood, he also himself likewise took part of the same; that through death he might destroy him that had power over death, that is, the devil and deliver them who through fear of death were all their life time subject to bondage, for verily he took not on him the nature of angels; but he took on the seed of Abraham that in all things he might be like his brethren and be to them, a merciful and faithful High Priest in things pertaining to God and to make reconciliation for the sins of the people." Three things are necessary in redeeming: First, he must be a kinsman; Second, the Redeemer must be able to redeem. Ruth 4:6, Jer. 5:34. St. John 10:11–18. Third, the Redemption is affected by the redeemer, paying the just demands in full. 1st Pet. 1:18, 19, Gal. 3:13. . . .

All this, as stated before, involved the forfeiture of the kinsman's own family name, and marred his inheritance; but it was recognized as a patriotic and social duty, overriding personal considerations. Now, this is just what Boaz did for Ruth, and what the nearer kinsman refused to do. Boaz merged his own personality and family in Ruth's family, making a real sacrifice, and thus he became her kinsman redeemer, and then, also, her husband. This is the beautiful type of our Lord Jesus Christ, our kinsman Redeemer. For us he has sacrificed His own divine rights. This is what the apostle meant when he said, "That being in the form of God, He thought it not a thing to be eagerly grasped and retained that He should be equal with God; but made himself of no reputation, and took upon Him the form of a servant, and was made in the likeness of men; and being found in fashion as a man, He humbled Himself and became obedient unto death, even the death of the cross." Christ gave us forever a place of dignity and right on yonder throne, where he was known as God and God alone. Henceforth, He is forever known as man, still divine, but not exclusively divine, but united to the person, flesh and form of a created being, and His whole inheritance merged in ours. He lay down His rights and His honours, and took up our wrongs and reproaches, our liabilities and responsibilities, and henceforth he has nothing but his people. He is the merchant man seeking goodly pearls, who, having found one pearl of great price, sold all that he had and bought that pearl. The Church, His Bride, is all He owns; He has invested everything in us. The Lord's portion is his people;

therefore, let us make up to Him what he has laid down; let us understand His sacrifice and love, and let Him find in us His sufficient and everlasting recompense. But the redeemer not only sacrificed his own inheritance, but also brought back the forfeited inheritance of the dead husband; and so our precious God has brought back for us all that we lost in Adam and added to it infinitely more—all the fulness of His grace, all the riches of his glory, all that the ages to come are yet to unfold in his mighty plan, victory over death, the restoration of the divine image, sonship with God, triumph over Satan, a world restored to more than Eden's blessedness and beauty, the crowns and thrones of the coming kingdom, and all the exceeding riches of His grace and kindness toward us which in the ages to come He is to show. All this and more is the purchase of his Redemption, says Dr. Simpson.

"In whom the tribes of Adam boast
More blessings than their father lost."

But the best of all the blessings brought by the kinsman Redeemer is Himself. Not only does he redeem the inheritance, but he purchases the bride and He becomes the Bridegroom. When Boaz bought the inheritance of Elimelech he took Ruth also in and she became his bride. And so our blessed Kinsman Redeemer is also our Husband. Not only does He come down into our nature in the incarnation, but He takes us up into his person in the wondrous betrothal which is to reach its consummation in the marriage of the Lamb. Once more we see in Ruth's example the pattern of a faith that dares to claim and enter into all the possibilities of its inheritance. It needed on the part of Ruth a very bold and decided act to claim her rights under the Levirate law. They would not have come to her as the snowflakes fall, but they had to be recognized and definitely claimed. And so her mother told her all about it, and showed her that she was doing no unwomanly or immodest thing to put herself at the feet of Boaz and in the place of which she was entitled and leave upon him the responsibility of accepting or refusing her. Still, it cost her many a struggle and many a tear before she robed herself in her wedding garments and, stealing through the eventide, lay down at the threshing floor of Boaz, putting herself and all that was dear to a woman's honour at his mercy. It was the abandonment of faith, but faith must always abandon itself before it can claim its blessing. It was thus that Mary, in later days, consented to risk her very reputation at the angel's message and believed for the mighty blessing that was to bring the world its Redeemer at the cost for a time of even Mary's reputation. "Behold the handmaid of the Lord," she cried, "be it unto me according to Thy word." And the answer came: "Blessed is she that believed, for there shall be an accomplishment of the things that were told her from the Lord?" And so faith must ever claim its promised rights. Every victory costs a venture, and the blessing is in the proportion to the cost. Faith must still see its inheritance under the promise and then step boldly forward and take what God has given. Salvation is not now bestowed as mercy to a pauper, but it is claimed in Jesus' name through baptism in water in Jesus' name, and the reception of the Holy Ghost by all who inherit his Brother's will. So we take His forgiveness and so we must take every blessing and answer to all prayer all along our way. God has given us the right to take this place of boldness. We are not presuming but we are honouring His word. We are not entering beyond our rights, but we are showing our confidence in our Father's truth and love by daring to take all He has dared to give. So let us have boldness to enter into the holiest by the blood of Jesus.

"And to its utmost fulness prove
The power of Jesus' name."

Finally the fruit of the union was the dynasty of David and the birth of Jesus Christ, the Son of man, the King of Kings, and the Lord of Lords. Ruth's faith brought her into a family of princes and a kingdom of glory. And so for us, too, redemption means a crown and a throne at the Master's glorious coming. But back of the throne and the crown lies the love story of redemption and the bold appropriation of faith. We must learn to know the Bridegroom now if we would sit with Him upon His throne then and share the glory of his millennial reign. Oh! shall we take Him as our Redeemer, our Husband, and our coming Lord, and have Him say to us, "Thy Maker is thy Husband and thy Redeemer the Holy one of Israel, the God of the whole earth shall He be called."

The Lord through uniting our human natures by the process of miscegenation—the mixing of the blood of Ham, Shem and Japheth—forever abolished the basis and principle of race prejudice, because if he is a kinsman to all having their blood in his veins, then whosoever hateth his brother, hateth his Lord, because whatever race that one who he hateth may be of, our Lord is of that race, whether Semitic, Hamitic, or Japhethic, although he is not wholly of any; he is not a Jew, a Negro, not a white man, that is, an Anglo-Saxon, but a relative of all. Praise the Lord. He is our Saviour, not a Jewish Saviour, nor a Negro Saviour, nor an Anglo Saxon Saviour, but a human, universal Saviour, (our kinsman) by virtue of the fact that the blood of Shem, Ham, Japheth, representatives of the entire human race, flows through his veins, therefore, all have the same interest and right in Him and none can say to another, "You have no part in Him."

"He is our Saviour" for He became our kinsman. Bone of our bones, and flesh of all flesh, that as we became one flesh in Him, He might by one spirit in us, make us one in Him. "For He is our peace, who hath made both one, and hath broken down the middle wall of partition between us. Having abolished in his flesh the enmity, even the law of commandments contained in ordinances; for to make in himself of twain one new man, so making peace. And [he] came and preached peace to you which were afar off, and to them that were nigh. And that he might reconcile both unto God in one body by the cross, having slain the enmity thereby. For through him we both have access by one spirit unto the Father; the church, a temple for habitation of God through the Spirit. Now therefore ye are no more strangers and foreigners, but fellow citizens with the saints, and of the household of God. And are built upon [the] foundation of the apostles and prophets, Jesus Christ himself being the chief corner stone. In whom, all the building fitly framed together groweth unto an holy temple in the Lord. In whom, ye also are builded together for an habitation of God through the Spirit."

We cannot make a difference between flesh, for we be [sic] brethren, 1st John 4:12. . . .

CHAPTER SIXTEEN

Charles Harrison Mason
(1866–1961)

L IVING ON A FARM in the South just outside Memphis, Tennessee, Charles Harrison Mason grew up in the shadow of slavery. His parents had been slaves all their lives and had just recently been freed when he was born in 1866. Virtually all the adults Mason knew had been slaves as well. That world was, of course, changing. Slavery was over and reconstructionist leaders were trying to build a new world. Many wanted to leave the past behind as fast as possible, but Mason believed some elements of slave religion needed to be preserved, especially its legacy of heartfelt faith and prophetic spirituality.

Slave religion was embodied faith, lived out morally during the day in the harsh grind of plantation life and drunk in spiritually at night in ring shouts, where believers sang and danced in the Spirit, accompanied by the sound of drums and whatever other musical instruments could be gathered together. Slave religion was also rural and agricultural, attuned to God's voice as expressed in natural phenomena such as oddly shaped fruits and vegetables, unusual animal behavior, peculiarly severe storms, or strange juxtapositions of events. It was that vitality of faith that Mason never wanted to lose: a faith that was realistic and socially critical on the one hand, but deeply aware of God's presence in the world and immersed in the body-shaking, soul-remaking power of the Spirit on the other.

Mason was known for his depth of faith as a young child, and that faith deepened when he was healed of a life-threatening fever at the age of fourteen. He was baptized shortly after his healing and set off to preach in southern Arkansas. In 1891, Mason was formally ordained by the Missionary Baptist Church, and in 1893, he enrolled at Arkansas Baptist College. Mason was troubled, however, by the higher critical approach to the Bible that was taught at the school and withdrew to continue preaching his old-fashioned gospel of holiness.

In the mid-1890s Mason met and became friends with a fellow holiness preacher named Charles Price Jones. Working in unison and encouraging each other, the two slowly built up a wide-ranging network of holiness congregations within the Baptist churches of the South. At some point during this time, Mason received a revelation from God (based on a New Testament phrase found in 1 Thessalonians 2:14) that this new group should be called the Church of God in Christ (COGIC). Mason and Jones formally registered the group as a denomination and began giving papers of ordination to ministers who joined the organization.

When the pentecostal revival broke out at the Azusa Street Mission in 1906, Mason caught a train to Los Angeles to check it out. He was very positively impressed and soon experienced the baptism of the Spirit for himself. After five weeks of tutelage under William Seymour, Mason returned home to share the good news with Jones. Jones rejected the new pentecostal message, however, and the two men argued over the direction of their church. Eventually each went his own way, and the denomination split in two. Mason's faction kept the name Church of God in Christ, while the Jones group became the Church of Christ (Holiness) U.S.A. Today COGIC is the largest pentecostal denomination in the United States.

The following selections come from a compendium of materials gathered together for the 1926 annual COGIC Holy Convocation. Mason did not do much writing himself, but many of his sermons were later summarized in print, and that is what appears here. These sermons illustrate Mason's rural roots, his critique of both racism and worldliness, his strong sense of calling as the head of his church, and his insistence that COGIC remain firmly trinitarian in opposition to oneness views of God that were percolating through the pentecostal movement.[1]

The following selections are from the *Year Book of the Church of God in Christ for the Year 1926*. (Compiled by Lillian Brooks Coffey. N.p.: [1926]).

---

[1] For more information, see Ithiel C. Clemmons, *Bishop C. H. Mason and the Roots of the Church of God in Christ* (Bakersfield, Calif.: Pneuma Life Publishing, 1996); and David D. Daniels, "Charles Harrison Mason: The Interracial Impulse of Early Pentecostalism," in *Portraits of a Generation: Early Pentecostal Leaders*, ed. James R. Goff and Grant Wacker (Fayetteville: University of Arkansas Press, 2004), 255–70.

Sermon in Part By Elder C. H. Mason

By ANNA SMITH, General Recording Secretary

Storms — Storms — Storms

The Lord will have His way in the storms, and the clouds are the dust of His feet. Nahum 1:2–3. Talk of His wonders and make known His deeds among the people. Ps. 105:1.

Some of the wise of today are saying God has nothing to do with the storm. But the Bible says: "The Lord will have His way in the whirlwinds and in the storms."

"God will rise up as in Mount Perazim and be wroth as in the Valley of Gibeon, that He may do His work, His strange work, and bring to pass His acts, His strange acts." Isaiah 28:21.

The word says that "the proud and the drunkards shall be visited of the Lord of hosts, with thunder and earthquakes and great noise, with storm and tempest, and the flame of devouring fire." Isaiah 29:86.

God with the hand of the storm shall cast down to the earth proud folks; and God shall trample them under His foot in the storm. Nahum 1:2–3; Isaiah 28:1–3.

Short-dress pride, low-necked pride, men proud over their success over others, lawyers proud over their arguments in sentencing some one for gain, judges proud over their power to send men into custody, men and women proud of their fine homes and automobiles, women proud of their powers of attraction that bewitches a man, turning [him] from his home, his wife and his children; man proud in his wickedness in taking to himself another man's wife, and bringing shame and disgrace to himself and to others; the rich man proud of his ascendancy over the poor, having gathered his gain by fraud and keeping back the hire from the poor. National pride bringing forth wars and polluting the land, causing blood to touch blood; all of these characters God will work with in storms, earthquakes, and great noise, and with flames of devouring fire.

While He was trodding the proud and the drunkards under His foot. I want here to relate some of the incidents of the storm which passed through five West States of America. Recently in passing through the eastern part of the West States of America, it destroyed in its wake over 800 people, injured 3,000; loss to property $15,000,000.

In Murphysboro, Ill., in His strange act put a woman in a well and the water felt as cotton under her feet, then in His strange way lifted her out, unhurt.

Another mother with twins was lifted up in a tree and was not hurt.

Again in His wrath He drove a scantling 2x6 feet through a tree; then in another tree He drove a scantling through and sent in a shingle through the scantling that went through the tree.

Who is like unto God?

Locomotives and steel cars were upturned, doing His work, His strange work.

It is said in one home a lady had lately installed a new gas range but God came and swept it out of the house and sent a coal stove in its place. Was that not one of God's strange acts?

"Come and see the works of God, He is terrible in His doing toward the children of men." Ps. 66:5. In a little town, DeSoto, where there was so much race hatred, I am told that a sign bearing these words was raised, "Negroes, read and run." God performed another one of His strange acts. This town was completely destroyed.

In confirmation of the Scriptures, after the storm was over, an open Bible was found by a telegraph operator, of Cairo, Ill., who went over inspecting the ruins, March 25. The Bible was lying face downward on the ground. Picking it up he declared it was opened on the 13th Chapter of Mark, starting with these words, "As He went out of the temple one of the disciples said unto Him; Master see what manner of stones and what buildings are here. And Jesus answering said unto him; Seeth thou these great buildings? There shall not be left one stone upon another that shall not be thrown down."

Another instance of a woman who was stripped of her clothing except her garters.

One of a chicken who was picked of its feathers. God says: "Thy nakedness shalt be uncovered, yea, thy shame shall be seen." Isaiah 47:3.

Again, in His anger in another storm He passed through Mississippi and lifting a feather bed from its place, emptying it in a pie, ready to be served; then carried away the tick, house and all. God working in a mysterious way.

A team of mules was lifted and placed upon the top of a house. Job. 9:10: "Behold He taketh away, who can hinder Him?"

A baby was taken up and was carried away and put down unhurt. A man also was carried away from his plough and when he came to himself he found he might have been more than 100 miles from home.

In a Mississippi storm a colored child was carried by the storm and placed in a white man's yard.

God's strange and terrible visitation [came] on man in the earthquake of September, 1923, [when] without a sign or any warning the house collapsed in a moment of time. Those which escaped the first shock were left frantic with fear, running here and there trying to find a place that would be safe to stand as the wrath of God caused the earth to rumble and quake. Earthquake and great noise, flames and devouring fire turned the proud, fascinating country of Japan into a place of death and destruction.

What a surprise to the people at ease; with the sun shining at noonday, with no thought of any disaster, and feel[ing] that the farthest thing from them was death, to be seized in a moment of time by the giant monster coming up [out] of the earth swallowing them without any time to repent or even think as to what the end would be. Matt. 24:44. "Therefore, be ye also ready: for in such an hour as ye think not the Son of man cometh." We can see from that how very necessary it is to be ready and not wait until we come to die.

Some of those that were saved, their bodies were stripped bare of all clothing and they wrapped themselves in anything they could find that would cover them.

The rich and the poor all suffered alike, God is no respecter of persons. Acts 10:34.

Apostleship in the Church of God in Christ

The Apostles in the church are called and made of God, and not of men. I Cor. 1:1. Nor by man. Gal. 1:1. Men may be called by an apostle and sent. Titus 1:5–8. The keys of the kingdom were given unto the Apostle; that whosoever he should bind on earth should be bound in Heaven and whosoever he should loose on earth should be loosed in Heaven. Matt. 16:17–19. The Apostles are set first in the church. 1 Cor. 12:28. When they have been breathed on and filled with the Holy Ghost they may forgive sin. St. John 20:21–23. Paul the Apostle commanded the church in Corinth to put out the evil doer, then after he had repented, Paul said to forgive him and he would do the same in the Person of Christ. 2 Cor. 2:6–10. The Church is built upon the foundation of the Apostles and Prophets. Eph. 2:20.

Bishops and Elders are made by the Apostles; but Bishops nor Elders never made nor make an Apostle in the Church of God in Christ. They are called and made of God. God sent Jesus and Jesus sent the Apostles. St. John 20:21. Apostles send Bishops ordained to ordain Elders and Deacons in the church. Titus 1:5–8. The Apostles commanded the multitude of the disciples to look out among themselves men full of the Holy Ghost and wisdom that they (Apostles) might appoint over that business, so they did. The Apostles ordained them for Deacons in the church. Acts 6:1–6. If one has been excluded from the church wrongfully by the Elders or members of the church, the Apostle may call to memory the deeds of the one that has done the wrong and restore one that was turned out to his right in the church. John, 5–10.

The words that God gave unto Jesus, Jesus gave unto the Apostles. St. John 17:8. The Revelations that God gave His son Jesus after the ascension, Jesus gave unto the Apostle John. Gave him to write and send it unto all the pastors and churches that were in Asia. Rev. 1:1–4. Oh, what Jesus in the Holy Ghost is doing through the Apostles in the church of today. Peter, James and John saw Jesus in His glory. No other man ever saw. Matt. 17:1–9. Paul the Apostle heard words that were not lawful for a man to utter. 2 Cor. 12:1–4.

Jesus through the Holy Ghost gave commandments unto the Apostle after He was taken up. Acts 1:7–26.

God's church has never been run by the majority of the people. God's words sent them by one, two, and three. His word is always right. One Noah with the word was right and ruled. All the world with its great multitudes died and left the church with one: Noah and his family. 1 Peter 3:19, 2 Pet. 2:5. So we see that God rules in one Abraham the father of all the faithful. One Lot in Sodom. One Moses in Egypt. One Joshua to stop the sun and break down the wall of Jericho. One Sampson in the spirit to rend a lion and eat honey out of his dead carcass. One David to kill the Giant of the Philistines and to sing the songs of the mind of God. And His Son who was to save His people from sin. Matt. 1:21. One Solomon, a king who was given wisdom to give words of truth about wise and fools; about rich and poor, high and low, old and young, male and female, free and bound. Oh, how much the more might be said about this one Solomon. One Isaiah saw the Lord high and lifted up and his train filling the temple; [that sight made him] fit to go [as] the messenger of the Lord to the great dogs, shepherds and blind watchman and fashionable women that rule over God's people. . . . To lift His voice like a trumpet, showing the people their sin.

God rules in one Jeremiah, sanctifying him before he came into the world. Jer. 1:5. One Ezra given to show the house of Isaiah that they would or should . . . be ashamed of their ways. Ezra 43:10.

One John the Baptist, forerunner of Christ, fulfilling the law. One Jesus died on the Cross and rose . . . from the dead that all who were dead in the graves might be raised up from the dead. One Jesus ascended up into Heaven for all and with all that may go up into Heaven. One Jesus sent the Holy Ghost on all that received Him. God's church is made one, of every nation, tongue and people that are upon the face of the earth. So the church is the body of Christ. Eph. 1:22. Christ is the head of the body, "the one church." Eph. 4:4–5.

God rules in one faith and in one Lord and in one baptism. . . .

The Sonship of Jesus

Jesus Christ is the Son of God. Matt. 1:21. He is not the Father of God but the Son of God, nor is He His own father, for no son has ever begotten himself, but all sons have fathers that begetteth them. So Jesus is the only begotten of the Father. John 1:14. God, His Father, took Him and made the world and all things therein. John 1:10. I must say here that I do not know anywhere in the

Bible that teaches that Jesus was or is the Father of God or His own father, but He is our Father. Of His own will begot He us with the word of truth that we should be a kind of first fruits of His creatures. James 1:18. So to believe that Jesus is the Son of God it is to give us eternal life with Him. John 3:15–16.

He is God's Son and is to save His people from their sins. Matt. 1:21; Isaiah 9:6–7. It is said of Him, "For unto us a son is given and the government shall be upon His shoulder; and His name shall be called Wonderful, Counselor, The Mighty God, The Everlasting Father, The Prince of Peace." This text does not say that He was His own father, but that He was His Son and Lord, having the nature of Him that was His Father. So as His Father was Everlasting, it makes Him (Jesus) Everlasting as God, His Father, and as much God as His Father was God. His Father sent Him into the world to save, and He was able to save, Isa. 6:13, being the Son of an Almighty Father, equal with His Father. Phil. 2:6. He is the Son in name. Matt. 1:21. He is the Son with power. Rom. 1:4. He is the Son in faith. Gal. 2:20.

He is the Son in glory, in the glory of the only begotten of the Father. John 1:14. He is the Son of God without a beginning of days, for before the days were, He was in the bosom of the Father, John 1:18, and the days were created by Him, so He began days, and the days did not begin Him. He had no end of life. Hebrews 7:3. He was put to death in His flesh but was quickened by the Spirit, and while His flesh was dead, He went and preached to the Spirits that were in prison with His endless life that was in the Father. 1 John 5:20.

Oh, what a wonder he gave His body up to death; and the grave at the Cross, and His Spirit up to the hands of His Father. Luke 23:46. He lived and died the Son of God. He was raised from the dead by the Father that begat Him who by Him do believe in God that raised Him from the dead. 1 Peter 1:21.

Elder R. C. Lawson, of Columbus, Ohio, when in St. Louis, Mo., in a convocation of the Church of God in Christ, said that he believed in the sonship of God and the fatherhood of God and the Holy Ghost; for God was manifested in the flesh, but after Jesus was put to death in the flesh that He was no longer the Son of God, and the Scripture nowhere taught that Jesus was any longer the Son, but was [now] the Lord that Spirit as in 2 Cor. 3:17 . . .

In a little while it was shown that the brother was wrong about Scripture reading. I listened to hear the brother say that he had made a mistake in his saying; but after he heard the Scripture read which showed that he was wrong, he went away without correcting his saying that he was wrong.

Now, let us see what sayeth the Scripture. Romans 1:3: The Spirit of Holiness with power, by the resurrection from the dead, said: "He was the Son of God." After His resurrection He Himself said that God was His Father. St. John 20:17–21.

Stephen, full of the Holy Ghost at his death, saw heaven open and Jesus standing at the right hand of God. Acts 7:5, 6.

Many years after the ascension of Jesus, John was taken up in the Spirit while on the Isle of Patmos and saw Him and heard Him say that He had washed us from our sins in His own blood and hath made us kings and priests unto God, His Father. He said God was His Father. He said, with His eyes like a flame of fire, that He was the Son of God. Rev. 2:18.

To us His name is Jesus, which is above every name, for He is the Savior of us all and God with us. The name Son is to God, His Father, and it is more excellent. Heb. 1:45. For unto which of the angels said He at any time, "Thou art My Son. This day have I begotten Thee"? Son expresses His relation to His Father and His relation as a brother to us. Heb. 2:11. For both He that Sanctifieth and they who are sanctified are all of one; for which cause He is not ashamed to call them brethren, saying: "I will declare thy name unto my brethren." Jesus knew His Father and His name, and the greatness of His name; so He came to declare God's name, His Father. He did and will declare it. John 17:6–26. Jesus' Father was greater than His Son. John 14:28. The Son Jesus dwelt in the flesh, and His Father dwelt in the Spirit of His Son Jesus. John 14:10. Jesus in the flesh died, but God in the spirit could never die. Are there three in the Godhead? Yes. Who are they? The Father, [the] Word and the Holy Ghost. These three are one. 1 John 5:7. Are there three that bear witness on earth? Yes. The Spirit, the Water and the Blood. These three agree in one.

Elder L. A. Bell, of Starksville, Miss., said that Jesus was the name of the Godhead, but we said to him that Jesus was the name of the Son and not the name of the Godhead, so God is the Father of the Godhead and Jesus is the Son of the Godhead and the Holy Ghost is the glory of all being in the Godhead.

O! What a wonder. Baptizing in the name of Jesus. Is it right?

Yes. But it is only right when it is done like Jesus said to do it. He said in Matt. 28:19, "Go ye therefore and teach all nations, baptizing them in the name of the Father and of the Son and Holy Ghost." This is the only way that Jesus commanded it to be done, or said while he was on earth, and He never did say after He went to heaven for it to be changed by anyone or at any time, for it was given to Him from God, His Father, just like it should be said. John 12:49–50.

"For I have not spoken of myself, but the Father which sent me; He gave me a commandment, what I should say, and what I should speak. And I know that His commandment is life everlasting; whatsoever I speak, therefore, even as the Father said unto me, so I speak." His Father said it just like Jesus spoke it, and He said it in the name of the Father and of the Son and of the Holy Ghost. I can say for one that I believe that it was said right then, and it is right now, and will be so until the end of the world.

What do we baptize for? We are baptized for the dead. 1 Cor. 15:9; Rom. 6:3–5, "Else what shall they do that are baptized for the dead?" Our baptism in the name of the Father, Son and Holy Ghost shows that while we were enemies we were reconciled to God by the death of His Son, so being reconciled we shall be saved by His life. Rom. 5:10. So we confess in baptism the Father, Son and Holy Ghost unto death; and in all life to live [the] will [of] the Father, Son and Holy Ghost.

The three that agree on earth say that there are three in heaven. Who can say that God and His Son and the Holy Ghost did not know how to count? They said, "Three in Heaven." But some of the wise today say they see it better. God saw "THREE" and said "THREE." But the "ONE IN THE GODHEAD PEOPLE" say they only see "one" and [there] could not be "three." God said "three" and could make them ONE. But we may see "one" and cannot make it "three."

The "One in the Godhead People" are undertaking to show God His wrong sayings. Who can understand His errors? Psa. 19:12. So if there are not "Three" in heaven as He said, then there are not "Three" in the earth as He said. John 5:7–8.

Jesus is the Son of God and is the only mediator between God and men. 1 Tim. 2:5. Jesus, God's Son, could be seen, but God, His Father, could or hath never been seen. John 1:18. "No man hath ever seen God at any time, the only begotten Son in the bosom of the Father, He hath declared Him." 1 John 4:12; Matt. 11:27. Danger!

He is an antichrist that denieth the Father and the Son. 1 John 2:22. "Whosoever denieth the Father the same hath not the Son." Verse 23.

So, to say that Jesus is not the Son of God is to make God a liar, because he believeth not the record that God gave of His Son. 1 John 5:10. One eternal life is in His Son. Verse 11. "He that hath the Son hath life, and he that hath not the Son of God hath not life." Verse 12.

We overcome the world when we believe that Jesus is the Son of God. 1 John 5:4–6. The Father sent the Son to be the Savior of the world. John 4:14. "Whosoever shall confess that Jesus is the Son of God, God dwelleth in him and he in God."

INDEX

DOUGLAS JACOBSEN is Distinguished Professor of Church History and Theology at Messiah College, Grantham, Pennsylvania. His other books include *Thinking in the Spirit: Theologies of the Early Pentecostal Movement* (Indiana University Press, 2003); *Re-Forming the Center: American Protestantism, 1900 to the Present* (with William Vance Trollinger); *Scholarship and Christian Faith: Enlarging the Conversation* (with Rhonda Hustedt Jacobsen); and *Gracious Christianity: Living the Love We Profess* (with Rodney J. Sawatsky). He holds a Ph.D. from the University of Chicago and is presently writing a global history of Christianity.

Ingram Content Group UK Ltd.
Milton Keynes UK
UKHW010614220323
418970UK00002B/144